China Tour Guide

Buddhism: *Rituals and Monastic Life*

Zheng Lixin

Translated by Ling Yuan

Foreign Languages Press   Beijing

First Edition   2007

Home Page:
  http://www.flp.com.cn
E-mail Addresses:
  info@flp.com.cn
  sales@flp.com.cn

ISBN 978-7-119-04490-3

© Foreign Languages Press, Beijing, China, 2007

Published by Foreign Languages Press
24 Baiwanzhuang Road, Beijing 100037, China

Distributed by China International Book Trading Corporation
35 Chegongzhuang Xilu, Beijing 100044, China
P.O. Box 399, Beijing, China

Printed in the People's Republic of China

Contents

Preface

Chinese Buddhism has a history of more than 2,000 years since it was first introduced into China. It features the coexistence of three language-family types of Buddhism, namely, Chinese, Tibetan, and Pali Buddhism that are found within a territory of 9,600,000 sq km. But the three language-family types of Buddhism spread into China in succession, and they are characterized by different forms and contents. Due to the coexistence of the three language-family types of Buddhism, China abounds in Buddhist literature and other materials, an accumulation perhaps unparalleled in the world.

The book *Buddhism: Rituals and Monastic Life* in the *China Tour Guide* series, written by Zheng Lixin, puts emphasis on each aspect of Chinese Buddhism. For example, this book gives a brief introduction to the history, sects, relationship between Chinese and foreign Buddhists, temples, four famous mountains, monks' societies and organizations, classics of Sanzang (*Tripitaka*), grotto arts, Buddhist festivals, major Buddhist activities, and Buddhist societies and organizations. This book is not only suitable for tourists at home and abroad, but also worth reading by anyone who wants to know about Chinese Buddhism. The book is written in an easy and fluent style with accurate historical records and some interesting legends and stories. As this book was soon to be published, Mr. Zheng wanted me to write some words, and I could not decline. To show my willingness and to accumulate virtue, I just wrote the above paragraph as the book's preface.

Dao Shuren

Vice-President of the
Chinese Buddhist Association

Foreword

With a chronicled history of some 5,000 years, China is one of the oldest civilizations in the world. The splendid Chinese culture has made important contributions to the progress and development of humanity, and holds forth the fascination of fabulous natural scenes and richly diversified characters and manners. Many of the scenic spots and sites of cultural and historical interest are associated with Buddhism.

Buddhism in this country falls into three language systems: Chinese, Tibetan, and Pali. The emphasis in this book is on Chinese Buddhism, with a brief introduction to Tibetan and Pali Buddhism in Chapter 1.

Buddhism spread to China from India during the Han Dynasty around the first century BC. However, it took some 600 years for Buddhism to become part of the Chinese cultural environment. While its basic creeds remain largely intact, major changes have taken place in both the spiritual and material life of the cloisters. Such changes were conducive to the dissemination and development of Buddhism, for dogmatism and conservatism would have gotten this religion nowhere in an alien land. After Buddhism met its demise in India, China became its second cradle and the origin for various sects in many other countries and regions.

Tourism is now booming in this country because of ongoing

reform and the opening up to the outside world. Visitors are arriving in droves, and many of them are curious about the religious life of the Chinese. This book is designed to satisfy that curiosity by telling a little about every aspect of Chinese Buddhism.

The emergence of the three language systems of Buddhism in China tallied with the three stages of development of Buddhism in India. While the Han-inhabited regions became repositories of Buddhism in the intermediary stage of its development during the first century BC, it was not until the seventh to eighth centuries that the early and late stages of Buddhism found their way into Yunnan and Tibet. The ups and downs of Buddhism in these three stages of development are dealt with in Chapter 1.

After Buddhism came to China, different sects began to emerge. The Tiantai sect was the first, and it was followed by seven others. Chapter 2 renders a brief account of the origin of each of these sects and their tenets.

Buddhism advocates the delivery of the multitude of people from misery through benevolence, and admonishes people to perform good deeds during their lifetimes. Buddhists in China have always maintained friendly cultural exchanges with their counterparts in other Asian countries. From Chapter 3 readers may learn some of the Buddha's teachings and gain some idea about Buddhist exchanges between China and the rest of Asia.

Chapters 4 and 5 take a look at the architecture, layout, and interior furnishings of Buddhist temples in this country, and provide the reader with a brief tour of the four holy mountains and some of the major ancestral establishments of the eight sects of Chinese Buddhism. As the saying goes, "Of all the renowned mountains under heaven, most are home to monks." These four mountains are not only peppered with monasteries and temples, but also each is endowed with a divine landscape. No visit to this country is complete without seeing these mountains. This is particularly the case for tourists who believe in Buddhism.

Chapter 6 answers a series of questions about the monks' organizational structure, commandments and prohibitions, their financial sources, and life in the cloisters.

The abundance of Buddhist canonical writings and translations are a crystallization of two millennia's diligent work by scholars at home and scholars from abroad. These books, known as the *dharma*, are one of Buddhism's *triratna* (three treasures, the other two being the Buddha and Sangha) as well as a component part of the Chinese cultural heritage. The origin and formation of these books, the translation work associated with them, and the composition of the *Tripitaka* are explored in Chapter 7.

Buddhist grottoes are found all over the land. One of them, the Dunhuang Grottoes, has had a history of 1,600 years since it came under construction during the Western and Eastern Jin dynasties (265-420), and compares favourably with the famous Ajanta Caves of India in terms of engineering size and artistic attainment in sculpture and mural painting. These grottoes give apt expression to the diligence and wisdom of the labouring people of ancient China. Chapter 8 introduces five major grottoes the traveler may wish to see.

The traveler is invariably enchanted by the ritualistic activities of Buddhist festivals. However, of all the festive and ceremonious occasions in a Chinese temple, only the ceremony that marks the birthday of Sakyamuni is relatively elaborate. This and some other rituals are dealt with in Chapter 9 as an orientation for those wishing to take a ringside look at what is happening in a Chinese monastery.

Chapter 10 acquaints the reader with Buddhist organizations

and undertakings in present-day China, with the spotlight on the Chinese Buddhist Association and its achievements.

Numerous Buddhist temples are found in urban and rural areas. Apart from those already mentioned in the previous chapters, a selection of fifty important temples is featured in the Appendix for the use of the prospective visitor.

Chi Lin Nunnery, Hong Kong

The Mahavira Hall of the
Guangji Temple, Beijing

A replica of an ancient Buddhist
statue given to the Chinese Buddhist Association by Buddhists in
Sri Lanka

Lingshan Giant Buddha behind the Xiangfu Temple, Wuxi, Jiangsu Province

The 1,000-handed Guanyin in Xiangguo Temple, Kaifeng, Henan Province

The Big Wild Goose Pagoda in Ci'en Temple, Xi'an, Shaanxi Province

Stone inscription of the 500 Arhats in the Baoji Temple, Pingxiang, Jiangxi Province

The dagoba in Qixia Temple, Nanjing, Jiangsu Province

The jade statue of Buddha in Yufo (Jade Buddha) Temple, Shanghai

Guanyin (Avalokitesvara) Cave on Mount Putuo, Zhejiang Province

The White Pagoda in Tayuan Temple, Mount Wutai, Shanxi Province

Statues in the Yungang Grottoes, Datong, Shanxi Province

Ming Dynasty bronze statue of Guanyin (Avalokitesvara) in the Lingshan Temple, Chaoyang, Guangdong Province

The Beamless Hall in Wannian (Ten-Thousand-Year) Temple on Mount Emei, Sichuan Province

"Light of the Buddha", a natural phenominon often seen on Mount Emei

The Giant Stone Buddha in Leshan, Sichuan Province

Buddhist statues in the Mogao Caves at Dunhuang in Gansu Province

Buddhist Pagodas in Ruili City, Yunnan Province

Potala Palace in Lhasa, Tibet

The Gilded Laughing Buddha in the
Tashilhunpo Monastery, Tibet

A Tangkha painting

Chapter 1

A General Situation of Chinese Buddhism

1. Introduction and Development of Han Buddhism

The term "Han Buddhism," or to be exact "Buddhism in the Chinese Language," can be attributed to the fact that after Buddhism was brought into China all its scriptures have been translated into Chinese.

Opinions differ as to exactly when Buddhism spread into China, but only two of them prevail.

One has it that Buddhism was brought into this country in 2 BC (1st year of the Yuanshou reign, Western Han Dynasty), when Yicun arrived from Indo-Scythae to dictate Buddhist scriptures to a man named Qin Jingxian.

The other is based on the legend that in 64 AD (7th year of the Yongping reign, Eastern Han Dynasty), Liu Zhuang, or Emperor Mingdi, dreamed one night of a golden man wearing a sparkling necklace who was flying over his palace. At morning court the following day, he asked his ministers what this incident implied. Fu Yi, the grand scribe, replied, "I heard that there is a god in the West whose name is Buddha, and he might be the person Your Majesty dreamed of." Convinced, the emperor dispatched an 18-member mission headed by Cai Yin to go to the West in search of the Buddhist doctrine. In 67 AD (10th year of the Yongping reign), the mission arrived in Indo-Scythae where they met two Indian monks, Kasyapamatanga and Gobharana. At Cai Yin's invitation, the two monks brought Buddhist scriptures and sculptures to Luoyang, the Chinese capital, where they began to translate the *Forty-two Chapter Sutra* into Chinese. Their arrival is thus thought to be the beginning of the dissemination of Buddhism in China.

It is difficult to tell which of the two ideas holds water. While scholars espouse the first opinion, the second is widely believed among Buddhists. However, given the narrow gap of seventy years between the two, both theories indicate that Buddhism first made inroads into China during the interregnum between the Western and Eastern Han dynasties.

In the beginning the Chinese regarded the Buddha as a god from some alien land, putting him on a par with the Yellow Emperor, Laozi, or immortals well versed in the art of divination[1], and the popularity of Buddhism was limited to the elite. However, it did not take long for Buddhism to acquire a following among the common people, despite the absence of canonical texts. It was not until the mid-second century that monks began to arrive from the Western Territories to preach the doctrines and translate the scriptures. According to history books, An Shigao, a prince of Parthia (present-day Iran), and Lokaksema from Indo-Scythae, were the two earliest monks to arrive as Buddhist translators. With more and more scriptures being translated into Chinese, Buddhism gradually presented itself to the Chinese not only as source of spiritual solace but also as a profound philosophy that played an important role in the development of civilization.

---

[1] Both the Yellow Emperor and Laozi are honored as founders of Taoism, and the "immortals" here refer to those Taoist alchemists who successfully achieved immortality and mastered the unpredictable art of divination.

During the Han Dynasty, the law banned people from relinquishing the secular world to become monks. But there were exceptions, and one of these was Yan Fotiao, a child prodigy from Huainan (in present-day east Fengyang County, Anhui Province). No historical records are extant to show who his master might have been, but he was regarded as the first Buddhist scholar in China to translate Buddhist scriptures, and he authored a number of treatises on Buddhism.

Buddhism had come a long way by the Three Kingdoms Period (220-265). The prohibition of the Hans against people becoming monks was lifted, and more and more temples were erected. But Buddhism was limited to the kingdoms of Wei and Wu, and remained little known to the kingdom of Shu in the remote southwest part of the country. Buddhism in the kingdom of Wei was highlighted by two major events. One was that in 250 AD (2nd year of the Jiaping reign), Dharmakala arrived and made Chinese Buddhist history by becoming the first Indian monk to lecture Chinese monks on the commandments and prohibitions. The other event was that Chinese monks began to embark on westbound pilgrimages in search of Buddhist doctrines. According to history books, in 260 (5th year of the Ganlu reign, Wei Kingdom), the Chinese monk Zhu Shixing began a solitary tour of the Western Territories. When he arrived at Khotan he obtained certain scriptures. His success exerted a great impact on pilgrims of later generations and unleashed a tidal wave of westward pilgrimages among Chinese monks during the Western and Eastern Jin dynasties (265-420).

The popularity of Buddhism in the kingdom of Wu was ascribed to two men's efforts. One was Zhi Qian, an Indo-Scythian who grew up in China and was educated in Chinese culture as a child. When Zhi Qian arrived in the kingdom of Wu towards the end of the Han dynasty, he showed his flair as a diplomat and translated many Buddhist sutras while there. The other man was Kang Senghui, a native of Soghdiana whose family lived in India for generations. He accompanied his merchant father and arrived in present-day Wuzhou, Guangxi, where he received a Chinese education during his childhood. When he became a teenager his parents died. He then became tonsured and started systematic studies of Buddhism in a temple. In 247 (8th year of the Zhengshi reign, Wei Kingdom), he traveled to Jianye (present-day Nanjing), capital of the Kingdom of Wu, where he won the confidence of the king of Wu, Sun Quan, who then built the Jianchu Monastery, the first of its kind in the kingdom. Sun Quan dedicated it to Kang Senghui. The construction of this monastery unveiled a period of prosperity for Buddhism in the Kingdom of Wu.

During the Western and Eastern Jin Dynasties (265-420), large numbers of Buddhist scriptures and classics were translated into Chinese, paving the way to a fusing of traditional Chinese culture with Buddhist philosophy. During the Western Jin Dynasty (265-316) Dharmaraksa emerged as the most prolific Buddhist translator of the time. An Indo-Scythian who lived with his family in Dunhuang, he was converted to Buddhism, traveled with his master to many kingdoms in the Western Territories, and in the process mastered thirty-six different languages. Returning to Dunhuang with a heavy load of Buddhist sutras that were popular in these kingdoms, he dedicated the rest of his life to translation, and rendered a total of 175 Buddhist scriptures into Chinese.

The Eastern Jin Dynasty (317-420) was ensconced in the safety of south China, keeping the 16 kingdoms up north at bay through the natural barrier of the Yangtze River. Mount Lushan and the city of Jianye (present-day Nanjing) emerged as two centers of Buddhism in the south, where many monks were engaged in the translation of Buddhist scriptures. In the North, Buddhism found its center in Chang'an (present-day Xi'an), where Kumarajiva and his team of Chinese and Indian scholar-translators rendered many scriptures into Chinese.

The increase in the number of Chinese translations of Buddhist scriptures gave rise to a new discipline of learning designed to rediscover the truth of Buddhism at a time when the metaphysical learning of Laozi and Zhuangzi was in vogue. That was why quite a few Buddhists were also versed in Taoism, and their knowledge was often a mixture of both religions. Zhi Dun (314-366) was an outstanding representative in this regard.

During the Eastern Jin Dynasty so many people embarked on pilgrimages to the West in search of the Buddha's holy words that this had become something of a campaign. One of the well-accomplished pilgrims was Fa Xian (c.337-c.422). In 399 (3rd year of the Long'an reign), he teamed up with Hui Jing and two other fellow disciples to set off from Chang'an for India in search of commandments and scriptures. Their 11-year journey brought them to more than thirty kingdoms. In India, they paid homage to Buddhist sites and obtained a number of scriptures and commandments. In Sinhala (present-day Sri Lanka), Fa Xian was moved to tears when he saw local merchants offering Chinese-made silk fans as sacrifices to the Buddha. He became so homesick that two years later he boarded a ship in Sinhala, and braving life-threatening risks on the sea returned to China in 412 (8th year of the Yixi reign, Eastern Jin Dynasty).

In the North, Kumarajiva was not the only prolific translator of Buddhist scriptures and classics. There were two others who played a pivotal role in this field. One was Fo Tucheng and the other is Shi Dao'an.

Fo Tucheng (232-348), a Buddhist from Kucha, arrived in Luoyang in 310 (4th year of the Yongjia reign, Western Jin

Dynasty) but war and turmoil dashed his hopes of building a monastery to disseminate Buddhism. At that time, General Shi Le's army was stationed in Gepo (north of present-day Xincai, Henan Province) and was terrorizing the area by the indiscriminate killing of innocent people, including quite a few monks. Fo Tucheng, showing great sympathy for the misery of the local people, risked his own life by going to see Shi Le at his headquarters. The general asked him what Buddhism could accomplish in divination. Fo, knowing that the general was a savage, impervious to reason, decided to impress him by his extraordinary powers. According to Volume III of the *Biographies of Preeminent Monks*, Fo filled a container with some water, lit some incense sticks and began to chant incantations. In no time a green lotus popped out of the water, emitting brilliant light and color. With this trick the monk caught the fancy of the general and won his confidence. He went on to persuade the general to stop the wonton killing and exercise the rule of virtue. Shi Le obliged, and as a result the lives of many people slated for decapitation were spared. She Le became the founder of the Kingdom of Posterior Zhao (319-351). His reign lasted for 14 years, and after his death he was succeeded by his son, Hong, but shortly thereafter the power was usurped by Shi Hu.

The new king, however, had great faith in Fo Tucheng, and never made a decision without consulting him. Thanks to Fo's effort, Buddhism flourished during the reign of Shi Hu, and construction of Buddhist monasteries became something of a fad. It is said that Fo alone had tens of thousands of followers, and more than eight hundred temples were built under his influence.

Shi Dao'an was a native of Fuliu in Changshan (northwest of present-day Quyang, Hebei Province), who became an orphan when his parents died young. After he was launched into his monkhood, he impressed his fellow monks with his photographic memory. However, his master was not impressed. Only after he became a disciple of Fo Tucheng did he earn respect for his talent. When he made a name for himself, he became the leader of a group of several hundred monks. However, he led an unsettled life due to war and chaos, and it was not until he arrived in Xiangyang (in present-day Hubei Province) that he settled down as a lecturer and writer. For his high moral and academic accomplishments he won the adoration of Emperor Xiaowu of the Eastern Jin Dynasty and Fu Jian, who made himself king of the former Qin Dynasty (350-394) in Chang'an. In 379 (4th year of the Taiyuan reign, Eastern Jin Dynasty), following his son's army conquering of Xiangyang, Fu Jian had Shi Dao'an moved to the Wuchong Monastery in Chang'an. While there, the monk took advantage of his talent and position to contribute a great deal to the dissemination of Buddhism. In the process, his reputation as an accomplished scholar and man of honor spread far and wide. Kumarajiva, living in the Western Territories at the time, held him in high esteem and extolled him as the "Sage of the East."

During the Southern and Northern Dynasties (420-589), China was torn apart by separatist regimes, and Buddhism embarked on different courses of development. In the South, emphasis was placed on decoding the philosophy of the Buddhist sutras, while in the North followers were devoted to the practice of *dhyana* (meditation) and *samadhi* (concentration). The emperors of the Southern Dynasties — Song (420-479), Qi (479-502), Liang (502-557), and Chen (557-589) — were all supporters of Buddhism, but none were more pious than Emperor Wudi of the Liang, who had previously been a Taoist. At a meeting of 2,000 monks and laymen in 504 (3rd year of the Tianjian reign), Wudi announced his decision to give up Taoism and convert to

Buddhism. He had monasteries built and Buddhist statues sculpted and enshrined, and he devoted himself to the study of Buddhist philosophy. On four occasions he renounced his monarchy and worked as a coolie in a local monastery, but on each occasion his court ministers paid a large sum in ransom to get him back on the throne. The Chinese monks' habit of eating only vegetarian foods had its beginning in the order of this emperor. After toppling the Liang Dynasty, the emperors of the Chen Dynasty continued to follow Buddhism and carried on with the dethroned Liang emperor's practices. During the Southern Dynasties, both the number of Buddhist monasteries and population of monks and nuns increased considerably, and the translation of Buddhist scriptures and writings went on uninterrupted. Major translators at the time included Gunabhadra (394-468) and Paramartha (499-569).

The development of Buddhism in the Northern Dynasties, that is the Northern Wei (386-534), Eastern Wei (534-550), Western Wei (535-557), Northern Qi (550-577), and Northern Zhou (557-581), had its fill of ups and downs. Most of the monarchs of these dynasties believed in Buddhism. Under their aegis, the construction of temples and translation of sutras thrived more than before, and the number of monks and nuns reached an all-time high of over two million. The world-famous Yungang and Longmen grottoes, and the unparalleled Yongning Monastery were constructed during this period and remain to this day a part of the precious Chinese cultural legacy. However, in the midst of this prosperity, Buddhism suffered two telling blows that Buddhists refer to as the "Disasters of the Dharma." These were the campaign launched by Emperor Taiwu of the Northern Wei Dynasty in 438 and the campaign by Emperor Wudi of the Northern Zhou Dynasty in 574 to eliminate Buddhism. Neither lasted long, but nevertheless incurred colossal losses to Buddhism.

The golden age of Buddhism came during the Sui (581-618) and Tang (618-907) dynasties. Yang Jian, founder of the Sui, was already working to resurrect Buddhism from the destruction wrought by Emperor Wudi during his days as prime minister of the Northern Zhou Dynasty. After he took the throne, he masterminded a renaissance of Buddhism in China. The Sui Dynasty was later overthrown by the Tang Dynasty, but Buddhism continued to grow. Actually sailing was even smoother during the Zhenguan reign of the Tang Dynasty, Li Shimin, or Emperor Taizong. With the lone exception of Emperor Wuzong of the Tang, all the Sui and Tang emperors were worshipers or supporters of Buddhism.

During the Sui and Tang dynasties new generations of outstanding personages emerged in the Buddhist circles, and an unprecedented number of Buddhist books were translated into Chinese. The celebrated monk Xuanzang alone translated 75 scriptures comprising 1,335 volumes in Chinese. Joining him in the effort was Yijing (635-713). The other major translators were from outside China. These included Siksananda (652-710) from the Western Territories, and Amoghavajra (705-774) from India. The work of these eminent translators vastly enriched the collection of Buddhist sutras in the Chinese language and became a component part of Chinese culture during the heyday of the Tang. Thus, after about six centuries of repeated adaptation to the local environment once it made its first inroads into China during the Han Dynasty, Buddhism gradually became fused with traditional Chinese culture. But it was not until the emergence of the eight sects during the Sui-Tang period that Buddhism completed its process of domestication and became a Chinese religion in form and essence.

It seems to be a norm that things turn into their opposites when they go the extremes. After a period of unprecedented prosperity during the height of the Tang Dynasty, Buddhism was in for serious destruction during the dynasty's waning years. This was because of a crackdown on Buddhism in 842 (2nd year of the Huichang reign), during which huge numbers of sutras were burned, numerous monasteries were closed down, monks were forced to return to a secular life, and Buddhism went on a decline.

Buddhism was somewhat revived during the early Song Dynasty (960-1279), but it never enjoyed the kind of prosperity it had during the Sui-Tang period. Emperor Huizong (1101-1125) of the Song Dynasty was initially opposed to Buddhism, but fortunately he changed his attitude before too long. The development of Buddhism during the Song Dynasty was characterized by the prosperity of a single sect, the Chan, but the Tiantai sect gained substantial growth as well. Another salient feature of Song-Dynasty Buddhism was its advocacy for both the Chan sect's practice of meditation in a crossed-legged sitting posture and the Jingtu (Pure Land) sect's practice of chanting the name of the Buddha.

The rulers of the Yuan Dynasty (1271-1368) advocated Lamaism, or Tibetan Buddhism. A number of eminent monks emerged during the Ming (1368-1644) and Qing (1644-1911) dynasties, but nothing could arrest Buddhism's general decline that began after the fall of the Tang Dynasty.

The study of Buddhism came somewhat back into its own by the late Qing Dynasty and early Republican years thanks to the efforts of some renowned scholars, and Buddhist seminaries were established to train high-caliber preachers. The result was that quite a few eminent Buddhist personages emerged during the Republican period (1912-1949). These included Dixian (1858-1935), Yuexia (1858-1917), Taixu (1889-1947), Hongyi (1880-1942), Xuyun (1840-1959), Yuanying (1878-1953), and

Yinguang (1861-1940), and the lay Buddhists Yang Wenhui (1837-1911), Ouyang Jingwu (1871-1944), and Han Qingjing (1884-1949), whose hard work and dedication gave hope to the revitalization of Buddhism.

After the founding of the People's Republic of China in 1949, the People's Government has adopted a policy of religious freedom. This has enabled Buddhists to enjoy the freedom of religious belief while devoting themselves to the prosperity of both the country and Buddhism.

2. Tibetan Buddhism: Introduction and Development

Tibetan Buddhism is the school of Buddhism predicated on scriptures that have been translated into Tibetan. Because its monks are known as lamas in the Tibetan language, Tibetan Buddhism is also called "Lamaism."

The development of Tibetan Buddhism falls into two stages. The first stage lasted for approximately 200 years from the mid-seventh century to the mid-ninth century; the second stage has continued to this day since the mid-tenth century.

Prior to the seventh century, the Tibetans had no written language. In the early seventh century, under the rule of the wise and far-sighted king Songtsan Gampo, Tibet began to grow in strength by gradually expanding its territory and unifying the tribes on the Qinghai-Tibet Plateau. To create a written language so that he could issue orders and exchange documents with neighboring countries, he selected a group of noble house children and sent them to study in Kashmir. Among these was Thonmi Sambhota, who excelled in linguistic studies and returned home to become the inventor of a grammar and written language for Tibet, thereby furnishing favorable conditions for the translation and dissemination of Buddhist literature.

The invention of this written language encouraged Songtsan Gampo to step up the introduction of Buddhism into Tibet. Under his leadership, translators teamed up to work on the scriptures, and the sculptures of the Buddha and other deities in the Buddhist pantheon were enshrined for local worshipers. To show goodwill to neighboring countries, he married Princess Bhrkuti of Nepal in the West and Princess Wencheng of the Tang Dynasty to the East. Both brides brought their countries' versions of Buddhist statues with them when they arrived in Lhasa. Construction of temples thus proceeded in Tibet for these statues. Songtsan Gampo also formulated laws according to the principles of Buddhism, and ushered Tibet into civilized society.

Several generations after the death of Songtsan Gampo, Buddhism entered another stage of robust growth under the rule of Tride Tsugtan (reigned 704-755), who married Princess Jincheng of the Tang Dynasty and sent people to study Buddhism in the interior of China. They eventually returned with large numbers of Buddhist scriptures. Development of Buddhism in Tibet, however, was not smooth sailing. It suffered setbacks at the hands of the stubborn followers of an indigenous religion, Bon. It was only after Tride Tsugtan's son, Trisung Detsan (reigned 755-797), took the throne, that Tibetan Buddhism revived. During the 762-766 period, the renowned Samye Monastery was built.

In 767, an Indian delegation of 12 *bhiksus* (mendicants) arrived in Tibet and held the first summons ceremony to introduce commandments in the Buddhist history of Tibet. Under the reign of Trisung Detsan, large numbers of Indian sutras were translated into Tibetan, and Tibetan Buddhism reached its zenith during this stage of development. It was also during this period that the compilation of the *Tripitaka* was completed, with many Indian and Chinese scholars joining their Tibetan counterparts in the translation of this colossal Buddhist work. Thanks to their concerted efforts they left a precious cultural legacy for the Tibetan people.

In 841, the king of Tibet, Lang Darma (?-842), masterminded a purge of Buddhists, incurring tremendous losses to the religion. As a result, for a little more than a century Buddhist monks virtually disappeared from the land of Tibet — they took refuge in the safety of the Kham region. The persecution of Buddhism ended in the early tenth century, when Tibetans began to arrive in Kham to learn the doctrines, and Tibetan Buddhism staged a slow comeback that marked the beginning of its second stage of development.

In 1042, the Tibetans invited Mahanayaka Atisa (982-1054) from India to preach on Buddhism. Atisa, translated as "Shusheng" in Chinese, was actually not the real name of the man who was the second of three brothers in the royal family of a tiny Indian kingdom. It was an honorary title bestowed on him by a king of Ngari. Translation and preaching were the tasks of Atisa's mission to Tibet, where he was only supposed to stay three years but remained there after the road of return to India was blocked by war in the border region of Nepal. In 1046, he settled in Nyetang, where he died at the age of 72. During his lifetime, Atisa translated more than a hundred Buddhist writings, which greatly replenished the literature of Tibetan Buddhism. As an important figure in the second stage of development of Tibetan Buddhism, his academic ideas had a far-reaching influence on the later development of Lamaism.

During the Yuan Dynasty (1271-1368), Emperor Kublai Khan appointed the celebrated Lama Phags-pa of Tibet as an imperial patriarch and entrusted him with the task of creating a written form for the Mongolian language. As a result, Buddhism at that time reached its acme in Tibet, and Tibetan Buddhism spread throughout Mongolia.

The Ming Dynasty (1368-1644) saw the emergence of another famous personage in Tibetan Buddhism. He was none other than Tsong-kha-pa, a native of Qinghai who began studying Buddhism in Lhasa after he was ordained as a monk. He rose to fame, wrote copiously, and went all out in boosting Tibetan Buddhism, acquiring quite a following and eventually emerging as the guru of Lamaism in its later stage of development. He revamped the religious system of Tibet so as to cope with rampant corruption and safeguard the integrity of Buddhism. He eventually convened a grand assembly and established the Gelupa sect, or Yellow Hat sect, so named because its members wear yellow hats. The Gelupa is the dominant sect of Tibetan Buddhism, having the largest number of followers and most lamaseries in Tibet.

During the course of five centuries of development after Buddhism first spread into Tibet in the eighth century, Tibetan Buddhism has branched into 11 sects: Bka'-gdems-pa, Bka'-brayud-pa, Sa-skya-pa, Jo-nang-pa, Shi-byed-pa, Zhi-byed-pa, Ko-tra-pa, Shangs-pa Bka'-brgyud-pa, Sha-lu-pa, Rnying-mama-pa, and Dge-lugs-pa (Gelupa).

The *Tripitaka* of Tibetan Buddhism consists of two parts. The first part is *Kanjur*, or *The Section of the Buddha*, which includes the holy words of the Buddha and the commandments and secret incantations he formulated. The second part is *Bstang'gyur*, or *The Section of Ancestors*, which is a collection of eulogies to Tibetan kings, and enunciations of sutras and incantations. Totalling more than 4,000 volumes, the Tibetan *Tripitaka* is a component part of the world's cultural heritage.

Two persons have figured prominently among the religious leaders of Tibetan Buddhism. These are the Panchen Lama and the Dalai Lama. Both have been regarded as reincarnations of Tsong-kha-pa's two disciples. Tsong-kha-pa was the reformist leader of Tibetan Buddhism. The current Panchen is the 11th reincarnate, and the current Dalai is the 14th.

The first Panchen Lama was Khedrub Je (1385-1438) born in the village of Chewo in Latu Toshong in Tsang (the part of Tibet that has Xigaze as its chief city). He became a novice and began learning the doctrines while a child. At 18, he showed his talent in writing. At 23, he became a disciple of Tsong-kha-pa. In 1431, he became the abbot of the Ganden Monastery. In 1438, he died at the age of 54, ending his life as a famed Buddhist scholar with a wealth of writings to his credit. The later generations of the Panchen Lama were all said to be his reincarnates. The current 11th Penchen Lama is still a young boy.

The first Dalai Lama was Gedun Truppa (1391-1474), born at the Shabtu Pasture near the Sakya Monastery in Tsang. The son of a poor family, he grazed cattle for other families as a young child. He began his monkhood at seven. At 25 he attended the lectures of Tsong-kha-pa. In 1426 he became a Lamaist preacher, and after he turned 40 he began to write. In 1447, he built the Tashilhunpo Monastery. In 1474, he died at the age of 84, going down in Tibetan history as a preeminent Buddhist scholar and author of many religious writings. It is said that the later generations of the Dalai Lama were all Gedun Truppa's reincarnates. The incumbent 14th Dalai went into exile in India during his 1959 rebellion in Tibet.[1]

---

[1] The material for this section was derived from Master Fazun's "Former-stage Buddhism in Tibet" and "Latter-stage Buddhism in Tibet," *China Buddhism*, Vol. I, pp. 134-158.

3. Pali Buddhism: Introduction and Development

Buddhism in the Pali language refers to the school of Buddhism whose scriptures are rendered in the Pali language. Pali Buddhism is also known as Southern Buddhism or the Southern Theravada.

Pali was a local dialect of ancient India. Without any written form, it has been rendered in different written languages. Thus the Pali scriptures of Buddhism in Sri Lanka, Thailand, and Myanmar are written out in the various alphabets of these countries, but the pronunciation is largely the same.

Pali Buddhism is popular in the southeast Asian countries as well as in the Dai-inhabited areas of Yunnan Province of China. Opinions differ as to when it found its way into Yunnan. An analysis of different historical accounts leads to the conclusion that Pali Buddhism first spread from Myanmar to present-day Xishuangbanna, Dehong, Simao, Lincang, and Baoshan areas in Yunnan some 1,300 years ago, roughly between the sixth and seventh centuries. This school of Buddhism is popular among the ethnic minority Dais, De'angs, Blangs, and some of the Vas.

The development of Southern Buddhism in Yunnan also falls into two stages. The first stage, from the seventh to the 12th century, saw the dissemination of this school of Buddhism from Myanmar. The first Buddhist temple in the province, the Wabajie Temple in Xishuangbanna, was erected in 615. Some simple prayer rooms also emerged at that time. During this period there was no written form for the Dai language, and the Buddhist sutras were preached and memorized by rote. The population of followers was small. They stayed together indoors during the rainy season and engaged in preaching in other seasons.

A large-scale war broke out between the Pugan Dynasty of Myanmar and Thailand in the 12th century. The ceaseless war forced the inhabitants of Xishuangbanna and neighboring areas to flee their homes, leaving their farmlands in waste. Pali Buddhism thus went into decline. The 12th century marked the end of the first stage of development of Southern Buddhism in Yunnan.

Pali Buddhism staged a comeback in Xishuangbanna after the 12th century. But the source of this was no longer Myanmar, but Chiengmai in present-day Thailand. The preachers from there brought Thai editions of the scriptures, and began the construction of temples, thereby enabling Buddhism to be fused with the local culture. A ritual system was formulated as well. Local scholars translated and annotated large numbers of Pali scriptures into Thai, which gained popularity among people who spoke the Dai, Lolo, and Lao dialects.

Southern Theravada consists of four sects: Run, Baizhuang, Duolie, and Zuodi. The Run sect is divided into the Baiba and Baisun subsects, and the Duolie sect comprises the Gongdan, Suteman, Runjing, and Mianzuo subsects. The difference between these sects lies in the degree of strictness with which the commandments are enforced, and the loudness or speed in which incantations are recited. Some of the sects originally came into being because members wanted to be different — they were not separated by controversies over religious concepts. Thus this division of the Southern Theravada of Yunnan into various sects is devoid of practical meaning. The following is an interpretation of the names of the four major sects.

The Chinese character "run" is a term of address used by the Dai people for the Lanna people living in the area around Chiangmai in ancient Thailand. They call that area "Mengrun," the people there "Thai-run," and the sect of Buddhism that spread from there the "Run sect." Having the largest following, the Run is the most influential of all Buddhist sects in Yunnan.

The word "baizhuang" in the Dai language means "monastic sect." But because the Dai transliteration of the word for "sect" is pronounced "bai," which sounds like the Dai word for "flee," the residents of the Dehong area call the Baizhuang sect the "fleeing monastic sect" — a misunderstanding caused by the similarity of pronunciation between the words "sect" and "flee" in the Dai dialect.

The word "duolie" is Myanmese, and is translated into the Dai language as "zhizhu," meaning "stop it." Legend has it that the founding father of the Duolie sect once violated the commandments, and his guru punished him by ordering him to hang a pot filled with water from his neck and to keep walking. A tiny hole the size of a needle point was bored into the bottom of the pot so that the water could slowly leak out. The poor monk was allowed to stop walking only after the pot ran out of water. It is said that he was walking in a grove of trees when the pot was drained of its last drop of water. He settled down there, built a monastery, and established the sect known as "Duolie," meaning "Stop it."

The word "zuodi" is the Chinese transliteration of the Myanmese word that means sincerity. Legend has it that the Zuodi sect broke away from the Duolie sect and became known for its strictness in observing the commandments.

The monasteries of Theravada Buddhism in Yunnan are of three levels. At the top level is the general temple of an administrative area, such as the general monastery of Xishuangbanna. At the middle level are the central monasteries of Bannas and Mengs, and at the bottom level are the village temples. For a long time these temples served as both religious sanctuaries and cultural centers where local people went to learn how to read and write from the monks. This situation changed after the establishment of schools. However, though the temples have retained only their function as religious sanctuaries and monk's abodes, they remain as centers for the dissemination and preservation of traditional culture, and as such retain their popularity in local communities. During Buddhist and folk festivals, followers make it a point of assembling in local temples to worship and celebrate. Different from their counterparts elsewhere in China, the temples in Yunnan are enshrined only with the likenesses of Sakyamuni.

The people living in areas in Yunnan where Theravada Buddhism is a popular religion follow more or less the same customs as the people in Myanmar, Thailand, and Laos. For example, boys are obliged to spend some time in a monastery before returning again to secular life. At a minimum, the duration of their stay is three months, but a boy may choose to stay in a monastery for his lifetime, which means he has to forsake marriage and dedicate himself to the Buddha for the rest of his life. Few people today, however, make this choice. Monks in Yunnan fall in two categories as they do elsewhere: *sramaneras* (novices) and *bhiksus* (mendicants). It was not until modern times that a tiny number of *sramanerikas* (female novices) joined the local religious ranks. There are as many as ten monastic or honorary titles for eminent *bhiksus* and abbots.

The Theravada's canonical classics are known as the *Pali Tripitaka* and consist of scriptures, commandments, and treatises. The title is the same as that in Chinese Buddhism, but the content is vastly different. The *Pali Tripitaka* furnishes valuable materials for a study of primitive forms of Buddhism and sectarian Buddhism and for the comparative research of Chinese and Tibetan Buddhism. Since ancient times quite a few scholars of the Dai-inhabited areas have been transliterating, translating, and annotating books of the *Pali Tripitaka* into their native language, leaving behind a major cultural heritage that, if systematically sorted out, could be of major importance for academic research and international cultural exchanges.[1]

---

[1] This section is based on Dao Shuren's article "The Southern Branch of Theravada Buddhism in Yunnan," Issue No. 1, *Fayin*, 1985.

Chapter 2

Sects in Han Buddhism

1. Tiantai Sect

The earliest sect to emerge in Chinese Buddhism was the Tiantai sect, founded by the prestigious monk Zhiyi (538-597) during the interregnum between the Chen (557-589) and Sui (581-618) dynasties. A native of Huarong (present-day Jianli, Hubei Province) whose style names were De'an and Zhizhe, Zhiyi is said to have had double pupils in each of his eyes. When he was 18 he became a novice under the tutelage of Monk Faxu of the Guoyuan Temple in

Zhiyi, founder of the Tiantai sect of Han Buddhism

Xiangzhou (present-day Changsha, Hunan Province) and began learning the commandments from another monk by the name of Huikuang. Two years later he was ordained with *Upasampana* (*Complete Commandments*). With a penchant for meditating on the *dharmaparyaya* (dharma door), he arrived at Dasu Mountain in Guangzhou (present-day Guangshan County, Henan Province) in 560 (1st year of the Tianjia reign, Chen Dynasty), where he soon won the favor of his master, Monk Huisi. In 567 (1st year of the Daguang reign, Chen Dynasty), he settled down in the Waguan Temple of Jinling (present-day Nanjing, Jiangsu Province), where he preached the methodology of *dhyana* (meditation) and began writing. In 575 (7th year of the Taijian reign, Chen Dynasty) he arrived at Tiantai Mountain (in present-day Tiantai County, Zhejiang Province) for his own meditation sessions. In 585 (3rd year of the Zhide reign, Chen Dynasty), Shu Bao, the last emperor of the Chen Dynasty, bestowed great respect on Zhi Yi by sending for him to lecture in the Hall of Supreme Being in Jinling. Then, after the downfall of the Chen Dynasty, he settled at Mount Lushan (in present-day Jiangxi Province). In 591 (11th year of the Kaihuang reign, Sui Dynasty), he was invited to Yangzhou to ordain the *Bodhisattva Sila* (*The Precepts of Bodhisattva*)[1] for Yang Guang, the son of Yang Jian, or Emperor Wendi, who had just been decorated as the King of Jin, with Yangzhou as his fiefdom. A year later he returned from Yangzhou to his native town of Jingzhou, where he built the Yuquan Temple on Yuquan Mountain in Dangyang. After the temple was completed he resided there for two years as a preacher. In 595 (15th year of the Kaihuang reign of the Sui Dynasty), he visited Yangzhou once again at the invitation of Yang Guang, and returned to Mount Tiantai in the ninth lunar month of that year.

Zhiyi was posthumously honored as the Grand Master of Tiantai on account of the long years he had spent on Mount Tiantai. Because he regarded Mount Tiantai as his domain, the sect he founded was named "Tiantai sect."

Historical records indicate that in his effort to establish the

---

[1] The *Bodhisattva Sila* consists of 10 commandments of cardinal importance and 48 commandments of secondary importance.

Tiantai sect, Zhiyi had the indispensable assistance of a disciple, Guanding (561-632), who took notes of all his lectures and remarks and compiled them into books to serve as the canons for this sect. The most important of these books are the *Penetrating Exposition on the Saddharma-pundarika-sutra* (*Lotus Sutra*), compiled on the basis of the "five graduated series of deeper meanings," *The Interpretative Commentary on Saddharma-pundarika-sutra*, and *Maha-samatha-vipassyna* that provides a methodology for self-cultivation.

The philosophy of the Tiantai sect originated in the teachings of Huiwen, a monk of the Northern Qi Dynasty (550-577). From his research into the *Mahaprajnaparamita-sastra* and the *Madhyamika-sastra* he derived the theory that "the three kinds of wisdom[1] of Buddhism can be obtained through one's own mind," and came up with the idea of "three kinds of enlightenment with one mind."[2] Huiwen's philosophy was inherited by his disciple Huisi, and when Zhiyi learned it from Huisi, he developed the theory that "the Great Chiliocosm or Universe exists in one mind"[3] The theory later became the guideline for the Tiantai sect.

The Tiantai sect is also known as the Fahua sect because it derives its major doctrine from the *Saddharmapundarika-sutra*. Following the theory of this sutra, members of the Tiantai sect

---

[1] According to the Tiantai sect, the three kinds of wisdom are: 1) earthly or ordinary wisdom; 2) supra-mundane, or spiritual (*sravaka* and *pratye ka-buddha*) wisdom; and 3) supreme wisdom of bodhisattvas and Buddhas.

[2] The three kinds of enlightenment with one mind refer to 1) study of all as void, or immaterial, 2) study of all as unreal, transient, or temporal; and 3) as the via media inclusive of both. If one achieves one kind of enlightenment, he can achieve the two other kinds as well.

[3] Derived from the "three kinds of enlightenment with one mind," this is another method of meditation of the Tiantai sect, meaning that the Great Chiliocosm exists only in one's mind.

divide the life of Sakyamuni into "five periods"[1] and summarize the instructions of different preachers into "eight classifications of the Buddha's teaching."[2]

The Tiantai sect became popular in Chinese religious life during its early days, but went on a decline by the mid-Tang Dynasty when other sects emerged. This prompted Monk Zhanran (711-782) to work to rejuvenate the Tiantai sect, and he produced a wealth of writings. But his efforts proved short-lived as most of the literature of this sect was damaged or missing as a result of the persecution of Buddhism under the 841-846 reign of Emperor Wuzong of the Tang Dynasty. Thanks to the efforts of some followers during the period that encompassed the Five Dynasties (907-960) and the Song Dynasty (960-1279), some of the missing materials were retrieved from Korea and Japan. The Tiantai sect then showed some signs of revival. Towards the end of the Ming Dynasty (1368-1644), a famous monk by the name of Zhixu (or Ouyi) delved into the study of the Tiantai sect, but he was not a follower of this sect, and his research covered the philosophies of other Buddhist sects as well. During the interregnum between the Qing Dynasty (1644-1911) and the Republic (1912-1949), the monk Dixian (1858-1935) made a name for himself as a self-styled advocate of the Tiantai sect, thus giving some hope to resurrecting the waning sect. Today, there is no lack of persons studying the teachings of the Tiantai sect, but few claim to be members.

---

[1] The "five periods" of time: 1) the period of preaching the *Avadamsaka Sutra*, 2) the period of preaching *Agama Sutras*, 3) the period of preaching *Vaipulya Sutras*, 4) the period of preaching *Pranna Sutras*, and 5) the period of preaching the *Lotus Sutra* and the *Nirvana Sutra*.

[2] The "eight classifications of the Buddha's teaching": Four modes of teaching: 1) direct teaching, 2) gradual teaching, 3) esoteric teaching, and 4) indefinite teaching; four periods of teaching: 5) Hinayana teaching, 6) interrelated teaching, 7) differentiated teaching, and 8) completed teaching.

2. Sanlun Sect

The Sanlun sect, also known as the "Three Sastras" sect, derives its name from three books, the *Mulamadhyamaka-karika,* the *Sata-sastra,* and the *Dvadasamukha-sastra.* Its founder was Jizang (549-623), an eminent monk who lived during a period that spanned the late Sui and the early Tang dynasties.

Jizang was a descendent of a man who had fled his native land of Pathia (present-day Iran) as a result of a family feud, and who first arrived at Nanhai (in present-day Guangxi) and then settled in Jinling (present-day Nanjing). Jizang himself was born in Jinling, and his name was given by Paramartha (499-569), the great Indian scholar who was translating Buddhist scriptures there.

During Jizang's childhood his father often brought him to lectures given by Falang (507-581) at the Xinghuang Monastery. At the age of seven, he was tonsured as a novice under the tutelage of Falang. At 19, he showed unusual talent for reciting Falang's lectures and he had already come a long way in his study of the Three Sastras. At the time, the country was torn apart by war between the failing Chen Dynasty and the rising Sui Dynasty. As a result many Buddhist temples were abandoned and monks became homeless. During the turmoil, Jizang scavenged missing Buddhist texts from the ruins of monasteries, and learned a great deal from what he found. After the Sui Dynasty restored peace to the Baiyue region (present-day Zhejiang and Fujian provinces), Jizang went to Huiji (present-day Shaoxing, Zhejiang Province), and settled in the Jiaxiang Temple. By that time he had achieved virtuosity in his cultivation of Buddhist theories, and he began teaching Buddhist doctrines in the temple. His lecturers were often attended by more than a thousand listeners. For this he was respectfully addressed as "Master Jiaxiang."

In 606 (2nd year of the Daye reign, Sui Dynasty), Yang Guang, or Emperor Yangdi, summoned him to Yangzhou and put him up in the Huiri Temple. Later he went to Chang'an (present-day Xi'an), where he was warmly received by the royal family and was settled in the Riyan Temple. His lecturers in Chang'an attracted listeners from various parts of the country.

In 618, when Li Yuan entered Chang'an as the founding emperor of the Tang Dynasty after conquering the Sui, Jizang was one of the ten eminent monks the emperor invited to run Buddhist affairs for him. During his lifetime Jizang was a prolific writer. Incomplete statistics show that he wrote at least 91 volumes on 21 subjects, most of which were about the doctrines of the Sanlun sect.

Of the three treatises that form the foundation of the Sanlun sect, the *Mulamadhyamaka-karika* and the *Dvadasamukha-sastra* were works by Nagarjuna (c. 3rd century), a major scholar of Mahayana Buddhism in India, and the *Sata-sastra* was the work of his disciple, Aryadeva (3rd century). At the center of the theories of these three treatises is the principle that all things arise from conditional causations without nature. The three classics were translated into Chinese by Kumarajiva (344-413), a celebrated monk from Kuqa. For this reason, Nagarjuna and Aryadeva are regarded as forefathers of the Sanlun sect. Kumarajiva is worshipped as a patriarch of a later time.

After Kumarajiva translated the three classics into Chinese, most of his disciples dedicated themselves to disseminating the doctrines contained in these works, but only one of the discipes, Shengzhao, was able to inherit Kumarajiva's ideas and to safeguard the purity of the theories of the three books. The books first circulated in the North, and found their way south of the Yangtze River with the arrival of Senglang at Mount Sheshan (present-day Xixia Mountain in the suburbs of Nanjing), where Senglang became the abbot of the Xixia Monastery. In 512 (11th

year of the Tianjian reign of the Liang Dynasty), Emperor Wudi
dispatched ten monks to the monastery to learn the three classics
from Senglang. Zengquan, the top student among the ten, later
became the master of a monk named Falang, who eventually
rose to fame and acquired a large group of followers on his own.
But none of Falang's followers compared favorably with Jizang,
who drew on the quintessence of the three books and founded
the Sanlun sect. Jizang's new interpretations of the three ancient
books were later dubbed the "New Three Classics."

The Sanlun sect's theories boil down to the belief that the
multitude of things in the universe, both material and spiritual,
came into being because of *hetupratyaya*, that is, internal and external causations. Only when all the necessary conditions become available can a thing come into existence. Otherwise
nothing can happen. For the same reason, all things owe their
existence to the availability of various conditions, and their own
identities are empty and unattainable. Such is the Buddhist philosophy: "All things are void."

The Sanlun sect divides the teachings of Sakyamuni into two
pitakas (collections) or three *dharma-cakras* (wheel of dharma). The
two *pitakas* refer to the Sravaka Canon that belongs to the Hinayana doctrine and the Boddhisattva Canon that belongs to the
Mahayana doctrine. In passing, the term "Hinayana" means "small
vehicle," such as a bicycle that is large enough to carry only one
passenger; whereas the term "Mahayana" means "large vehicle,"
such as a train that can carry many people at the same time. "Hinayana," which developed before the rise of Mahayana Buddhism
in first century BC, is a derogative term used by the followers of
Mahayana Buddhism in jeering at Buddhists of the earlier period
on the grounds that they were preoccupied with their own eman-
cipation while leaving other people alone in the ocean of misery.

The three theories are the fundamental dharma-cakra, the incidental dharma-cakra, and the from-the-incidental-to-the-fundamental dharma-cakra,[1] which exactly classify the Buddha's teachings in a chronological manner.

The Sanlun sect had its heyday when it was first created during the Sui Dynasty, but it began to decline after the mid-Tang Dynasty, following the emergence of the Huayan (Avatamsaka), Ci'en, and other sects, at a time when "a hundred flowers were blossoming and a hundred sects of thought were contending." The reason behind the decline of this sect is perhaps its delineation of the theory of "the void and unattainable," which was so thorough that human beings either found it unacceptable or were simply scared of it. The lack of successors is another reason for its decline. As a matter of fact, there was no lack of people engaged in the study of the Sanlun sect, but few regarded themselves as followers. This situation remains to this day.

3. Huayan Sect

The Huayan sect, also called the Xianshou or Avatamsaka sect, is predicated on the *Buddhavatamsaka-mahavaipulya-sutra* (*Garland Sutra*). Its founder was Fazang (643-712), an eminent monk of the Tang Dynasty.

---

[1] The preachings of the Buddha are symbolized by *dharma-cakra*, meaning "wheel of dharma." The fundamental *dharma-cakra* refers to the first sermon the Buddha delivered to some bodhisattvas on the *Buddhavatamsaka-mahavaipulya-sutra* (*Garland Sutra*) in the Deer Park and showed them Ekayana (the One Vehicle) on the second 7th day after he achieved Buddhahood. The incidental *dharma-cakra* means "all other teachings" he preached for the next 45 years, during which time he lectured on the *Triyana* (the three vehicles which carry living beings across samsara or mortality to the shores of nirvana) to different audiences. At a dharma-flower ceremony prior to his entry into Nirvana, the Buddha preached the *Saddharma-pundarika-sutra*, in which the "branches and leaves" of the truth are reunited with the root; hence the term, "from-the-incidental-to-the-fundamental *dharma-cakra*."

Fazang, founder of the Huayan sect of Han Buddhism

Fazang, a native of Soghdiana who was styled as Xianshou, grew up in China and was educated in Chinese culture as an intelligent, boy prodigy. At 17, he went to Mount Taibai and became a disciple of the famous monk Zhiyan (602-668). He won his master's favor by excelling in his studies of the *Garland Sutra*. In 670 (3rd year of the Zongzhang reign, Tang Dynasty), Fazang passed an imperial examination and won the opportunity to be sworn into his monkhood at the imperial court. Empress Wu Zetian personally selected ten famous monks to preside over the ordination ceremony for him and named him "Xiaoshou." For a while, he was part of the celebrated monk Xuanzang's team of Buddhist translators, but he quit after failing to see eye to eye with Xuanzang on some translation problems. Together with Yijing, who had just returned from his studies in India, he joined Siksananda (652-710) in translating the 80-volume *Buddhavatamsaka-mahavaipulya-sutra*. After this work was finished he participated in a translation workshop organized by Yijing.

A prestigious Buddhist during the Tang Dynasty, Fazang personally bestowed the Bodhisattva Commandments on two Tang emperors, Zhongzong (reigned 705-709) and Ruizong (reigned 710-712). For this he was decorated as an "Imperial Tutor." With his wide knowledge and high moral accomplishments, he made great contributions to the development of Buddhism during his lifetime. He left behind a wealth of works, most of which were findings on his research into the *Buddhavatamsaka-mahavaipulya-sutra*. He became the father of the Huayan sect.

Though the Huayan sect was founded by Fazang, the idea for it was Du Shun's.

Du Shun (557-640), also known as Fashun, was an expert on *dhyana* and *samadhi*. Legend has it that he was also in possession of certain divine skills. Li Shimin, or Emperor Taizong of the Tang Dynasty, adored him and bestowed on him the title "Heart of the Emperor." Hence his nickname, "Venerable Heart of the Emperor." According to historical records, Du Shun had the following divine skills:

(1) Once, Du Shun asked a patron to donate a meal for a large crowd. The man prepared enough food for 500 people, but unexpectedly, more than 1,000 arrived. The patron flushed with embarrassment and did not know what to do. Du Shun comforted him and asked him to go ahead and serve the meal as if nothing had happened. The result was that all those present were able to eat their fill.

(2) A herdsman by the name of Zhang Hongchang took the cows and horses he had raised to the market, but these animals were so ferocious nobody dared to buy them. When Du Shun saw what was happening, he murmured into the ears of the cows and horses, which, as if having seen the point, immediately became docile and obedient.

(3) Du Shun and his disciples were practicing austerities and meditating on the Buddha's holy words in a monastery where they had to grow their own vegetables. But the vegetable garden was infested with insects, making it impossible for them to sow the seeds. When Du Shun heard about this, he went to the garden and said something to himself. After that the garden

was disposed of all the insect pests.

These anecdotes may sound ridiculous to a layman, but Buddhists have never doubted their credibility, because they firmly believe that the force of divinity is a real thing.

Du Shun classified the teachings of Sakyamuni into five divisions,[1] and formulated five forms of meditation. Zhiyan inherited and built on the ideas of Du Shun. But it was Fazang who summarized all the research results of the *Buddhavatamsaka-mahavai-pulya-sutra* and established the Huayan sect.

The Huayan sect has adopted the five kinds of teachings established by Du Shun as its guidance. Actually, the doctrines of this sect cover all the Five Divisions of Buddhism and the Ten Sects,[2] the Six Characteristics,[3] and the Ten Metaphysical Entrances of Thought.[4] The universe is all-inclusive. All the things in it, be they *samskrta* (active beings) or *asamskrta* (non-active beings), have their origins in *pratityasamutpada* (con-

---

[1] The five divisions of teachings according to the Huayan sect are: the Hinayana Teachings for Savakas, which interprets nirvana as annihilation; the Primary Teachings of the initial stage of Mahayana, with two sections — the realistic and the idealistic; the Terminal Teachings of Mahayana in its final stage, teaching the universal Buddhahood; the Teachings for Immediate Comprehension, applied in Mahayana as the key to immediate enlightenment by right concentration of thought, or faith; and the Complete Teachings of the Huayan sect, combining all the rest into one all-embracing vehicle.

[2] That is, the ten sects of thought in Buddhism.

[3] The six characteristics found in everything: whole and parts, unity and diversity, entirety and its fractions.

[4] The Ten Entrances: 1) All phenomena are present simultaneously and correlate with each other; 2) The relationship between them is like the endless Indra Net; 3) The visible phenomena exist within one unit; 4) Even the smallest particles retain their own nature while mutually penetrating. 5) Dharmas in ten epochs are manifest without separation; 6) Dharmas in all traditions have virtues whether pure or impure; 7) Each thing and all other things inter-penetrate, but do not lose their own character; 8) Various dharmas exhibit phenomenal identity, free from resistance; 9) All dharmas exist as the reflection of the Tathagata's mind; 10) Profound theory can be illustrated and perceived with things.

ditional causations), interact with one another in harmony, and form what looks like a multileveled and inexhaustible network. From the perspective of the nature of the various doctrines, one is all, and all is one, and the relationship between all things is one of harmony and mutual incorporation, with no distinctions made between them. Such a relationship is not only one of interdependence between the phenomenal and the noumenal, but also interdependence among the phenomenal. That is why the Huayan sect is called the sect of perfect harmony without impediments.

After the Huayan sect was established during the Tang Dynasty, it spread extensively, but its dissemination was cut short by Emperor Wuzong's persecution of Buddhism during his reign (841-846) of the Tang Dynasty. All the literature of this sect was lost as a result, though some of it was later retrieved from Korea and Japan during the Song Dynasty. Some people were devoted to the study and rejuvenation of this sect during the Yuan, Ming, and Qing dynasties. Among those in modern times were Yuexia (1858-1917) and Yingci (1873-1965). In 1914 (3rd year of the Republic), Yuexia established Huayan University in Shanghai and Hangzhou, and made his contributions to the Huayan sect by training a contingent of successors.

4. Ci'en Sect

The Ci'en sect, that is, the Dharma Laksana or Vijnanavada sect, was founded by Xuanzang, the celebrated Buddhist translator who once resided in the Ci'en Monastery of Xi'an, and his disciple Kuiji (632-682).

Xuanzang (600-664), a native of Goushi (present-day south Yanshi County, Henan Province) with the surname of Chen,

Xuanzang, founder of the Ci'en sect of Han Buddhism

lived in a monastery during his childhood with his elder brother, Changjie, who was a monk. At the age of 13 he also became a monk and began studying Buddhist doctrines. As he grew up, his religious knowledge also grew. In 622 (5th year of the Wude reign, Tang Dynasty), he received his ordination in the commandments and began traveling and calling on established Buddhist masters. Puzzled by contradictions and discrepancies in the Buddhist instructions then available in this country, he hit upon the idea to study in India. In 629 (3rd year of the Zhenguan reign, Tang Dynasty), Xuanzang began his pilgrimage to the West. In 633 (7th year of the Zhenguan reign, Tang Dynasty), having weathered all the hardships of the road, he arrived at central India's Nalanda Monastery, the Buddhist and cultural center of India, and started learning the philosophy of Yogacara under the tutelage of Silabhdra (c. 6th-7th century), a famous Buddhist scholar who happened to be the abbot of the monastery. During his stay in India Xuanzang was able to travel widely, and for his superb accomplishments in his studies, Indian Buddhist scholars honored him as a Mahayanadeva, or Deity of Mahayana. In 649 (19th year of the Zhenguan reign, Tang Dynasty), he returned to China with a full load of scriptures and treatises in Sanskrit. With the support of the imperial court, he put together a translation workshop, and personally translated 75 scriptures in 1,335 volumes, an unprecedented feat in Chinese Buddhist translation history. One of his translations was the *Vijnanamatrasiddhi-sastra* (*Treatise on the Establishment of the Doctrine on Consciousness Only*), which became the foundation for the Ci'en sect that he established. But it was through the efforts of his disciple Kuiji that the Ci'en sect finally stood on its own as an independent religious sect.

Kuiji, a man of Chang'an with the secular surname of Chiwei, was a son of a noble house who began reading Confucian classics and writing as a child. His talent was not lost on Xuanzang, who offered to accept him as a disciple in 648 (22nd year of the Zhenguan reign, Tang Dynasty). It is said Kuiji's parents were happy about the offer but that their son thought otherwise. Finally he raised three conditions for accepting the offer: first, he would never abstain from worldly desires and feelings; second, he would be allowed to eat meat; and third, he would be allowed to eat in the afternoon. All these conditions violated Buddhist taboos. Xuanzang feigned consent in order to obtain this gifted disciple, but his true intention was to educate the boy after he became a monk. The following story shows the result of this education.

For a time Kuiji was known as the "Monk with Three Carts," a nickname he earned during a lecture tour in which he employed an impressive procession of three carts. While the chart that led the way was packed with scriptures and reference books, he himself rode on the cart in the middle and had the third cart loaded with his concubine, maidservants, and food. Midway along the road he came across a respectful old man, who, attract an exchange of pleasantries, asked him what was loaded on the first cart. After he received the answer, the old man asked what was on the cart at the back. Kuiji was nonplussed by the questioning, but, feeling compelled to give a reply, he told the old man the truth. The man smiled faintly, and said, "Your Excellency is such a well-known Buddhist master, yet you are preaching Buddhist doctrines by bringing your concubine and servants along. Doesn't that clash with the holy teachings?" Kuiji was so embarrassed that he immediately asked his concubine and servants to go home, and traveled on alone with the cart loaded with sutras.

Despite this unseemly tale about his nickname, Kuiji's reputation remains untarnished. He was a famed scholar and Xuanzang's most trusted student. In Chinese Buddhist history, he was the "Master Explainer of a Hundred Scriptures." It was through his efforts that the Ci'en sect emerged as a major Buddhist sect in China.

At the heart of the Ci'en sect is the philosophy of idealism that had its origin in the teachings of Maitreya, Asanga, and Vasubandhu, who lived during the 4th and 5th centuries in India. Vasubandhu was the author of the *Vijnaptimatrasiddhi-trimsaikakarika-sastra (Idealism in Thirty Lines),* which was later studied and enunciated by ten masters. While in India, Xuanzang studied Vijnanavada under Silabhdra. After his return to China, his study was concentrated on the theories of Dharmapala (c. mid-6th century) on Vasubandhu's work. Incorporating the theories of the other nine masters, he compiled the *Vijnaptimatrata-siddhi-sastra,* which became the canon of the Ci'en sect.

It is the belief of the Ci'en sect that the "three realms originate from the mind, and the cornucopia of laws are geared to realism." That is to say, all things in the universe are converted into reality through the heart's perception. There are eight major perceptions, of which *alaya-vijnana* (storage consciousness), whose store of seeds spawn all the things in the universe, is the most important. The Ci'en sect's doctrine boils down to the *pancadharma* (five dharmas),[1] three aspects of the nature of things (*trisvabhavata*),[2] eight *parijnana* (kinds of consciousness),[3] and two categories of anatman (non-ego).[4] In this sect the Buddha's teachings fall into three periods of time: Bhava Canon (the teaching of reality of ego and things), Sunya Canon (the teaching of unreality of ego and things), and Madhyama Canon (the teaching of the mean, that mind or spirit is real while things are unreal). The Ci'en sect's analyses of conception are so meticulous that they are akin to modern psychology.

The fact that the Ci'en sect has been a subject of academic study since its founding during the Tang Dynasty perhaps has something to do with the prestige of Xuanzang. However, this did not protect it from the destructive blow sustained during Emperor Wuzong's crackdown on Buddhism. Its literature fell into oblivion as a result, and some of it was not retrieved from Japan until the modern times. During the interregnum between the Qing Dynasty and the Republic, there was an upsurge in the study of the *Vignanamatrasiddhi-sastra*. Today, the treatise is a compulsory course for students at the Chinese Buddhist Seminary.

---

[1] The five dharmas (laws) govern 1) phenomena; 2) their names; 3) ordinary mental discrimination; 4) corrective wisdom, which corrects deficiencies and errors; 5) absolute wisdom, reached through the understanding of the law of the absolute.

[2] *Trisvabhavata* consists of three aspects: the illusory (*parikalpita*), the dependent (*paratantra*) and the perfected (*parinispanna*).

[3] The eight kinds of consciousness include the five senses of 1) seeing (*caksur-vijnana*), 2) hearing (*srotra-v*), 3) smelling (*ghrana-v*), 4) tasting (*jihva-v*), and 5) touch (*kaya-v*), as well as 6) intellect or the mental sense (*mano-vijnana*), 7) the discriminating and constructive sense (*klista-mano-vijnana*), and 8) the basis from which come all "seeds" of consciousness (*alaya-vijnana*).

[4] The two categories of *anatman* (no-ego) means 1) there is no permanent human ego, or soul; and 2) no permanent individuality in or independence of things.

5. Chan Sect

The Chan or Dhyana sect is a major sect of Chinese Buddhism whose establishment was made possible through the efforts of Huineng, an eminent monk of the Tang Dynasty.

Huineng (638-713) was a native of Fanyang (present-day Zhuoxian, Hebei Province) whose secular surname was Lu. His father was an official who was demoted to Xinzhou (present-day Xinxing County, Guangdong) on the South China Sea, and died when Huineng was a child. The family fortune declined as a result. After he grew up, he had to sell fagots to provide for his mother. One day, overhearing someone recite the *Vajracchedika-prajnaparamita-sutra (Diamond Sutra)*, he became impressed with its good meaning. Huineng asked the man who had taught him the scripture, and learned that the teacher was

Master Hongren at a place known as Huangmei. He reported this to his mother, and asked for her permission to go to Huangmei and seek out the truth. His mother consented, but Huineng did not set out on his journey north until he had raised enough money and supplies for her. When he arrived in Huangmei, Hongren (602-675) asked him where he came from and what was the purpose of his visit. He answered that he came from south of the Five Ridges

Huineng, the sixth patriarch of the Chan (Zen) sect of Han Buddhism (present-day Guangdong and Guangxi) and that he wanted to become a monk. When Hongren said that men from south of the Five Ridges had no aptitude for Boddhahood, Huineng replied, "Men may come from south or north, but the capacity to comprehend Buddhism knows no geographical distinction." Hongren, impressed by the reply, immediately knew that he was facing a man who could be taught and would likely amount to something, and he soon arranged for Huineng to work in a rice-husking workshop.

Eight months later Hongren decided that he would choose from his disciples someone who could inherit his mantle by asking each of them to compose a hymn on their understanding of the Buddhist doctrines. Shenxiu, his top disciple, came up with a verse that said, "I have a body like the bodhi tree and a heart like the mirror on a pedestal. I want to clean them from time to time, so as to keep them free from dust." Huineng, on seeing the monk pasting up the verse on the wall while reading it aloud, immediately improvised a piece in response, "The bodhi never has a tree, nor has the mirror a pedestal. The heart of a Buddhist is calm and clean — how can they be contaminated by dust?" Not knowing how to read and write, Huineng asked a fellow monk to write down this composition beside Shenxiu's. When Hongren read the two pieces, he immediately knew that Huineng had a better understanding of Buddhism. That night, he invited Huineng to his abode and passed on to him the most secret part of his instructions, and gave him a monastic habit as a token of his trust.

Huineng immediately went on a journey back home that very night when he learned the secret to the Buddhist doctrines. Upon his arrival in the South, he followed Hongren's instructions and consigned himself for 15 years to an anonymous life among a team of hunters. While the hunters ate meat, he adhered to a vegetarian's diet by picking out the vegetables mixed in meat dishes. During a visit to the Faxing Monastery (present-day Guangxiao Monastery of Guangzhou) as a lay Buddhist, he attended Monk Yinzong's lecture on the *Mahapari-nirvana-sutra*. He saw two monks among the audience who were arguing about whether a stream moved because of the wind or by itself. As the two of them became all worked up over the argument, Huineng chipped in, "Why don't you stop arguing? The stream moves not because of the wind nor by itself — it moves because both of your hearts are moving." Yinzong the lecturer was taken aback when he overheard the remark. "I have long heard of the arrival of a master from Huangmei," Yinzong said, coming down from his podium. "Are you that distinguished guest?" Huineng showed him the gift his teacher had given him. Yinzong was impressed and he arranged for the lay Buddhist to settle down in the Faxing Monastery and ordained him as a monk. After living in the Faxing Monastery for a period of time, Huineng moved to the Baolin Monastery (present-day Nanhua Monastery) in Shaozhou. Once, delivering a lecture in the Dafan Monastery at the invitation of the provincial governor Wei Qu, he brought the house down. His disciple, Fahai, recorded the lecture and compiled it into what is today's widely read classic, *Analects of the Sixth Chan Patriarch Huineng*.

In 705 (1st year of the Shenlong reign, Tang Dynasty), Emperor Zhongzong (reigned 705-710) sent a messenger to Nanhai (present-day Guangdong) to summon Huineng to the capital city of Luoyang. Huineng turned down the invitation on the basis of being a long forgotten hermit, his old age, and his poor health. A very sympathetic Zhongzong bestowed on him a kasaya, a patchwork outer vestment, and large quantities of daily supplies.

Throughout his life Huineng was devoted to disseminating

the Chan doctrines in the South. His unique interpretations of the doctrines had a tremendous influence on the development of the Chan sect, and because of this he is regarded as the de facto patriarch of it.

The traditional history of Buddhism, however, regards the Indian monk Bodhidharma as the father of the Chan sect. After he arrived in China, his theories were passed down along the following the line: Huike (487-593), Sengcan (?-606), Daoxin (580-651), Hongren (602-675), and Huineng. So Huineng was the sixth and last patriarch of the Chan sect. This line of heritage was composed by Qisong (1007-1072), a preeminent monk of the Song Dynasty. As a matter of fact, the Chan prior to Huineng was merely a discipline of learning rather than a sect of Buddhism.

During his lifetime Huineng had a large team of disciples, and the three most influential among them were Xingsi (?-740), Huairang (677-744), and Shenhui (686-760). Xinsi was a native of Luling (present-day Ji'an, Jiangxi Province) who became a novice while yet a child. After he obtained the secret instructions from Huineng, he returned to Luling and settled in the Qingju Temple on Qingyuan Mountain. His mantle, carried forward by his disciple Xiqian, or Monk Shitou, later evolved into three of the five subsects of the Chan: Caodong, Yunmen, and Fayan. Huarang (677-744) came from Ankang (present-day Ankang, Shaanxi Province) and became a monk at age 15. After he studied for a time under Huineng, he settled on Mount Hengshan, the Southern Mountain Sanctuary, and recruited Daoyi as his disciple.

Daoyi (709-788) was a native of Shifang, Hanzhou (present-day Shifang, Sichuan Province) and arrived at Mount Hengshan during the Kaiyuan reign of the Tang Dynasty and practiced meditation all day long. Huairang, who lived nearby in the

Guanyin Temple, immediately knew this was a young man of promise and paid him a visit. Seeing Daoyi meditating, Huairang asked what he was doing, sitting there like that. Daoyi said he was trying to attain enlightenment and achieve buddhahood. At this reply Huairang said nothing but picking up a brick started grinding it against a stone. Daoyi, curious, asked, "Why do you grind the brick?" Huairang answered, "To turn it into a mirror." Daoyi, even more bewildered, asked again, "How can a brick become a mirror?" Huairang answered, "knowing that a brick cannot become a mirror, can meditation alone turn you into a Buddha?" Daoyi was taken aback, and he asked Huairang for advice. After the encounter Daoyi became Huairang's disciple, and, inheriting his teacher's methodology, finally emerged as the patriarch of the Weiyang and Linji subsects of the Chan sect. Later the Yangqi and Huanglong subsects merged as the Linji sect. Thus the Chan sect became a sect of Chinese Buddhism with five branches and seven subsects.

Shenxiu, a disciple of Hongren, continued to disseminate Chan teachings after his master's death and, with the monks at the eastern capital of Luoyang and western capital at Xi'an all becoming his followers, exerted a great influence on the religious life in north China. When Shenhui, a disciple of Huineng, arrived in the North from present-day Guangdong, he was somewhat resentful of what was happening there, and he began advocating that Huineng's southern branch of the Chan sect was better than Shenxiu's northern branch. He set up a *pancaparisad* (quinquennial assembly)[1] at the Dayun Temple of Huatai (present-day Huaxian County, Henan Province) for a debate between the two branches.

---

[1] *Pancaparisad*, the quinquennial assembly where men and women, old and young, share the alms both in kind and in spirit on an equal footing; it is also an occasion for confession, penance, and remission.

During the debate the conclusion was reached that the southern branch was for immediate enlightenment and should thus be called the "instantaneous subsect of Chan," and that the northern branch was for gradual enlightenment and should thus be called the "progressive subsect of Chan." Hence the Chan sect was divided into two geographical branches. However, as the instantaneous subsect spread northward, Shenxiu's northern subsect went on a decline and gradually disappeared. In all this, Shenhui played a major role. Yet his southern subsect also met its demise by the sixth generation. At the same time, another southern branch of Chan headed by Huairang gradually spread to the North.

The five branches and seven subsects of the Chan sect each flourished at different periods of time, but the Linji subsect was the most influential, with the Caodong subsect ranking second. For a time the adage among Buddhists in China was: "While the Linji subsect of Chan has the entire country under its influence, the Chaodong subsect manages to control half the country."

The creeds of Chan sect (Dhyana sect) are transmitted from mind to mind, without recourse to language, words, or writings, and above all, without the use of any scripture. Chan advocates attaining Buddhahood by discovering one's own innate Buddha nature. Legend has it that once Sakyamuni brandished a bouquet of flowers during an audience at the Nirvana Assembly. While most of the audience were bewildered by this gesture, only Kasyapa, one of Sakyamuni's ten disciples, smiled in tacit understanding of the Buddha's intentions. That transmission of the Buddha's holy words by the mind has been inherited through the ages, and the 28th-generation disciple, Bodhidharma, brought this method to China. It is the belief of the Chan sect that man's mind is pure and clean to start with, but such purity fails to manifest itself because it has been obliterated by worldly worries. Once the mind obtains the straightforward guidance of the knowledge of benevolence, it can immediately see its true nature and achieve Buddhahood.

Because the Chan sect chose to dispense with written scriptures, it suffered no loss of literature during the persecution of Buddhism under the reign of Emperor Wuzong of the Tang Dynasty. That is why during the long period from the Five Dynasties to the Song Dynasty (907-1279), the sect was able to achieve the acme of its development. After the Song Dynasty, however, some of its subsects gradually went on a decline.

The tradition of the Chan sect to do without recourse to writing was challenged by the emergence of quite a few books on the quotations of Chan masters after the Song Dynasty. This was something unheard of in previous Chan history. However, it is precisely because of these quotations that posterity has been able to cherish Chan literature as a major component of the cultural heritage of Chinese Buddhism, so much so that in modern times the celebrated Buddhist scholar Taixu maintained that the "Chan Pitaka" should be added to the *Tripitaka* of Chinese Buddhism. By the "Chan Pitaka" he meant precisely the collection of quotations of Chan masters.

6. Vinaya Sect

The Vinaya (Disciplinary) sect is also called the "Vinaya sect of the South Mountain" because its founder, the prominent Tang monk Daoxuan, lived on Zhongnan Mountain in the South. Daoxuan (596-667) came from Wuxing in present-day north Zhejiang. He began reading Confucian classics while a child and by nine was able to compose poetry and rhapsodies. At 16 he began his monastic life with Monk Zhijun as his master,

Daoxuan, founder of the Vinaya
Sect of Han Buddhism

and at 20 he was bestowed with the Upasampanna (Complete Commandments). He then came under the tutelage of Zhishou, an erudite in the *viyana* (monastic rules), who taught him the commandments and the *Dharmagupta Vinaya*. However, after he finished one round of study of the *vinaya* he decided that was not what he wanted. Instead, he wished to start learning Chan Buddhism. His master was not reconciled to this and demanded that he repeat his lesson 20 times on the *Dharmagupta Vinaya* before starting his Chan lessons. The master's word was final, and he had no choice but to continue to study under Zhishou. In 624 (7th year of the Wude reign, Tang Dynasty), he went to Zhongnan Mountain and settled in the Baiquan Monastery. Shortly afterwards, he went on an itinerary to collect different theories of Buddhist discipline. On the basis of the *Dharmagupta Vinaya*, he drew on the strengths of different sects of Buddhism and came up with his own understanding of the *vinaya*, thereby creating the Vinaya sect of the Southern Mountain.

The *vinaya* is a code of conduct for Buddhists. For lay Buddhists there are the *Pancasila* (*Five Commandments*) and the Eight Commandments. There are the *Sikasapada* (*Ten Prohibitions*) for *sramaneras* (novices), 250 commandments for *bhiksus* (mendicants) and 500 commandments for *bhiksunis* (nuns). The

Chinese Buddhists began to be disciplined in the commandments during the Jiaping reign (249-254) of the Kingdom of Wei during the Three Kingdoms Period, when the Indian monk, Dharmakala (3rd century) translated *The Heart of Sanghika-vinaya* and started training Chinese monks in the commandments. Translations of more canonical writings on the commandments emerged in the years that followed. During the Southern and Northern dynasties (420-589), studying the *vinaya* became quite popular among Chinese Buddhists. The *Dharmagupta Vinaya* was translated into Chinese by Sramana Buddhayasa from Kubha and Zhu Fonian, a Chinese monk translator. The *Dharmagupta Vinaya* was put together by Dharmagupta one hundred years after Sakyamuni achieved nirvana by garnering passages from the canons of Theravada that he thought were identical to his own viewpoints, and his compilation comes in four parts: commandments for mendicants, commandments for nuns, the code for peaceful life, and the code for houses and miscellany.

Famous persons who made names for themselves in the study of the *Dharmagupta Vinaya* prior to Daoxuan were Facong and Huiguang, both of whom lived during the reign of Emperor Xiaowen of the Northern Wei Dynasty (471-499). During the Tang Dynasty, joining Daoxuan in preaching the *Dharmagupta Vinaya* were Fali (569-635) of the Riguang Temple at Xiangzhou and Huaisu (625-698) of the Dongta Temple of the West Taiyuan Monastery. These three masters all wrote works on the creed, and they held different opinions on the embodiment of commandments. By "embodiment of commandments" is meant the function a Buddhist acquires to forestall erroneous thoughts and to prevent evil in his heart when he is ordained with the commandments. According to Fali, the embodiment of commandments is neither *rupadharma* (physical phenomenon) nor mental dharmas. Daoxuan, under the influence of

Xuanzang's Yogacara theory, believed that the embodiment is a mental thing. Huaisu, on his part, held that it is a physical phenomenon. Their depositions on the *Dharmagupta Vinaya* were known as the "Three Major Commentaries," which circulated in society at the same time, but only the Vinaya sect of South Mountain founded by Daoxuan has been able to survive to this day.

The Vinaya sect of South Mountain divides the teachings of the Buddha into two categories, that is, the classics designed to educate the multitudes, such as *Agama Sutras*, and *Pranna Sutras*, which provide the code of conduct for the multitudes.

The Vinaya sect of South Mountain has had its ups and downs like other religious sects in Chinese history. It flourished when someone was advocating and disseminating it. Otherwise, it just went downhill. By the Yuan-Ming interregnum the Vinaya sect of South Mountain sank to an all-time low, and it did not show signs of a revival until the early Qing Dynasty, when Jiguang, the abbot of the Longchang Monastery on Baohua Mountain in Jurong County (Jiangsu Province), and a disciple of Ruxin, who was then preaching the *Dharmagupta Vinaya* at the Linggu Temple of Jinling (present-day Nanjing), converted his monastery into a grand domain for the preaching of the Vinaya Sect principles only. The facility was later continuously expanded thanks to the efforts of Jiguang's disciples, and it soon achieved a nationwide reputation as the uninterrupted venue for two major summons ceremonies (one held in spring and the other in autumn) for the ordination of commandments every year.

During 20th century Hongyi (1880-1942) came to the fore because of his studies and dissemination of the *Dharmagupta Vinaya*. Born in Tianjin to a rich family whose ancestral home was in Zhejiang, Hongyi devoted himself to *vinaya* studies after he became a monk in 1918, the seventh year of the Republic. He was the author of *A Record of Forms of Bhiksu Rules in the Four-division Vinaya* and *Some Important Contents of the Southern Mountain Vinaya Prepared for Reading at Home*. He was held in high esteem by Buddhists at home and abroad for his exemplary practice of the commandments.

7. Jingtu Sect

The Jingtu (Pure Land) sect, also known as the Sukhavativyuha sect or Lotus sect in China, is named for the Pure Land, the aspired destination for a monk in meditation. It was established in China by Shandao during the Tang Dynasty.

Shandao (613-681), whose secular surname was Zhu, was a native of Linzi (present-day Zibo, Shandong Province). In his study of Buddhist classics, he found that the Dharma Door for Reciting the Buddha's Name was the most convenient and easily achieved of all Buddhist commandments to be mastered, and thus he became a convert of the Jingtu sect. He once went all the way to Mount Lushan to explore the

Shandao, founder of the Jingtu (Pure Land) sect of Han Buddhism cultural heritage left by the prominent Eastern-Jin monk Huiyuan. In 641 (15th year of the Zhenguan reign, Tang Dynasty), he settled at the Xuanzhong Temple in Bingzhou (present-day Taiyuan, Shanxi Province) to learn the creeds of the Jingtu sect from Daochuo. In 645 (19th year of the Zhenguan reign) Daochuo died, and Shandao then went to Chang'an to disseminate the Dharma Door for the Reciting of Buddha's Name. Practising the most stringent type of austerities and meditation, he devoted all his time to chanting the name of the Buddha except when he was out begging for alms. It is said that he copied 100,000 volumes of the *Amitabha Sutra* (*Sutra of Buddha of Boundless Light*), and drew 300 or so pictures that tell stories about the Jingtu sect. He was also the author of five works on the dharmaparyaya (dharma door) to the Pure Land, which established him as the father of the Jingtu sect in China.

The Pure Land is the Paradise of the West. According to the *Amitabha Sutra,* it is a place of sublime beauty and the people living there are happy and don't know what pain is. Access to the Pure Land is through chanting Amita Buddha's name as many times as possible. Chanting Amita Buddha's name calls for the union of the three behaviors, that is to say, one should personally pay homage to the Amita Buddha, always chant his name, and always bear him in one's mind. Shandao developed a whole collection of methods and set a series of requirements for his followers. According to him, those practicing the Dharma Door for the Reciting of the Buddha's Name should first set their minds at ease. Setting their minds at ease, calls for sincerity, profundity, and *parinamana* (readiness for the transference of one's merits to somewhere). After one has focused one's mind on these three aspects and has begun self-cultivation, one is bound to arrived in the Pure Land so long as one persists in chanting the name of the Amita Buddha. There are not many theories to speak of in this sect of Chinese Buddhism, which advocates nothing but self-cultivation by chanting the Amita Buddha's name.

Chanting the name of the Buddha is a way of self-cultivation, and self-cultivation is one of the *trisiksa* (three studies) that is a must for all sects of Buddhism despite differences in methodology. When chanting the name of the Buddha one is required to dispel all worldly thoughts and concentrate on a certain point — the point of the Amita Buddha. To perform well in chanting the Buddha's name is *samadhi* (concentrating on Buddha).

In China the Dharma Door for Chanting the Buddha's Name was initiated by Huiyuan, a monk who resided on Mount Lushan during the Eastern Jin Dynasty. Huiyuan (334-416), a native of Loufan (present-day Daixian County, Shanxi) with the secular name of Jia, was a disciple of the famed monk Dao'an. Because of his rich knowledge and moral integrity, he was able to recruit many social dignitaries to study under his tutelage. These included Liu Yimin of Pengcheng (present-day Xuzhou, Jiangsu), Lei Cizong of Yuzhang (present-day Nanchang, Jiangxi), Zhou Xuzhi of Yanmen (Daixian County, Shanxi), Bi Yinzhi of Xincai (in present-day Henan), and Zongbing of Nanyang (present-day Henan). By the time Huiyuan established the White Lotus Society with 18 prominent personages at Mount Lushan, he had recruited 123 local people, who gathered to offer sacrifices to a statue of Amita Buddha, and collectively chanted his name with the hope that after their death they would be reborn in the Pure Land.

By the Southern and Northern Dynasties, another eminent monk emerged in the Jingtu sect. Tanluan (476-542) began his religious life as a Taoist intent on finding a pill of longevity. He once went all the way to the Maoshan Mountain in the South to seek the instructions of Tao Hongjing,[1] and returned to the North with ten volumes of the Tao's book *Classics on Immortality*. When he came across Bodhiruci (5th-6th century) during a visit to Luoyang, he asked the Indian monk if there was any book on longevity. Bodhiruci told him there was no such thing as immortality because every person in this world dies, but there were ways to prolong one's life. The monk give him a copy of *Amitayur-dhyana Sutra* (*Discourse Concerning Meditation on Amitayus*), telling him that this was the Buddhist book on long life, and asked him to practice self-cultivation according to what the book said. Tanluan, enlightened, destroyed the *Classic on Longevity*, and concentrated on the study and practices of the Pure Land sect. He eventually rose to fame, and the ruler of the Northern Wei Dynasty (386-534) adored him as the "Celestial Luan."

Both Huiyuan and Tanluan silently chanted the name of the Amita Buddha. It was not until Daochuo of the Sui and Tang dynasties began chanting the name aloud that Buddhists everywhere did likewise. Daochuo (562-645), a native of Wenshui in the Bingzhou Prefecture (present-day Wenshui, Shanxi Province) whose secular surname was Wei, also began his religious life as a Taoist. During a visit to the Xuanzhong Temple up the Shibi Mountain in 609 (5th year of the Daye reign, Sui Dynasty), he read a stone tablet inscription on how Tanluan chanted the name of the Amita Buddha and practiced the doctrines of the Pure Land sect of Buddhism. He was so moved by Tanluan's assiduousness that he converted to this sect. After that he made

---

[1] Tao Hongjing (456-536), whose style name was Tongming, was a native of Molin in Danyang (in Jiangsu Province). A Taoist scholar and medical expert, he used to be an official of the Southern Qi Dynasty (479-502). After the Northern Qi was toppled by the Liang Dynasty (502-557), he became a hermit in the Maoshan Mountain, where he repeatedly turned down the offer of Xiao Yan, emperor Wudi of the Liang, to leave the mountain and serve him. The emperor, however, often consulted him on major issues. Hence Tao's nickname, "Prime Minister in the Mountains."

it a point to chant the name of the Amita Buddha 70,000 times a day. He would count the times of his incantation with beans or with a string of golden rain nuts, thus becoming the first Buddhist in China to use a rosary in religious meditation. With his great personality, Daochuo acquired quite a following in and around Wenshui, and his chanting the name of the Amita Buddha aloud became a fashion. His disciple, Shandao, inherited the method and turned this name chanting into a sect of Chinese Buddhism, the Jingtu sect.

The Jingtu sect's method is simple and feasible to practice. What appeals most is its belief that with the power of the Buddha people can achieve reincarnation in the Pure Land of the Amitatha Buddha with *karmas*. The literature of the Jingtu sect is generally limited to three sutras and one treatise, and there are three theories on its differential instructions.

The Jingtu sect has been thriving for more than one thousand years since its establishment. In modern times Ven. Yin Guang was the most influential personage in this sect. Even today, the sect remains most influential and has the largest following among all the Buddhist sects in China.

8. Esoteric Sect

The Esoteric sect of Buddhism, known in China as the Zhenyan (True Word) sect, was founded during the Kaiyuan reign (713-741) of the Tang Dynasty. Its founders were three Indian monks in China, Subhakarasimha, Vajrabodhi, Amoghavajra, who were collectively known as the "Three Major Scholars of Kaiyuan."

Subhakarasimha (637-735), a scion of an Indian royal became clan, a military commander when he was only ten years old,

Amoghavajra, one of the founders of the
Esoteric sect of Han Buddhism

and he ascended the throne when he was 13. After he quelled an armed rebellion launched by his younger brother who was jealous of him, he abdicated the throne and went on the road to pursue a religious life. He first studied Buddhism at a temple in a coastal area of South India, then he traveled to Magadha where he was recruited to the Nalanda Monastery to study Tantrism. In 716 (4th year of the Kaiyuan reign, Tang Dynasty) Subhakarasimha arrived in Chang'an, where Emperor Xuanzong revered him and made him a "Patriarch." A year later he began translating Buddhist scriptures. Upon learning that the Huayan Monastery in Chang'an held some Sanskrit versions of the Buddhist sutras brought back by Chinese monks returning from studies in India, he received the blessing of the emperor and went to the monastery with his disciples to return with a number of such books. In 724 (12th year of the Kaiyuan reign), he followed the emperor to Luoyang where he resumed his translation work at the Xianfu Temple. The four sutras he translated there were all Tantric classics, one of which was the *Mahavairocana-sutra*, the fundamental canon of the Esoteric sect. Because of this Subhakarasimha is regarded as the father of the Esoteric sect of Chinese Buddhism.

Vajrabodhi (669-741), a south Indian born into the Brahman

caste, was a child prodigy able to recite ten thousand words a day. He began his religious life as a student at the Nalanda Monastery. Later, he traveled to Simhala (Present-day Sri Lanka), where he boarded a ship going to Pulau Sumatera in present-day Indonesia. His journey eventually brought him to Guangzhou in 719 (7th year of the Kaiyuan reign, Tang Dynasty). Emperor Xuanzong received word of his arrival and summoned him to Chang'an. A major Tantric master, Vajrabodhi acquired many followers and presided over the *abhisekana* ritual (consecration by pouring water on the heads of followers). The books he translated on Tantric methodology and rituals laid a solid foundation for the introduction of Tantrism into China.

Amoghavajra (705-774), a northern Indian (another theory says he was from Simhala) born of the Brahman caste, arrived in China as a young child with his uncle. He became a disciple of the Indian preacher Vajrabodhi at 13, achieved his monkhood at 15, and was awarded the Mendicant Commandments at 20. For his high intelligence and photographic memory, he won the favor of his mentor, Vajrabodhi, who died in 741 (29th year of the Kaiyuan reign). A year later (1st year of the Tianbao reign, Tang Dynasty), Amoghavajra carried out his mentor's will by leading a 37-member Chinese delegation on a pilgrimage to Simhala, where his studies covered both the open and Esoteric sects of Buddhism. At the end of the journey, which brought him to India, he returned to Chang'an, put together a workshop to translate large numbers of Sanskrit Buddhist scriptures and treatises into Chinese, most of them Tantric classics, and emerged as one of the four major translators in Chinese Buddhism history. He then established his own domain for the Esoteric sect of Chinese Buddhism.

A salient feature of the Esoteric sect is the establishment of an altar on which to practice austerities and to recite the

Honored One's spell (mantra). Chinese versions of the Tantric mantra and classics had become available as early as the Three Kingdoms Period (220-265), when some monks from India or the West Territories, well-versed in the mantra, were already spreading Tantrism in China. Among them were Fu Tucheng (232-348) and Bodhiruci (5th-6th century), who were masters of the mantra. A legend about Bodhiruci's mantra-reciting power has it that one day, when he went to fetch water from a well without bringing a pail, he found the water level in the well was so low that it was impossible to draw water from it. He tossed a tiny poplar tree twig into the well and recited the mantra again and again for some time. Before long the water began to rise until it reached the brim of the well, allowing him to ladle out the water with his hands. The Chinese monks who were watching were naturally surprised, and they called him a sage. Bodhiruci hastened to explain that he was no sage at all, and that things like this were not uncommon in India though they were unknown to the Chinese. He declined to pass on the secret to the Chinese for fear that odd things like this would have a pernicious influence on society.

At that time Buddhism was still a novelty to the Chinese, the number of esoteric scriptures translated into Chinese were few and far between, and no monks were working to introduce this sect of Buddhism into China. That was why Tantrism failed to become a sect in its own right during Bodhiruci's time. The situation changed during the Kaiyuan reign (713-755) with the arrival of the three Tantric masters — Subhakarasimha, Vajrabodhi, Amoghavajra. Thanks to the work of this trio, Esotericism emerged as one of the sects of Chinese Buddhism.

The Esoteric sect in the Han-inhabited regions of China falls into two categories, the *vajradhatu* (diamond element) and the *garbhahatu* (womb treasury). Vajra, or diamond, means solidity, which is a property to be utilized; while the womb denotes sustainability and concealment. The profound meanings of both categories are too complicated to be described in a tourist book such as this — they call for meticulous studies provided by esoteric masters.

The Esoteric sect of the Chinese tradition, like other Buddhist sects, was subjected to suppression under Emperor Wuzong of the Tang Dynasty. The crackdown was followed by the war and turmoil of the Five Dynasties (907-960), and as a result the once prosperous Exoteric sect gradually disappeared from the Chinese landscape. The Chinese Esoteric sect, however, had spread to Japan, where it is as thriving today as before. In modern times, Ven. Chisong (1894-1972) devoted himself to rejuvenating the Esoteric sect in China. He made two trips to Japan to learn the secrets with the intention of bringing the sect back to China. His efforts, however, failed.

The Esoteric sect being followed in China today is actually borrowed from Tibet and is therefore different in both tradition and content from the original Esoteric sect introduced into China by the aforementioned Indian monks.

The Esoteric sect was introduced into Tibet from India during the 7th century. After Tibet became part of China during the Yuan (1271-1368) Dynasty, the Yuan emperors all became pious followers of this sect. Tantrism, however, was placed under government control during the Ming Dynasty (1368-1644), but by the Qing Dynasty (1644-1911), for political purposes, the imperial court held this school of Buddhism, followed by the Tibetans, in high esteem. During the Republican years, the Tibetan school of Esoteric Buddhism was able to spread far and wide through the interior of China.

Chapter 3

Buddhist Relations Between China and the World

1. China and India

Both China and India have ancient civilizations. Their territories are linked, but they have strikingly different cultural traditions. Buddhism, however, has played a major role in bridging that cultural gap and keeping the two great nations close together over the last several millennia.

Buddhism emerged in India between the sixth and fifth centuries BC. Theories differ as to when it spread into China. One theory has it that eighteen *sramanas* (monks) including Sramana Srifang arrived in China with Buddhist scriptures during the reign of Qinshihuang (221-210 BC). Obviously they came to this country for the purpose of disseminating Buddhism, but because of their strange looks they were sent back before they could do anything. It happened that the arrival of Srifang in China coincided with the historical fact that Asoka, the king of the Mayura Dynasty of India, was dispatching large numbers of priests to neighboring countries. Though historical records about this arrival of Indian monks in China are nowhere to be found, it was likely that Srifang was among those dispatched.

Another legend has it that Emperor Mingdi of the Eastern

Han Dynasty responded to a dream and dispatched Cai Yin as his envoy on a pilgrimage to India, escorted by Kasyapamatanga and Gobharana who were to translate the *Forty-two Chapter Sutra* (for details, see Section 1, Chapter 1), but this theory is disputed among historians. In 1998, Chinese Buddhist circles held a grand ceremony to celebrate the 2,000th anniversary of the introduction of Buddhism into China. This means that 2 BC, or the first year of the Yuanshou reign of Emperor Aidi of the Western Han Dynasty, is officially regarded as the year when Buddhism found its way into China.

The introduction of Buddhism into China boosted personnel exchanges between India and China. While Indian Buddhists arrived in China mainly to preach and translate scriptures, Chinese monks went on pilgrimages to India to search for more Buddhist scriptures and to pay homage to the holy landmarks of Buddhism. It can be said that Buddhism provided the avenue by which China and India came close together.

Numerous monks have come and gone between the two nations during the past two thousand years. It is hence impossible for a book of this size to enumerate them one by one. All we can do is to provide a brief introduction to some of those who figured prominently in the Sino-Indian Buddhist relations. First, some monks from India.

Kumarajiva (343-413). Born in Kuqa in a family of Indian descent, Kumarajiva began his religious life at age seven with his mother. He went to Kubha to study the doctrines at age nine, and, having excelled in his studies and shown his gift of speech in debates, returned to Kuqa at age 12. Before long he made a name for himself by his erudite knowledge of Mahayana and Hinayana classics. In 382 (7th year of the Taiyuan reign, Eastern Jin Dynasty), he was captured by the Former Qin general Lu Guang and taken to Liangzhou (present-day Wuwei, Gansu

Province) by the Former Qin's army. During the 17 years he spent in Liangzhou, Kumarajiva learned local customs and habits, as well as the Chinese language, and prepared himself for a career as a Buddhist scriptural translator. In 401 (5th year of the Long'an reign, Eastern Jin Dynasty), he arrived in Chang'an and won the respect of the emperor, Yao Xing. With his arrival, Chang'an became the Buddhist center of north China, and he became the leader of a team of Chinese and foreign scholars who translated large numbers of major scriptures, commandments and treatises into Chinese, thereby vastly replenishing the Buddhist literature in Chinese and opening a new chapter in the development of Chinese Buddhism. For his tremendous contributions to Sino-Indian cultural exchange, Kumarajiva is regarded as the foremost of the four major sutra translators in the history of Chinese Buddhism.[1]

Paramartha (491-569). This Indian monk was preaching Buddhism in Funan (present-day Cambodia) before he arrived at Nanhai (present-day Guangdong) in 546 (12th year of the Datong reign, Liang Dynasty). Two years later, he went to the capital of the Liang Dynasty (502-557) at present-day Nanjing, Jiangsu Province, and soon won the favor of Xiao Yan, or Emperor Wudi. However, his life of settled peace and contentment was short lived because of the mutiny launched by General Hou Jing against the emperor. Paramartha became homeless and had trouble making ends meet. But despite these hardships, he translated large numbers of Buddhist scriptures and treatises and became one of the four major translators of Buddhist scriptures in the history of Chinese Buddhism.

Amoghavajra (705-774). Arriving in China as a child to

---

[1] The other three major translators of Buddhist scriptures were Paramartha, Xuanzang, and Amoghavajra.

receive his education in Chinese culture, Amoghavajra became a monk in China. He eventually rose to fame by rendering large numbers of Indian Buddhist scriptures into Chinese and becoming one of the major founders of the Esoteric sect of Chinese Buddhism (for details see Section 8, Chapter 2).

Among the Chinese monks who made pilgrimages to India were:

Faxian (336-422), a native of Wuyang (Xiangqiu County, Shanxi Province) with the secular surname of Gong, became a monk while a child. The plan to make a pilgrimage to India became his cherished dream after he was bestowed with the commandments at age twenty. In 399 (3rd year of the Long'an reign, Eastern Jin Dynasty), together with three companions he set off from Chang'an and began an arduous journey to India. The toughest part of the journey was when they were traveling across the Gobi desert, a no-man's land where there were no birds in the sky nor animals roaming about. Having endured all the adversities and survived the traps of many a drifting sand dune, he eventually arrived at Patuliputra, capital of Magadha. While there he studied and copied sutras and treatises for a while before traveling further south to Sinhala, the "Lion Country." He returned to China in 412 (8th year of the Yixi reign, Jin Dynasty). A year later, working together with the Indian monk Buddhabhadra (359-429), he translated six scriptures and treatises. Basing himself on his itinerary to more than thirty countries, he wrote the immortal book *Faxian's Pilgrimage to India*. At the time, quite a few Chinese went on pilgrimages to India but because of harsh conditions along the way few were heard from again. Faxian, however, emerged as one of the most accomplished pilgrims among them.

Xuanzang began his journey to the West in 629 (3rd year of the Zhenguan reign, Tang Dynasty). He stayed in the Nalanda

Monastery for many years, where he established a high reputation throughout India. He eventually returned to China with a massive load of Sanskrit classics, some of which he translated into Chinese. He even translated Laozi's *Tao De Jing* into Sanskrit, and the *Mahayana-sraddhotpada-sastra* by the Indian philosopher Asvaghosa from Chinese into Indian language, thereby making historic contributions to Sino-Indian Buddhist exchanges. (For details see Section 4, Chapter 2.)

Yijing (636-713), a native of Fanyang (present-day Zhuoxian, Hebei Province) was tonsured as a monk at the age of fifteen. His admiration for the noble deeds of Faxian and Xuanzang in journeying to India to enable the dissemination of Buddhism in China inspired him to make the same trip. In 671 (2nd year of the Xianheng reign, Tang Dynasty), he set off from Yangzhou and boarded a ship at Fanyu, Guangdong, thereby beginning his solitary journey to India. Two years later he arrived in east India where he first roamed the country to see famous Buddhist scenes and sights and then settled in the Nalanda Monastery as a student. Eleven years later, having studied various schools of Indian Buddhism and having collected 400 or so Sanskrit versions of Buddhist literature, he began his journey home. In 695 (1st year of the Zhengsheng reign of Empress Wu Zetian), he arrived at Luoyang to the personal welcome of the empress. His translations and works amounted to 239 volumes in 61 titles, second only to the achievements of Xuanzang.

The Buddhist ties between China and India went on uninterruptedly for more than a thousand years from the Han to the Song dynasties. It was not until the 12th century when India was invaded by an alien nation and Buddhism was suppressed there that the two nations' exchanges in this field were interrupted.

In the early 20th century Indian Buddhism showed signs of a revival. Buddhists from some Asian countries began to build temples in India. In the 1940s, Chinese Buddhists joined in this effort, hoping to restore the Sino-Indian Buddhist relations after the interruption of several centuries. In January 1940, a Chinese Buddhist delegation headed by Master Taixu visited India, and was accorded a warm welcome in Calcutta when they visited the Maha Bodhi Society, the Bangla Buddhist Association, and the International University founded by the celebrated poet Rabindranath Tagore (1861-1941). The visit laid a good foundation for restoring the Buddhist relations between the two nations.

In 1956, the Chinese Buddhist Association received an international Buddhist monks' delegation headed by India's Ven. Ananda Kusalyayana. Another Indian monk member of the delegation was Jagdis Kasyapa (1908-1976). That same year a Chinese Buddhist and cultural delegation visited India. The Chinese Buddhist Association received the Indian Buddhist scholar Rahula in 1958, and another Indian Buddhist scholar, Chandra Nanda, in 1983. These mutual exchanges gradually brought the Buddhists of both countries close together again.

2. China and Sri Lanka

Buddhist relations between China and Sri Lanka figure prominently in China's Buddhist relations with foreign countries. The two nations started exchanges in this field as early as the Eastern Jin Dynasty (317-420). According to Volume 54 of the *Book of Liang*, when the king of Sinhala (present-day Sri Lanka) learned that the emperor of China worshipped the Buddha and his doctrines, he dispatched an envoy to deliver a 1.38-metre-high jade statue of the Buddha to China. The envoy traveled first by sea, and it took him ten years to arrive at the Chinese capital located at present-day Nanjing in 406 (2nd year or the Yixi reign, Eastern Jin). At about the same time, in 410 (6th year of the Yixi reign), the Chinese monk Faxian left India and arrived in Sinhala. During Faxian's two-year stay there, he called on famous monks, collected Buddhist classics, and attended a grand parade of the Buddha's tooth sarira. By the time he left Sinhala and began his journey back to China in 412 (8th year of the Yixi reign), he had already cultivated a reputation for himself. Faxian today remains a household name in Sri Lanka, where there is the Faxian Cave, probably the former residence of the Chinese monk during his stay in that country.

During the Southern and Northern Dynasties (420-589), eight Sinhalese *bhiksunis* visited Songjing (present-day Nanjing), the capital of the Southern Dynasty. Shortly afterwards, another group of eleven Sinhalese nuns headed by Tissara arrived in China to preside over a ceremony in which Chinese nuns were to receive the commandments from two Nikayas of Sangha. Chinese Buddhists built a temple for the nuns from Sinhala and named it the Tissara Temple, an event which has since become a legend of Sino-Sri Lanka Buddhist exchanges.

The Indian monk Amoghavajra (705-775) was said to be a native of Sinhala. In 742 (1st year of the Tianbao reign, Tang Dynasty), he led a Chinese delegation on a journey to study in Sinhala. When he returned to Chang'an four years later, he organized a workshop to translate scriptures and became the father of the Esoteric sect of Chinese Buddhism.

During the Song Dynasty (960-1279), China retained a close Buddhist relationship with Sinhala. It was not until Western colonialists invaded the country that the frequent exchanges of visits between the monks of the two nations were interrupted.

The Sino-Sri Lanka Buddhist relations came into their own once again in the 1930s when Ven. Narada, a famed abbot of the

Vajrarama Monastery of Colombo, visited Shanghai, where he established wide contacts with local Buddhists and made the decision to accept five Chinese monks to study in Ceylon. In 1940, the eminent monk Taixu headed a Chinese delegation on a visit to Ceylon, and talked to Dr. Gunapala Piyasena Malalasekera (1899-1973), leader of the All Ceylon Buddhist Congress, about ways and means to establish a World Fellowship of Buddhists. In 1942, Ven. Fafang, a disciple of Taixu, arrived in Ceylon to preach the doctrines of Mahayana Buddhism. In 1946, the Han-Tibetan Buddhist Academy of China and the Maha Bodhi Society of Ceylon reached an agreement. As a result two Chinese students went to study in Ceylon and three Ceylonese students arrived in China. In 1950, Ven. Fafang was invited to Ceylon University as a lecturer on Chinese Buddhism.

The Sino-Sri Lanka Buddhist relationship became even closer after the founding of the People's Republic of China. In 1956 the Ceylon Buddhist circles launched a campaign to compile an English version of *Encyclopedia of Buddhism* to mark the 2,500th anniversary of the nirvana of Sakyamuni. The Chinese Buddhist Association responded by forming a panel of writers who contributed manuscripts on Chinese Buddhism. In 1961, at the request of Ceylon's Buddhist circles, the Chinese Buddhist Association escorted the Buddha's tooth sarira to Ceylon to be worshiped by local monks. In 1979, the visiting prime minister of Sri Lanka, Ranasinghe Premadasa, presented a reproduction of an ancient statue of the Buddha to the Chinese Buddhist Association. Since then, the two countries have exchanged visits of Buddhists to step up their bilateral relationship. In 1986, five Chinese Buddhist Seminary students arrived in Sri Lanka, while Buddhist students from Sri Lanka were enrolled in Peking University. Thanks to the frequent exchanges, Sino-Sri Lanka friendship has steadily been enhanced.

3. China and Nepal

The Buddhist relations between the two good-neighbor countries of China and Nepal have come a long way. A legend that is still popular in Nepal has it that in remote antiquity what is today's capital city of Kathmandu was a lake surrounded by mountains. It was Manjusri who wielded his sharp sword and slashed open the mountains to the south, draining the water and turning the lake into land. Whatever its origin, one thing is certain about this legend — it shows Nepal's close ties with China and Chinese Buddhism, for Manjusri is a major bodhisattva of Mahayana Buddhism and his domain was Mount Wutai of China.

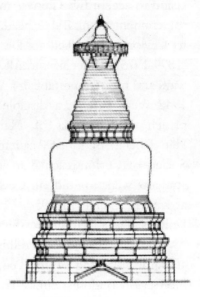

The model of the White Dagoba designed by the Nepalese architect Aniko for the Miaoying Temple in Dadu (now Beijing) of the Yuan Dynasty

More than 2,500 years ago, Suddhodana's son, Siddhartha Gautama (565-486 BC), was born in Lumbini in Nepal. Gautama later embarked on a religious life, and, through the practice of a series of austerities, achieved Buddhahood. For this he is deified as "Sakyamuni," or "Sage of the Sakya Clan." After 45 years of travels and preaching, he founded Buddhism. Since Buddhism was introduced into China in first century BC, Lumbini, the birthplace of Sakyamuni, has become the mecca for Chinese Buddhist pilgrims.

In 405 (1st year of the Yixi reign, Eastern Jin Dynasty), Faxian, the Chinese high monk who was studying in India, paid a visit to Lumbini, becoming perhaps the first Chinese to do so. *Faxian's Pilgrimage to India* rendered a detailed account of his visit to Lumbini and Kapilavastu.

While Faxian was studying Buddhism in India, Buddhabhadra, a well-known monk who belonged to the same caste as Sakyamuni, was preaching and translating Buddhist scriptures in China. One of his translations, the sixty-volume *Buddhavatamsaka-mahavaipulya Sutra (Garland Sutra),* became a major scripture for Chinese Buddhism. After Faxian returned, Buddhabhadra joined him at the Daochang Monastery in present-day Nanjing where they translated six major scriptures and commandments.

When Xuanzang was studying in India, he did the same as Faxian had done. In 633 (7th year of the Zhenguan reign, Tang Dynasty), he arrived in Nepal for a visit to Lumbini and Kapilavastu. According to his eyewitness account in the *Records on the Western Regions of the Great Tang Empire*, the places were clustered with Buddhist establishments, and there were more than 2,000 monks devoted to the study of both Mahayana and Hinayana Buddhism.

In the seventh century, King Songtsan Gampo of Tibet married Princess Wencheng of the Tang Dynasty and Princess Bhrikuti Devi of Nepal. As both princesses were Buddhists, they helped promote exchanges between China and Nepal and opened up a shortcut for Chinese pilgrims to go to India by way of Tibet and Nepal. It was precisely by this route that the three hundred or so Chinese monks dispatched by the Northern Song Dynasty arrived in India to pursue Buddhist studies.

Nepal is world famous for its handicrafts. During the Yuan Dynasty, Nepalese craftsmen were invited to build a gold pagoda for Phags-pa in Tibet. One of these craftsmen was the famed artisan Aniko, who later arrived in Dadu (present-day Beijing), capital of the Yuan Dynasty, where the imperial court entrusted him with the task of casting Buddhist statues, painting, and building construction projects. The White Dagoba of the Miaoying Temple in Beijing's West District was designed by him and constructed under his supervision.

In over half a century since the founding of the People's Republic, Buddhist relations between China and Nepal have progressed a great distance. In 1956, at the invitation of Ven. Amrita Nanda, a fifteen-member Chinese delegation with Shes-rab-raya-mtso as leader and Zhao Puchu as deputy leader attended the fourth session of the World Fellowship of Buddhists in Nepal. In 1959, the Chinese Buddhist Association invited a six-member delegation of the Nepalese Society for the Rejuvenation of Buddhism, headed by Ven. Amrita Nanda, to pay a month-long visit to various parts of China, thereby greatly enhancing the understanding and friendship between the Buddhists of both countries. Shortly after the Nepalese delegation returned home, the Chinese embassy at Kathmandu donated a fund on behalf of the Chinese Buddhist Association to the Nepalese government for the construction of a science center.

The exchanges between Chinese and Nepalese Buddhists have continued unabated since China adopted the policy of reform and opening up to the outside world. More visits have been exchanged. In 1997, five Nepalese *sramanerikas* were ordained to the *bhiksuni* commandments in Guangdong.

To promote Sino-Nepalese friendship, the Chinese Buddhist Association built a Chinese-style monastery in Lumbini, which was completed and consecrated in a grand ceremony in the year 2000.

4. China and Myanmar

Theravada Buddhism prevails over the religious life of Myanmar, but no conclusive historical evidence is extant as to the exact time for the introduction of Buddhism into Myanmar. Legend has it that in the third century BC, King Asoka of the Mayura Dynasty in ancient India dispatched Buddhist preachers to neighboring countries and regions, including a so-called "Golden Region," but whether this is a reference to Myanmar is yet to be authenticated. Another theory has it that Buddhism spread into Myanmar from Sinhala during the fifth century AD. Both theories attest to the long history of Buddhism in Myanmar. In Volume Ten of his *Records on the Western Regions of the Great Tang Empire*, Xuanzang mentioned that in a country called Sriksetra, Buddhists were making a living by soliciting alms. The *Biographies of Famous Tang Pilgrims to Western Regions* written by Yijing, who lived in an age slightly later than Xuanzang, said that a Chinese monk and a native of Jiangling (in Jingzhou in present-day Hubei Province) by the name of Tanguang once visited the region of Arakan in western Myanmar, and he won the respect of the local king by offering him a copious tribute.

In the seventh century Theravada Buddhism was introduced from Myanmar into the Dai-inhabited areas of Yunnan. In 792, the younger brother of the king of Myanmar, known at the time as the kingdom of Pyu, visited China and delivered Buddhist music scores to the Tang imperial court. Buddhism met its demise in Myanmar as a result of the Thai-Myanmese war in the 12th century. But shortly afterwards, Theravada Buddhism once again found its way from Thailand into Yunnan by way of Myanmar. (For details, see Section 3, Chapter 1). Historical records show that in the 18th century, the king of Myanmar dispatched an envoy to deliver Buddhist statues and Buddhist scriptures in Myanmese to the emperor of China — highly likely written in the Pali language spelled in the Myanmese alphabet.

The founding of New China in 1949 saw new growth in the Sino-Myanmese Buddhist relationship. In 1955, a ten-member Chinese Buddhist Association delegation, headed by Shes-rab-rgya-mtsho, visited Myanmar at the invitation of Myanmese Buddhist circles. Most members of the delegation were well-known personages. They gave their Myanmese friends quite a few gifts, including Buddhist sariras, a Chinese edition of the *Tripitaka*, monastic robes in Han and Tibetan styles, alms bowls, and staffs. In September of the same year, a 12-member Myanmese Buddhist delegation, headed by U Thien Maung, arrived in Beijing to escort a Buddha's tooth sarira from China to Myanmar for public display. The Chinese Buddhist Association held a grand farewell ceremony in Guangji Monastery, which was attended by more than a thousand people from various walks of life, and appointed Zhao Puchu as the head of a Chinese delegation to go along with the Myanmese delegation on the journey to Myanmar. When the airplane carrying the Buddha's tooth sarira arrived in Yangon, President Ba U and Premier U Nu were at the airport to personally carry the golden stupa enshrined with the sarira from the airplane. When the float loaded with the sarira drove through the city, the entire population of Yangon came out into the streets to greet it. During the sarira's eight-month display, more than one million people paid homage to it. To see the Buddha's tooth sarira from China had been a dream cherished by the Myanmese people for many generations, and when the dream came true at last, shortly after the founding of the People's Republic of China, the enthusiasm for this was immeasurable.

In May 1956, a delegation of the Chinese Buddhist Association arrived in Myanmar following an invitation to attend the closing ceremony of the sixth grand summons ceremony[1] in commemoration of the 2,500th anniversary of the nirvana of Sakyamuni. When the Chinese delegation headed by Hubameng, a religious leader of the ethnic Dai background, escorted the Buddha's tooth sarira back to China, the government of Myanmar sent U Khin Maung Phyu, secretary-general of the Myanmese government, and two others to accompany the delegation until the sarira arrived in Kunming.

In October 1958, the Chinese Buddhist Association presented a replica of the Buddha's tooth sarira to Myanmar at the request of the Buddha Sasana Council of Myanmar. Later, a pagoda was erected in the region of Myitkyina in north Myanmar to enshrine the gift as a symbol of Sino-Myanmese friendship.

China's current policy of reform and opening up to the outside world has brought the Buddhists of the two nations even more closely together. In 1994 and 1996 respectively, the Buddha's tooth sarira was again publicly displayed in Myanmar, and the Chinese Buddhist Association dispatched a number of young monks to study Theravada Buddhism in Myanmar.

Obviously the Buddha's tooth sarira has also played a major role in the Sino-Myanmese Buddhist relationship. Their shared love of the sarira is indeed a bond to bring Buddhists of both countries closely together.

5. China and Cambodia

Buddhist relations between China and Cambodia began during the Southern and Northern Dynasties in the fifth century.

---

[1] At this grand summons ceremony, taking place for the sixth time in Buddhist history in 1956 in memory of the nirvana of Sakyamuni, an unprecedented number of 2,500 monks participated in proofreading and annotating the Pali edition of the *Tripitaka*.

Cambodia was known as Funan at the time. According to volume 58 of the *Book of the Southern Qi Dynasty*, an Indian monk by the name of Nagasena, was residing in China's Nanhai (present-day Guangdong). He had once arrived in Funan by ship and talked to the king about the prosperity of Buddhism in China. The king, delighted by what he heard, entrusted Nagasena to bring a letter of credence and gifts to Xiao Ze, Emperor Wudi of the Southern Qi Dynasty (479-502) in 484 (2nd year of the Yongming reign). The event probably marked the first Buddhist contact between China and Cambodia. Shortly afterwards, Sanghapala (459-524), a Cambodian monk known in his country for his academic accomplishments, arrived at the Chinese capital in present-day Nanjing, settled down in the Zhengguan Temple, and joined the Indian monk Gunabhadra (394-468) in the study of Mahayana Buddhism. After the Southern Qi Dynasty fell, Sanghapala went into hiding and lost contact with the public.

When Xiao Yan seized political power and became Emperor Wudi of the Liang Dynasty (502-557), he converted to Buddhism and began searching for talented Buddhists. In 503 (2nd year of the Tianjian reign, Liang Dynasty), another Cambodian monk, Mandra (5th-6th centuries), arrived in China to deliver many Sanskrit Buddhist scriptures and gifts to the Chinese emperor. In 506 (5th year of the Tianjian reign, Liang Dynasty), Emperor Wudi found the whereabouts of Sanghapala, brought him out of his hermitage, and allowed him to resume his translation work. It was said he translated a total of 38 volumes in 11 Buddhist sutras and treatises (another theory puts it at 10), a small number of which were probably done together with Mandra. In 519 (18th year of the Tianjian reign) and 539 (5th year of the Datong reign), the king of Cambodia twice paid tributes to Emperor Wudi. When the emperor learned from one of the Cambodian envoys that Funan was in possession of the Buddha's hair sariras, he dispatched Monk Shi Baoyun to go along with the envoy back to Cambodia to ask the Cambodian king for a portion of the sariras and to invite a famous Cambodian *Tripitaka* expert to come preach in China.

It so happened that the famous Indian monk Paramartha was in Funan at the time, and with the consent of the Cambodian king, he was invited to China. Paramartha eventually emerged as one of the four major Buddhist translators in China and made great contributions to the development of Buddhism in this country. After the Chen Dynasty (557-589) seized power from the Liang Dynasty, more Cambodian Buddhists arrived in China as translators. Judging from the scriptures translated by Parmartha and other Cambodian monks in China, the same type of Mahayana Buddhism was dominating the religious life of Cambodia at the time.

During the sixth century, Funan was renamed Chenla. In Volume Ten of his *Records on the Western Regions of the Great Tang Empire*, Xuanzang mentioned Isana City as the capital Chenla, but because he had never been to that country he was not able to give an eyewitness account of the place. In the early ninth century, the king of Chenla began construction of Angkor City, which eventually assumed its present shape after the hard work of several generations. Today, Angkor, with its central monastery having the same name, is the pride and emblem of the Cambodian people.

After the 12th century, Chenla became Cambodia, and due to the influence of Thailand and Myanmar, the Cambodian people were gradually converted to Theravada Buddhism, which resulted in the disappearance of Mahayana Buddhism in that country.

Exchanges between the Buddhists of China and Cambodia were meager over the last few centuries, but the situation improved somewhat after the founding of New China in 1949. In

May 1957, at the invitation of the Cambodian Buddhist circles, a Chinese delegation headed by Chisong arrived in Cambodia for a ceremony to mark the 2,500th anniversary of the nirvana of Sakyamuni. During this ceremony, members of the Chinese delegation came into wide contact with their hosts, including leaders of the two major local Buddhist sects. In June 1958, a Cambodian Buddhist delegation headed by Ven. Preah Huo Tat was warmly received by Chinese Buddhists when they visited China. Both events marked the restoration of Sino-Cambodian Buddhist relations after an interruption of several decades.

6. China and Thailand

The Buddhist ties between China and Thailand enjoy a time-honored history. As early as the fifth century, the tribesmen of present-day Thailand believed in Buddhism or Brahmanism, and those who followed Buddhism were in touch with Buddhists in China. The Khmer monks inhabiting the Mekong River valley, for example, often came to China to preach, while Chinese monks reciprocated by paying return visits.

According to Chinese history books, there were four countries in western Thailand — Lang-ya-hsiu, P'an-P'an, Ch'ih-t'u, and Dvaravati — in ancient times, and all of them had contacts with China.

In 515 (12th year of the Tianjian reign, Liang Dynasty), the king of Lang-ya-hsiu dispatched an envoy who brought a letter of credentials to the Liang emperor to foster friendly relations. Beginning from 529 (3rd year of the Datong reign, Liang Dynasty), P'an-t'u repeatedly sent envoys to present gifts such as models of pagodas, agalloch eaglewood (*Aquilaria agallocha*), sariras, and bodhi tree leaves to the Liang court. Buddhism enjoyed a wide popularity in Ch'ih-t'u, and Emperor Yangdi (Yang Guan) of the Sui Dynasty (581-618) once dispatched a minister by the name of Chang Jun to visit the country with gifts, to the delight of the king, who reciprocated by sending his son to the Sui court with gifts. An envoy from Ch'ih-t'u arrived in China with objects for divination in 638 (12th year of the Zhenguan reign, Tang Dynasty), and another envoy visited China with ivory and big pearls in 649 (23rd year of the Zhenguan reign), and China repaid the goodwill with gifts of thoroughbred horses. A Chinese child monk by the name of Dachengdeng settled down in Dvaravati as a child with his parents. While there he was tonsured and became a monk, and once returned to Chang'an, where Xuanzang personally ordained him with commandments.

Some of these countries held vital access to India for Chinese monks traveling by sea after the seventh century. This was the same route followed by the Chinese monks, Yilang of Yezhou, Yihui of Luoyang, and Daolin of Jingzhou on their way to India, according to the *Biographies of Famous Tang Pilgrims to the Western Regions,* and they all visited Lang-ya-hsiu. Yihui actually died there.

In 1387 (12th year of the Hongwu reign, Ming Dynasty), the kingdoms of Sien and Lavo were unified, and the new nation was known as "Siam," a name that remained until it was changed to "Thailand" in the 12th century. After the founding of New China, Sino-Thai Buddhist relations achieved major development, and received a great impetus in 1975 with the establishment of diplomatic relations between the two nations.

In 1956, with the tacit consent of the Thai government in the absence of a diplomatic relationship with China, four Thai students studying in India visited China as members of a seven-nation International monks' delegation at the invitation of the Chinese Buddhist Association. During their one-month visit, the students wrote articles introducing Buddhism in China to those in their homeland, enabling the Buddhists of Thailand to gain some understanding of the Chinese government policy of religious freedom, and playing a good role in promoting friendly relations between Chinese and Thai Buddhists.

After the adoption of the policy of reform and opening up to the outside world, mutual exchanges between Buddhists of China and Thailand have become more frequent. In June 1980, a Thai Buddhist monks' delegation visited China, while Zhao Puchu, leader of the Chinese Buddhist Association, and Li Rongxi, council member of the association, were attending a standing committee session of the World Conference on Religion and Peace (WCRP) in Bangkok, where they also called on local Buddhist leaders.

In May 1981, an official from the department of religious affairs of the Ministry of Education in Thailand led a five-member Buddhist delegation to visit China at the invitation of the Chinese Buddhist Association.

In April 1982, in celebrating the 200th anniversary of the establishment of Bangkok as the capital city, the religious circles of Thailand issued an invitation to the Chinese Buddhist Association to attend the celebrations and receive a precious gift — three large bronze statues of the Buddha. The Chinese Buddhist Association dispatched a delegation headed by Zhengguo to accept the statues.

In June 1993, the Thai Sangharaja (patriarch) visited China, and in 1995, the Buddha's finger sarira was sent from China to Thailand to be worshipped by Thai Buddhists. These two events were extolled as unprecedented in the history of Chinese-Thai Buddhist relations. Today, some Chinese monks are studying Theravada Buddhism in Thailand.

Generally speaking, the Buddhist relationship between China and Thailand has never been closer than it is today.

7. China and Indonesia

Indonesia today is basically an Islamic country. In ancient times, however, Buddhism was popular in this island nation. This was particularly the case in Java and Sumatra. Java is known variously in Chinese history books as Yavadi, Jaya, Java, and Holing. The relationship between Chinese and Indonesian Buddhists dates back to the fifth century.

In 412 (8th year of the Yixi reign, Eastern Jin Dynasty), Faxian, a famed Chinese monk on a westbound pilgrimage in search of Buddhist doctrines, stopped at Java for five months on his way back to China from Sinhala. According to Faxian's *Pilgrimage to India*, Brahmanism held sway in Java at that time, and the influence of Buddhism was negligible. It was not until the arrival of the celebrated Indian monk Gunavarman that Buddhism began to thrive there.

It is said that on the eve of the arrival of Gunavarman in Java, the mother of the king of Java dreamed of the arrival of a Taoist on board a spaceship. The next morning Gunavarman arrived. The mother queen was both surprised and delighted, surprised that her dream had come true, and delighted because she had acquired an excellent teacher. She later became a follower of the Indian monk, who ordained her to the *Pancasila* (*Five Commandments*), thus making her a real Buddhist. Her son, the king, however, did not believe in Buddhism and so she began to persuade him. "The two of us became mother and son because of fate," she said. "Now that I have been converted to Buddhism and received the *Five Commandments*, I'm afraid our mother-son relationship will come to an end during my lifetime if you continue to disbelieve in it." The son, for fear of hurting his mother's feelings, had no choice but to beseech Gunavarman for ordination of the *Five Commandments*, though it took quite a long time before he became a pious Buddhist.

At that time, a neighboring nation was invading across the border region of Java. The king turned to Gunavarman for council. "The treacherous enemy is trying to take advantage of its superior military force and dispatching troops to invade my country," he told his master. "If I send troops to fight them, the casualties are bound to be staggering, but if I choose not to meet them tit for tat, my country runs the risk of annihilation. What is to be done? As your disciple, I wonder if you can give me a good idea?" His master already had an idea. "The violent enemy should definitely be countered," he said, "but at the same time let us fill our hearts with benevolence and refrain from senseless killing." The king took his master's instruction and launched a counterattack. Amidst a boom of militant drums, the sky reverberated with battle cries. The engagement did not take long before the enemy beat a hasty retreat. During the battle the king was injured by an arrow, but his master cured the wound in no time with his holy dew. The experience gave rise to the king's desire to leave home and become a monk. He summoned his ministers and told them to choose a new king because he wanted to abdicate and become tonsured as a monk and to live the rest of his life in a monastery. Not believing what they had heard, the ministers fell on their knees. One of them said, "If Your Majesty leaves the throne, our people will have no one to fall back on when we are confronted with a vicious enemy nation. Without Your Majesty's blessings and protection, what will become of the people? Doesn't Your Majesty have mercy on the multitude as a man of benevolence? We would like to risk death to plead with you not to leave and become a monk. Please stay on as our king."

The king, touched by the sincerity of his court ministers, began to have second thoughts about his decision. Then he raised three demands — first, the entire nation should worship Gun-

avarman; second, the entire country should refrain from slaugh-
tering animals; and third, all the property in storage should be
used to aid the sick and relieve the poor. If these demands were
met, he said, he would stay. The ministers were delighted, and
they all agreed to accept the demands. As a result, the people
throughout the country received ordination by Gunavarman and
became Buddhists, and Buddhism in Java began to thrive.

The Propagating Buddhism by Gunavarman in Java was
known to all the Buddhists in China. In 424 (2nd year of the
Jingping reign, Song Dynasty), the well-known monks Huiguan
and Huicong met Emperor Wendi (Liu Yilong) and suggested
that Gunavarman be invited to China to preach. The emperor
consented, and instructed the regional chief of Jiaozhou, in present-day north Viet Nam, to dispatch a ship to Java to fetch
Gunavarman. Huiguan immediately sent Fazhang, Daochong,
Daojun, and some other monks to go with a letter to the king of
Java, asking his permission to release Gunavarman. When the
mission arrived at Java, however, Gunavarman had already left
for somewhere else. The mission was thus unaccomplished.[1]

According to Volume 97 of the *Book of Songs*, in 435 (12th
year of the Yuanjia reign), the king of Java sent a mission to
China to deliver a letter of credentials, offer religious objects,
and solicit friendship. The letter of credentials received by the
Chinese side contained a full account of the popularity of Buddhism in his country. During the 436-520 period (from the 13th
year of the Yuanjia reign of the Song to the 1st year of the
Putong reign of the Liang), Java repeatedly sent missions to
China to present gifts and seek friendly relations.

---

[1] Before the Chinese mission arrived in Java, Gunavarman had already left the
country and embarked on a journey aboard a merchant ship. A windstorm rose
midway on the journey, sending the ship adrift to Guangzhou, where he landed. In 431
(8th year, Yuanjia reign, Song), he arrived in Jianye (present-day Nanjing).

During the Tang Dynasty (618-907), Sino-Indonesian Buddhist relations grew even closer. Many Chinese monks on their way to India visited Java or Sumatra, and some of them even stayed there permanently. One of these was Yijing, who stayed in Srivijaya, a kingdom in Sumatra, for six months studying the Indian language before resuming his journey to India. Eleven years later, having studied in India for 11 years, Yijing visited Srivijaya once again, where he devoted himself to translation and writing for six years. It was not until 695 (1st year of the Zhengsheng reign of Empress Wu Zetian) that he left for home. During the Kaiyuan reign (713-741) of the Tang Dynasty, the esoteric master Vajrabodhi (669-741) also stayed for a while in Srivijaya on his way from Sinhala to China. In 781 (2nd year of the Jianzhong reign, Tang Dynasty), the Java monk Bianhong arrived in Chang'an with religious gifts for Chinese monasteries. He settled down in the Qinglong Monastery to study Tantrism from Monk Huiguo.

The Sino-Indonesian Buddhist ties continued uninterrupted during the Song (960-1279) Dynasty. In 983 (8th year of the Taping Xingguo reign), the Chinese monk Fayu stopped over in Srivijaya on his way back to China from a pilgrimage to India. When Fayu went to India again, the imperial court of the Song entrusted him with a letter of good will to the king of Srivijaya.

After the fifteenth century, Islamism became the major religion of Indonesia, and Buddhism went into decline. The Buddhist ties between China and Indonesia faded as well. Buddhism still exists in Indonesia mainly among the Chinese residents there. In March 1965, a Chinese Buddhist delegation headed by Zhao Puchu visited Indonesia. In the 1970s, Lee Rongkun, an Indonesian Buddhist of Chinese descent, visited China. Since then, however, contacts between the Buddhists of the two countries have been few and far between. Whether the relationship can be restored to its former glory depends on the development in bi-lateral relations.

8. China and Korea

Buddhist ties between China and Korea date back to the fourth century. At that time, the Korean Peninsula belonged to three countries, Koguryo, Shinla, and Baekje. Individuals were sent or came on their own to China to learn Buddhism. Some of these people chose to stay after they finished their studies, while the others returned to preach Buddhism

Official records date Sino-Korean Buddhist relations back to 372 (2nd year of the Xian'an reign, Eastern Jin Dynasty), when Fu Jian, who had made himself emperor of the Former Qin Dynasty in Chang'an, sent envoys and monks to Kogurya with gifts of Buddhist statues and scriptures. The mission was warmly received, and the king of Kogurya sent an envoy to the Former Qin Dynasty to express his gratitude. This exchange triggered a constant stream of people from these three Korean countries to arrive in China to learn Buddhism, and the arrivals reached an all-time high during the Sui and Tang dynasties.

During the Sui and Tang dynasties, different sects emerged in Chinese Buddhism and each of them acquired some followers in Korea. In 628 (2nd year of the Zhenguan reign, Tang Dynasty), the Kogurya monk Todung arrived in Chang'an to study under Jizang, the patriarch of the Three Sastras sect. He ended up in Japan as a Dhamma Pakati preacher. Shinbang, a famed monk from Koguryo, distinguished himself in his study in China during the Tang Dynasty, and was summoned by the emperor to join Xuanzang's scripture translation workshop at the Hongfu Monastery. Another monk from Koguryo, Wonchik, a Vijnanavada scholar and disciple of Xuanzang, enjoyed the same prestige as another of Xuanzang's disciples, Kuiji. In 638 (12th year of the Zhenguan reign), the Koguryo monk Chachang arrived in Chang'an with a dozen or so disciples to study the *vinaya* (monastic rules) and preach the commandments. The *Tripitaka* he brought back to his country was the first of its kind in Korean history. In 661 (6th year of the Xianqing reign, Tang Dynasty) another monk from Koguryo, Uisang, became a classmate of Fazang, the *de facto* father of the Huayan sect, at the Zhixiang Monastery on Zhongnan Mountain. While there, both of them studied the *Garland Sutra*. After he returned to his country he became the patriarch of the Huayan Sect of the East Sea.

Many Korean monks studied Esoteric Buddhism in China. In 632 (6th year of the Zhenguan reign), the Koguryo monk Myonglang arrived in China to study miscellaneous Tantrism. In 635 (9th year of the Zhenguan reign), he returned to become the father of the Tong-hae-shin-in sect. Many Koguryo monks studied Tantrism in China during the Kaiyuan reign (713-741) of the Tang Dynasty.

But even more Korean monks came to China to pursue Chan studies. According to historical records, Pomlang arrived during the early Tang Dynasty to study under Daoxin, the forth-generation patriarch of the Chan sect. When Pomlang's disciple Shinhaeng came to China, he became a student of Zhikong, a disciple of Shengxiu. The *Quotations of Buddhists in the Jingde Reign of the Dynasty* mentions many Korean monks who were studying Chan Buddhism in China.

One of them is particularly worth mentioning. He was Gim Kyokak, a scion of the imperial family of Shinla, who arrived in China during the mid-Tang Dynasty and settled down on Mount Jiuhua in present-day Qingyang County, Anhui Province. He soon won the respect of local Buddhists. Three years after his death in 803 (19th year of the Zhenyuan reign, Tang Dynasty), his remains, contained in a sitting posture in a stone receptacle, remained in perfect condition, prompting local Buddhists to believe that he was the reincarnation of Ksitigarbha. Thus Mount Jiuhua became one of the four major mountain sanctuaries of Chinese Buddhism and a mecca for tens of thousands of pilgrims from all over the world.

During the late Tang Dynasty Chinese Buddhism suffered a major setback at the hands of Emperor Wuzong. His crackdown on Buddhism was followed by an endless war and turmoil during the Five Dynasties and ten Kingdoms Period, causing great losses to religious literature. Many of the lost scriptures and treatises found their way to Korea. That is why after the Five Dynasties many precious works of Buddhist literature were retrieved from Korea, and because of that Chinese Buddhists have a lot for which to thank their Korean counterparts.

Sino-Korean Buddhist relations continued into the Song Dynasty. In 989 (2nd year of the Duangong reign, Song Dynasty), the king of Koguryo sent the monk Yoka to China to ask for an edition of the *Tripitaka*, a request that was readily granted by Zhao Gui, Emperor Tazong. The rulers of the Liao and the Jin dynasties also gave gifts of the *Khitan Tripitaka* to Koguryo.

Many monks in Koguryo were skilled at copying Buddhist sutras with gold powder. This ability was not lost on the rulers of China. The Yuan Dynasty (1271-1368), for example, twice sent scouts to that country to select such copiers. On both occasions, a team of more than one hundred copiers was put together and brought to China to copy the scriptures. It took about two years to finish copying the *Tripitaka* in gold. Unfortunately, these precious copies are nowhere to be found today.

After the Yuan Dynasty, Korean Buddhists developed a method for practicing both Chan and Pure Land Buddhism at the same time, probably due to the influence of the Chinese Buddhist practice at the time. After the Japanese invasion of Korea, Sino-Korean Buddhist relations were gradually torn apart.

Following World War II, the Korean Peninsula was divided into two countries. While Buddhist contacts across the boundary between China and North Korea were sporadic at best, exchanges between China and the Republic of Korea were non-existent. It was not until diplomatic relations were established between China and the Republic of Korea that Buddhists from both sides restored their contacts. The late Zhao Puchu, president of the Chinese Buddhist Association, visited the Republic of Korea, while major leaders of the Buddhist Religious Group Association and of the various Buddhist sects, paid repeated visits to China. Members of the Tiantai sect in the Republic of Korea founded an ancestral memorial hall at the Guoqing Monastery on Tiantai Mountain, Zhejiang Province. In 1995, a 33-member South Korean Buddhist delegation attended a Sino-South Korean-Japanese Conference on Friendly Buddhist Exchanges in Beijing. These activities helped cement the ranks of Buddhists of these countries.

9. China and Japan

The Buddhist relations between China and Japan date back to the mid-sixth century. In 552 (2nd year, Tianzheng reign of the Liang Dynasty), the king of Baekje had some Chinese editions of Buddhist scriptures and statues presented to Japan as gifts. The event marked the beginning of Buddhism in Japan. After that the Buddhists of China and Japan were in direct contact with each other. While the Japanese came to China to study Buddhism, Chinese monks went to Japan to preach.

With the emergence of various sects, Buddhism reached its zenith during the Sui and Tang Dynasties in China. This attracted many Japanese to China to learn about Buddhism during the 593-628 period (from the 13th year of the Kaihuang reign of the Sui Dynasty to the 2nd year of the Zhenguan reign of the Tang Dynasty). In 607 (3rd year of the Dayi reign, Sui Dynasty) Prince Shotoku of Japan, who advocated Buddhism and worshiped Chinese culture, dispatched an envoy to China to establish friendly relations. The following year he began sending people to China to learn Buddhism. More Japanese monks arrived in China later on, and their pursuits went beyond Buddhism to cover all Chinese culture.

In 625 (8th year of the Wude reign, Tang Dynasty), the Korguryo monk Keikan began his lectures in Japan on the Sanlun (Three Treatise) sect, but he failed to establish it in Japan. It was not until the return of some Japanese monks from studies in China that this sect was established there. More Japanese returned later from China, and as a result the Yogacara, Huayan, Chan, Pure Land, Tiantai, and Esoteric sects were established one after another. The one exception was the Vinaya sect, which was founded in Japan by the Chinese monk Ganjin.

Ganjin (688-763), a native of Jiangyang (present-day Yangzhou, Jiangsu Province), was an expert in *vinaya*. During the Kaiyuan reign of Emperor Xuanzong of the Tang Dynasty, he set out on a journey to Japan to preach commandments with a 21-member entourage at the invitation of the Japanese monks Eiei and Fusho, but the journey fell through. His four other attempts to go to Japan failed too, due to natural causes in some cases and man-made hurdles in others. Towards the end of his fifth abortive attempt he lost his eyesight, but his determination to visit Japan remained undeterred. Finally, in 753 (12th year of the Tianbao reign, Tang Dynasty), he embarked on his sixth journey at the age of 66 and succeeded in reaching Japan. He was accorded a warm welcome there and was put up in the Tadaiji Monastery at Nara, where it did not take long for him to begin preaching the commandments to his disciples, including the Japanese emperor, members of the imperial family, and commoners. In 757 (2nd year of the Zhide reign, Tang Dynasty), the emperor of Japan had the mansion of a deceased prince converted into a monastery and dedicated it to Ganjin. This was none other than what is now the Tosho Daiji Temple in Nara, and it became his domain. Shortly afterwards, he had altars established at the Yakushiji Temple in Shimotsuke and at the Kannonji Temple in Tsukushi. These, along with the Tosho Daiji Monastery, are known as the three major commandment altars of Japan.

While preaching Buddhism, Ganjin also brought the culture of the high Tang to Japan. Some of the disciples who went with him to Japan were experts in sculpture, handicrafts, and architecture. The Tosho Daiji Monastery in Nara, for example, is a fine example of high-Tang architecture, and its pattern was later followed by various other Buddhist sects when building their own sanctuaries. This phenomenon was indicative of China's cultural influence in Japan. The statue of Ganjin enshrined in the Tosho Daiji Monastery and wrought by one of his disciples is regarded as a national treasure of Japan, and the man himself has been deified by the Japanese people as the "Blind Sage."

Among the Japanese monks who studied in China during the Tang Dynasty was the outstanding Kukai, who studied Esoteric Buddhism from Huiguo at the Qinglong Monastery in Chang'an. In 806 (1st year of the Yuanhe reign, Tang Dynasty), he returned to Japan with 216 Buddhist classics and began disseminating Esoteric Buddhism. He founded Japan's headquarters of the Esoteric sect at Koyazan, and became the author of 150 or so books, thereby making a name for himself as a great master in disseminating the holy words of the Buddha.

Saicho and his disciple, Gishin, also rose to prominence in their studies of Buddhism in China. After the two of them arrived in China in 804 (20th year of the Zhenyuan reign, Tang Dynasty), they studied the Tiantai creed from their Chinese masters, Daosui and Hangman, and then received training in Esoteric Buddhism from Shunxiao at the Lingyan Monastery in present-day Shaoxing, Zhejiang Province. A year later they returned to Japan, bringing 230 Buddhist classics with them. Saicho was the author of 280 books, and extolled as a master preacher. Another of Saicho's disciples, Enjin, arrived in China in 838 (3rd year of the Kaicheng reign, Tang Dynasty) for a visit and studies of Esoteric Buddhism. He returned to Japan with 583 Buddhist scriptures in 847 (1st year of the Dazhong reign, Tang Dynasty). It became a custom for Japanese visiting China to return home with some Buddhist books.

Most of the Buddhist scriptures and treatises were destroyed during Emperor Wuzong's suppression of Buddhism during the Huichang reign (841-846), and even more losses were incurred during the war and turmoil of the Five Dynasties (907-960). Only the Chan sect, which passed its knowledge on through verbal transmission without recourse to writings, survived the melee and became the only sect of Chinese Buddhism to thrive after the Five Dynasties. In 1191 (2nd year of the Shaoxi reign, Southern Song Dynasty), the Japanese monk Eisai returned to Japan after having been trained in the meditation practices of Chan Buddhism by the Chan monk Huaichan of the Linji subsect, and established the Rinzai sect in his own country. Eisai's disciple, Dogen, came to China in 1223 (16th year of the Jiading reign, Southern Song Dynasty). Returning to Japan in 1227 (3rd year of the Baoqing reign, Southern Song Dynasty) from studies of the meditation practices of the Caodong subsect under the tutelage of Rujing at the Tiantong Temple in Ningbo, Zhejiang Province, he devoted himself to disseminating Chan Buddhism and established the Soto-shu sect (Japan's answer to the Caodong subsect) at the Eiheiji Temple. Following the Song Dynasty, exchanges between the monks of China and Japan continued to grow unabated.

In 1654 (11th year of the Shunzhi reign, Qing Dynasty), the Chinese monk Yingyuan arrived in Japan to preach Chan Buddhism at Nagasaki and Uji. Yingyuan (1592-1673) was a native of Fuqing in Fujian province and abbot of the Wanfu Temple on Huangbo Mountain. While in Japan, he built the Manfukuji Temple (named after the Wanfu Temple), established the Oboku-shu sect (named after Huangbo Mountain), and laid down the rule that the abbotcy of the Manfukuji Temple should be filled by a monk from China, a rule that was terminated by the 13th abbot. The Manfukuji Temple transplanted the traditions, monastic systems, and rituals from its Chinese counterparts, and some of these have remained unchanged to this day. In 1655 (12th year of the Shunzhi reign, Qing Dynasty), Mu'an arrived in Japan at the request of his master, Yingyuan, to assist him in running the Manfukuji Temple. He proved a great help in this, and after he became abbot of the temple, he went in for large-scale construction work and expanded the temple into a colossal affair. The Oboku-Shu sect, headquartered in the Manfukuji Temple today, still exerts a considerable influence on Japan's religious life.

Towards the end of the Qing Dynasty, Yang Wenhui, a lay Buddhist of China, took it upon himself to rejuvenate Buddhism by printing and publishing Buddhist scriptures. Many Japanese Buddhists helped him by collecting scriptures and treatises that had been missing in China and sending these back to China.

After the founding of New China, Buddhists exchange between China and Japan continued uninterrupted despite the fact that the two nations had no normal diplomatic relations. During the Asian and Pacific Peace Conference held in 1952, Zhao Puchu entrusted the Japanese delegates to bring a Buddhist statue to Japan as a token of peace and friendship. This gesture drew a warm response from Japanese Buddhist circles, which immediately wrote a letter of gratitude to Zhao. This was the first exchange between Buddhists of the two nations after the end of World War II. Beginning from that year, friendly Japanese Buddhists worked to collect the remains of Chinese martyrs who had died in Japan and sent them in separate shipments back to China. In 1957, the Chinese Buddhist Association received a goodwill delegation formed by various Buddhist sects in Japan, and a joint communique was issued to mark the event. This opened a new chapter in friendly religious exchanges between the two nations. In 1963, Buddhists from China and Japan jointly commemorated the 1,200th anniversary of the death of Ganjin. In 1964, Japanese Buddhists sent a delegation to attend a ceremony held by the Chinese Buddhist Association to commemorate the 1,300th anniversary of the nirvana of Xuanzang and consecrated a stupa enshrined with the Buddha's tooth sarira.

After Sino-Japanese diplomatic relations returned to normal, Buddhists from both countries stepped up their friendly exchanges. Activities such as the 1980 parade of the statue of Ganjin in his motherland are growing in scale and frequency. Further development will be achieved in Sino-Japanese Buddhist relations during the 21st century.

Chapter 4

Architecture of Chinese Buddhist Temples

1. Origin and Development

The temple where monks reside, practice self-cultivation, and propagate Buddhist creeds had its origins in religious life during Sakyamuni's age.

During Sakyamuni's lifetime, it was a custom in Indian society that *sramanas* should settle down and live in the forest. Before Sakyamuni achieved Buddhahood under a pippala tree, he had practiced austerities in the forest of a snowclad mountain for six years. After falling in with five mendicants who had previously deserted him and, in Deer Park preaching to them his first sermon on the Law, he continued to live in the forest. With his prestige mounting steadily, the ranks of his disciples also grew and they began to hope that Sakyamuni would have a permanent residence so that they could visit him and listen to his lectures. One of these was Bimbisara, king of Magadha and a devoted Buddhist, who built the Veluvanaramaya, or Bamboo Grove Monastery, in the city of Rajagrha and had Sakyamuni and his disciples move in. Shortly afterwards, a rich merchant by the name of Sudatta built the Jetavanaramaya, or Jeta Grove Monastery, in the city of Savatthi and dedicated it to Sakyamuni.

What prompted Sudatta to build the monastery was his meeting with Sakyamuni on a business trip to Rajagrha. During the meeting he invited Sakyamuni to give a lecture in Savatthi, and promised to build him and his entourage a monastery. When the meeting and trip were over, Sudatta returned to Savatthi and looked for a site for the construction of the monastery he had promised to build. When he visited the Jeta Garden, he was impressed by its picturesque scenery and peaceful environment and so he decided that this was the place he wanted. However, the garden was the private property of Prince Jeta. Sudatta found the prince and talked to him, offering to buy part of the garden at whatever price the prince might demand. The prince loved the garden so much that he flatly refused the acquisition proposal. Sudatta, however, was not discouraged. He continued to pester the prince. The prince, thinking that it wouldn't hurt to make a joke, offered what looked like an impossible price. "Sudatta," he said, "I'll let you have the garden if you can completely cover the ground of my garden with gold coins — that is the only price I will accept, and I'll not take anything less than that." The prince thought that this would discourage the merchant and he would then keep his mouth shut. What the prince did not expect was that Sudatta was delighted by the offer. "Well, if you really mean that, you should not go back on your word. I'll do as you like, covering the ground of your garden with gold coins."

Sudatta lost no time in dispatching a team of porters to transport gold coins from his treasury, and he quickly filled the garden with them. Prince Jeta was dumbfounded for he had never expected that the merchant was so wealthy. Upon further learning that the man bought the garden at this monumental price not for his own enjoyment but to build a monastery for Sakyamuni and the monks, the prince decided to perform a philanthropic deed as well. He readily agreed to sell the garden, but he would accept only half of the gold coins and donate the other half to provide for Sakyamuni and his disciples. The deal being thus struck, Sudatta had a large monastery built in the garden and named it "Jetavanaramaya." Sakyamuni lived there for a long period of time and delivered many lectures there.

The Veluvanaramaya and the Jetavanaramaya are the two earliest monasteries in the history of Buddhism. But at the time they were not known as "monasteries'" but rather as "sangharama," meaning "residence shared by Buddhists and laymen."

It is said that Buddhism was introduced to China in the first century by two Indian monks, Kasyapamatanga and Gobharana. When the two of them had arrived in this country, they were put up at the Court for Dependencies, a government institution for the reception of foreign guests. Later, the government had a residence built for them outside the Xiyong Gate in Luoyang and named it "White Horse Temple." Since then "temple" became a special term for a place lived in by monks.

The White Horse Temple was the first Buddhist monastery in the history of Chinese Buddhism. Its name was attributed to two stories. One is that when the two Indian monks arrived, they had their scriptures carried on the back of a white horse. The other is that when a king of ancient India was about to demolish the Caturdesa Sangharama in order to seize its tremendous amount of wealth, a white horse suddenly descended on the scene and neighed plaintively while galloping around the pagoda of the temple. This aroused the sympathy of the king, who gave up his idea of destroying the monastery and renamed it the White Horse Monastery. Since then every sangharama in India was named after the white horse, and so was the first Buddhist temple built in China. But which story is true depends on the reader's judgment.

With the popularization of Buddhism, the number of its

followers increased and more temples were constructed to accommodate them. According to Volume Three of the *Apology for Buddhist Truth* by the eminent Tang monk Falin, there were a total of 180 temples in Luoyang and Chang'an during the Western Jin Dynasty (265-316), and the number snowballed to an amazing 1,768 during the Eastern Jin Dynasty (317-420). The number kept growing during the ensuing Southern Dynasties, reaching 1,913 during the Song Dynasty (420-479) founded by Liu Yu, 2,015 during the Qi Dynasty (479-502) founded by Xiao Daocheng, and 2,954 during the Liang Dynasty (502-557) founded by Xiao Yan. The number might have been even greater during the Northern Dynasties. Nobody knows for sure how many monasteries and temples there are in China today, but the number can definitely be counted in the tens of thousands.

Buddhist monasteries were rather simple in their exteriors and interiors in the early days, but they grew increasingly in magnificence and elaborate details with the progress in science and culture. There is certainly nothing wrong about building gorgeous and glittering monasteries, especially from the perspective of "dignifying the national territory and rendering a human touch to the buildings." The imposing looks of a monastery not only appeal to the masses, but also embody the quintessential elements of Chinese culture. For tourists, they are irresistible attractions.

A monastery is not only for the use of monks. It is also a center for disseminating culture and educating people. In underdeveloped regions, people wanting to know how to read and write may go to local monasteries to be educated by the monks there. This was the situation in pre-1949 Tibet and in the Dai-inhabited areas of Yunnan. The situation has changed with the development of culture and education but monasteries, no matter where they are located, remain cultural and artistic entities of such a high caliber that they deserve to be marveled at.

2. Form and Layout

Buddhist establishments in China fall into two categories: monasteries and temples. Monasteries refer to those of large size and impressive architecture, whereas temples are small in size and their buildings far less imposing. This book takes a look at the architectural characteristics of monasteries.

The first monastery in China was built by the famed Chan master Huaihai (720-814) of the Tang Dynasty. A disciple of Daoyi (709-788), he carried out his master's unaccomplished will and built a monastery to receive and provide lodgings for the monks on Baizhang Mountain in present-day Jiangxi Province. He called it a *conglin* or *chanlin*. But his monastery was supposed to meet the everyday needs of its monk residents. It was simple in structure, and had a chamber for the abbot, a hall for preaching the dharma, a Sangha hall for meditation, and monks' dormitories. There was no hall of the Buddha out of the belief of the Chan sect that one's own mind is the Buddha and so there is no need to worship an idol built of clay or wood. Huaihai obviously did not build a hall of the Buddha because of the line in the *Vajracchedikaprajnaparamita-sutra*:

> "If by form one looks for the Buddha
> Or by the sound of the voice seeks me,
> This person walks the wrong path,
> And is unable to see the Buddha."

The absence of a Buddha's shrine in Huaihai's monastery not only accords with the sutra, but also with the practice of early Indian Buddhism — the sangharama did not have a Buddha shrine either.

Prior to the Song Dynasty (960-1279), Buddhist monasteries in China fell into several categories according to their purposes. Some were for preaching and some were for the enforcement of monastic discipline. The monasteries of different sects differed in interior furnishings. However, after the Song Dynasty these sects began to merge into the mainstream. For example, there was the integration of the Samadhi practice (i.e., meditation in tranquility) of the Chan sect with the doctrines of the Pure Land sect. The differences in the construction of monasteries diminished in this process. That is why the monasteries built after the Song Dynasty were more or less all of the same specifications and design.

A monastery of a fair size consists of a group of ancient buildings. Generally it faces south. The architecture is quintessentially Chinese, marked by unaffected simplicity and natural poise. The buildings are arranged in three lines. Aligned along the axial line are the centerpieces — the front gate hall or the Hall of Three Doors.[1] the Hall of Heavenly Kings, the Mahavira Hall, the Avalokitesvara Hall, and the Vairocana Hall (or Bhaisajyaguru Hall). The ancillary buildings are arranged along the eastern and western lines and serve practical purposes, such as a reception hall, a dining room, a warehouse, an abbot's chamber, a preaching hall, a meditation hall, and an ancestral hall. If more ancillary buildings are needed, they can be erected behind the eastern and western flanks, or another courtyard can be added beyond either one of the two lines. Some monasteries have ponds in front of them where fish in captivity can be free to swim, and a square inside the front gateway with bell and drum towers on both sides. The Tripitaka Pavilion is usually on the second floor of the posterior hall. The Guangji Monastery of Beijing follows exactly this layout — minus the pond for fish. See the diagram below:

---

[1] The "three doors" refer to *samathi*, which entails discipline, intent contemplation, and perfect absorption.

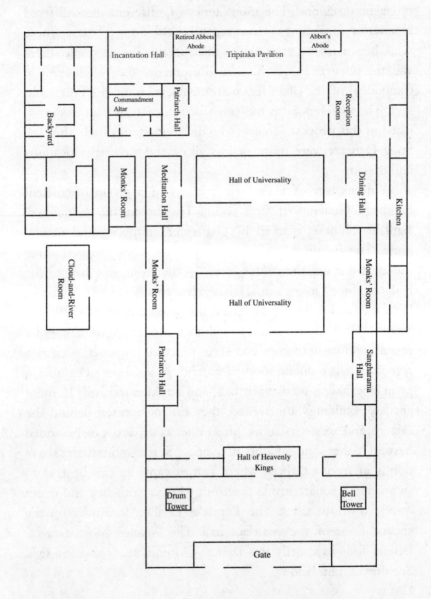

The layout of the Guangji Monastery in Beijing

The pond for fish in captivity is not indispensable to every monastery. Built mostly for symbolic purposes, it is generally situated in front of the gate hall, and its size varies. In its center will be a tiny isle atop which are tiny pavilions or some other small buildings. Buddhism advocates equality of all living beings and is opposed to the harming of life. The presence of the pond in which to set captive fish free is an embodiment of the Buddhist spirit of mercy and love of life. In the olden days, the Buddha's birthday in the fourth lunar month was often marked by a congregation standing by the pond to release birds, fish, and turtles into nature — an occasion Buddhists regarded as a good opportunity to accumulate virtue during their lifetimes.

In the beginning the pagoda was the centerpiece of any monastery, with houses built around it. With the passage of time, however, this was gradually replaced by the Buddha's Hall. Wherever a pagoda was needed, it was erected outside the monastery. In ancient India the pagoda was known as a "stupa," meaning "grave." Out of their reverence for the Buddha, his disciples came up with a new design and turned the stupa into a monumental structure in the shape of an inverted urn. This kind of stupa is popular in Buddhist countries in southeast Asia. After Buddhism spread into China, elements of Chinese architecture were blended into the construction of the stupas, and the result was a rich variety of pagodas. All the pagodas in China, no matter where they are found, are associated with Buddhism.

So much for the Buddhist monasteries in Han-inhabited regions. In Tibet and other Tibetan-inhabited regions, the monasteries follow an entirely different design. A Tibetan monastery is of such colossal size that it looks like a tiny town with a population of hundreds to thousands. The Dai-inhabited areas in Yunnan, however, are different in that the pagoda remains the centerpiece of a Buddhist monastery. The buildings surrounding the pagoda are simply dormitories for monks, and the only hall on the premises is dedicated to a single statue of the Buddha. This layout is similar to that of monasteries in the Buddhist countries of south Asia because the Dai people follow the same school of Buddhism as do those countries.

3. Devine Statues and Interior Decoration

The statues of divinities enshrined in Buddhist monasteries are more or less of the same ensemble in various parts of China, but differences may exist in a Mahavira Hall. The following is an introduction of these statues beginning from the Gate hall.

The Gate hall is the entrance to a monastery, and a visitor is invariably greeted by statues of General Heng and General Ha as they enter the gate. These two generals, portrayed as gigantic and ferocious warrior statues, are guardian spirits in Buddhism. However, not every monastery has the privilege of being protected by these two mighty generals.

The Hall of Heavenly Kings houses six statues. Facing the gate and occupying the center of the floor is the statue of Bodhisatta Maitreya. Maitreya was a native of south India and a disciple of Sakyamuni, who once told Maitreya that he would become a Buddha but would continue to be known as Maitreya. However, the image of Maitreya enshrined in the Hall of Heavenly King in various monasteries is that of a plump monk with a smiling face holding a bag in his hand. Actually the image was derived from that of a bag-carrying monk by the name of Qici who lived in present-day Fenghua in Zhejiang Province during the Five Dynasties (907-960) and who was held in high esteem by the local people. It is said that prior to his death, Qici was heard saying, "The Maitreya is indeed who he is. With his identity

split into hundreds of millions of bodies, his presence is ubiqui-
tous so that he can teach people whenever it is necessary, but it is
only natural that people in the mundane world do not know who
he is." From these lines people regarded Qici as the reincarnation
of Maitreya, and statues of him were thus erected everywhere.
Legend has it that prior to the Ming Dynasty (1368-1644), monasteries in this country were not in the habit of enshrining a
statue of Maitreya. Later, when Zhu Yuanzhang rose in an armed
rebellion against the Yuan Dynasty, he expanded his forces by
using the influence of the Maitreya cult. When he established the
Ming Dynasty and became Emperor Taizu, he showed his gratitude to Maitreya by having statues of the bodhisattva erected in
monasteries throughout the country. Whether this legend tallies
with history remains to be proven.

The eastern and western sides of the Hall of Heavenly Kings
are enshrined with the statues of the four Heavenly Kings. In
ancient times, when science was still underdeveloped, the Indians
regarded the entire world as an ocean. In that ocean stood the
insurmountable Mt. Sumeru, which was attached to another
mountain whose four peaks were each occupied by a Heavenly
King and were thus known as Gatur-maharaja-kayikas (Heaven
of the Four Deva-Kings). Mt. Sumeru was surrounded by the
Four Catur-dvipa or Lokapalas (Continents) ruled by the four
Deva-Kings. Dhrtarastra, the Deva King of the Eastern Lokapala, protected his territory and people by holding a *pipa* in his
hand and is thereby deified as the God of Music. Virudhaka, the
Deva King of the Southern Lokapala, helped people do good
and accumulate merits. This statue thus holds a sword to protect
the people inhabiting the Southern Lokapala. Virupaksa, the
Deva King of the Western Lokapala, observed the world with
his eyes peeled and this statue holds a dragon that coils in his
hand to protect the people of the Western Lokapala. Dhanada,

the Deva King of the Northern Lokapala, had the ability to safeguard the people's wealth, and this statue holds an umbrella in his right hand to protect the people inhabiting the Northern Lokapala.

Behind the statue of Maitreya and standing facing north, wearing armor, and holding a vajra (a sturdy weapon of ancient India) in his hand, is the statue of Skanda, a guardian god under the command of Virudhaka. Because the name of Skanda has a sound that can be confused with one of the twenty deva-kings in Buddhist scriptures, he is also known as Deva-King Skanda. His statues began to appear in monasteries of Chinese Buddhism after the Song Dynasty. It is said that while the Northern Loka-pala is not governed by the Buddhist law, Skanda's responsibility is to maintain Buddhist rule in the east, south, and west lokapalas. Hence the saying, "The sphere of influence of the law-protecting Skanda Deva-King covers three Lokapalas." Skanda is portrayed as facing the front door of the Mahavira Hall, and gazing at the arrivals and departures with eyes that can easily discern good and evil.

The Mahavira Hall is the center of a monastery, and meant to be enshrined with a statue of Sakyamuni. Because the term "Mahavira" implies the noble character of the Buddha, the hall is naturally dedicated exclusively to the statue of Sakyamuni. However, because of the fact that Chinese Buddhism belongs to the Mahayana (i.e., the Great Vehicle) form, whose pantheon includes more than one Buddha, some monasteries are obliged to put statues of other Buddhas together with that of Sakyamuni in the Mahavira Hall.

Sakyamuni used to be Prince Siddhartha of Kapilavatthu, a tiny kingdom of India in ancient times. After he achieved complete enlightenment and became the Buddha, he was called Sakyamuni, meaning "Sage of the Sakya people." In Buddhist statues Sakyamuni is portrayed in a sitting or standing position. He has different sitting postures. If he sits cross-legged holding palms in hand coupled in front of his chest, this is known as the "Image of Meditation." If he places his left hand in front of himself while hanging his right hand below his knees and pointing at the ground, this is known as the "Posture of Touching the Earth" or the "Image of Attaining Enlightenment." There is a story behind the "Posture of Touching the Earth."

When the Buddha sat on the vajra throne under the Bodhidruma (*Ficus religiosa*) tree and was about to achieve buddhahood, Mara, the evil one, appeared on the scene to make trouble. Asserting that the Buddha did not deserve the honor of sitting on the throne, the demon wanted him to leave. The Buddha refused to budge, retorting that he deserved the seat because in his life he had sacrificed himself and performed plenty of good deeds for the multitudes of people. The evil one asked, "How can you prove what you've done?" The Buddha then pointed a finger at the earth and said, "The earth can testify because all I have done was done on earth." Mara was thus convinced and gave up the idea of dethroning the Buddha. Such is the origin of the "Posture of Touching the Earth."

Another kind of statue has the Buddha sitting on his throne with his legs crossed and the soles of his feet turning upward, while his left hand is placed horizontally at his left front side and his right hand extends upwards with the index finger forming a ring in what is known as the "Posture of Preaching the Dharma," or the "Image of Preaching the Dharma."

The old man standing by the left side of this statue of Sakyamuni is Mahakassapa, and to his right is a young man, Anada. Both were the Buddha's most favored disciples who made indelible contributions to the dissemination of Buddhism.

The one and only standing pose of Sakyamuni in Buddhist

sculptures has him hanging his left hand down in what is known as the "Posture of Willing to Grant," or extending his right hand upward in the "Posture of Vaisaradya (Self-Confidence)." In either posture the Buddha is trying to dispel his followers' misgivings by promising them that he is capable of satisfying all their desires and delivering them from their miseries. It is said that King Udayana of ancient India created this posture of the Buddha in a sculpture carved out of white sandalwood. Hence the name, "Sandalwood Statue." Chinese imitations are known by the same name.

The Mahavira Hall of many temples is enshrined with the trikaya (threefold body) of the Buddha and the Buddhas of the past, present, and future. The former refers to the Dharmakaya (embodiment of Truth and the Law) of Vairocana, the Sambhogakaya (reward body) of Locana, and the Nirmanakaya (incarnation) of Sakyamuni. The latter includes the Buddhas of the Three Vertical Forms, that is, Kasyapa, Sakyamuni, and Maitreya, and the Buddhas of the Three Horizontal Lands, that is, Baisajya-guru-vaidurya-prabhasa (Buddha of Medicine) of the Land of the Bhaisajyaraja, Amitabha of the Sukhavati Western Paradise, and Sakyamuni of the Saha Endurance Land. In a few monasteries, the Mahavira Hall is enshrined only with the Dharmakaya of Vairocana. In the Pure Land sect, it is the domain of Sakyamuni or the Three Amita Saints of the West — Amitabha, Avalokitesvara, and Mahasthamaprapta. Amitabha is portrayed as holding a tiny lotus throne on the palm of his hand in a posture to greet those bound for the Western Paradise.

The Buddha in the Mahavira Hall is also flanked by 16 arhats (enlightened saintly men), who are disciples of the Buddha, sometimes with the addition of two more later arrivals. Legend has it that when the Buddha was achieving nirvana, he instructed his disciples to preside over the dharma and not to enter nirvana until the birth of Maitreya, the Buddha of the future. It is said that in Sinhala in ancient times there lived a monk known as Nandimitra, who wrote the book *Records on the Continuity of Dharma*, in which he recorded the deeds of the 16 arhats disseminating the law of Buddhism, which was translated into Chinese by Xuanzang, the celebrated Tang-Dynasty monk. In honor of both the author and the translator, Buddhists in China erected statues for them and placed them among the arhats. Thus the ranks of arhats swelled to 18. Another theory has it that beside Nandimitra and the other addition is a repetition of the original 16 statues.

In the rear of the Mahavira Hall, standing behind the Buddhist sages are the trinity of Manjusri riding on the back of a lion, Samantabhadra mounted on an elephant, and Avalokitesvara riding a mythological animal known as *"hou."* In some monasteries the position is occupied by a statue of Avalokitesvara standing on an island in the ocean in the company of Sudhana, a virgin boy referred to in the *Buddhavatamsaka-mahavaipulya-sutra* (*Garland Sutra*), and Nagakanya, a virgin girl mentioned in the *Saddharmapundarika-sutra* (*Lotus Sutra*).

The Avalokitesvara Hall, also known variously as the Hall of Mahakaruna (Great Mercy) or Hall of Universality, is reserved exclusively for a statue of Avalokitesvara, who assumes the image of a woman in Chinese Buddhism known as the Goddess of Mercy (Guanyin). However, because Avalokitesvara is a patron of great magnanimity and great mercy and takes it upon himself to deliver the multitudes from misery, he assumes an unpredictable array of identities. According to the saying in the *Saddharmapundarika-sutra* (*Lotus Sutra*): "By what form of body people can be saved, immediately the Bodhisattva manifests that body to preach the dharma to save them." Thus Avalokitesvara assumes whatever identity is needed to answer the call of the one who is to be delivered from misery. Avalokitesvara's body is thus portrayed in the following forms:

Arya-avalokite'svara (Sacred Avalokitesvara), in which he assumes the identity of a person with one head on two shoulders, sitting on crossed legs and holding a lotus flower in his hand, with a figurine of Amitabha embedded in the center of his crown.

Pandaravasini (Avolikitesvara in a White Robe), in the identity of a beauty holding a holy-water vase and a poplar twig in her hands.

Avalokitesvara with a Free Mind, a lady sitting on one leg, with the other leg hanging down in a posture of leisure and repose.

Ekadasa-mukh-avolokitesvara (Eleven-faced Avalokitesvara). Of these eleven faces, three stare down on the evil ones, three are benign-looking faces that teach the good ones, and three are quiet faces providing guidance for those belonging to the supra-mundane. As each of the three categories of people belong to the Trilokya, or Three Realms,[1] so altogether nine faces are needed. Above these nine faces are the face of solemnity and smiles, meaning that only with awe and a ready willingness can education be provided to the multitudes of people and become effective. Atop all these faces is the Buddha face, which gives expression to both good and evil, and quiet and composure. The different facial expressions are designed for the convenience of guiding the multitudes of people to buddhahood.

Sahasrabhuja-sahasranetra-avalokitesvara (Thousand-Arm-Thousand-Eye Avalokistevara). In this form, Avalokistevara puts the multitudes under the protection of her thousand hands while

---

[1] Three Realms 三界. This represents the world outlook of the Mahayana Buddhism, which classifies the world into three realms, that is, *Kamadhatu* (Ream of Desire), *Rupadhatu* (Material Realm), and *Arupadhatu* (Immaterial Realm). Each realm has its own multitude of people who need the guidance and education of Buddhism.

keeping the mundane world under a thousand watchful eyes. Both the hands and the eyes are manifestations of Avalokiste-vara's great magnanimity and mercy. Each eye grows in the palm of a hand.

Forty-eight-arm Avalokistevara. Each arm has a special con-notation, and all of the arms are designed for the good of the multitudes.

The Hall of Ksitigarbha of a Buddhist temple is generally of small size, and the statue of Ksitigarbha is portrayed as sitting or standing. In his right hand he holds a staff that is a symbol of his love for the people, and in his left hand he has a pearl, indi-cating he is able to meet all the desires of people. However, the image of Ksitigarbha in various parts of China is often mixed with the likeness of a Korean monk by the name of Gim Kyokak.

The Hall of Samgharama is a memorial hall dedicated to those who have rendered meritorious deeds on behalf of Bud-dhism. In this hall, the statue of Prasenajit, a contemporary of Sakyamuni who converted to Buddhism, is flanked by Siddhartha to the left and Prince Jeta to the right.[1]

The Hall of Patriarchs, also known as the "ancestral hall." Different sects have different sages enshrined in this hall. For example, in the Chan sect this hall is always housed with images of Bodhidharma (菩提达磨?-293), Huineng (慧能 638-713) and Huaihai (怀海 720-814).

Some monasteries have a Hall of 500 Arhats. Mention of these arhats is found in some Buddhist scriptures, but none of them has a name. In this hall, however, all of them have names scraped together from multiple sources, and some are sheer fab-rications. The first Hall of 500 Arhats probably appeared in a monastery built during the Five Dynasties (907-960) by the king

---

[1] See Section 1 of this chapter.

of Wuyue at the Fangguang Temple in the Tiantai Mountain. In 954 (1st year of the Xiande reign, Later Zhou Dynasty) the Chan priest Daoqian began erecting statues of the five hundred arhats at the Jingci Temple of Hangzhou. The idea may have originated from the fact that after the Buddha achieved nirvana, five hundred of his disciples gathered at Rajagrha. The priest established the hall presumably to commemorate the event. But the truth of this happening cannot be verified.

The various halls in a monastery are, as a rule, furnished simply with a table placed before a saintly statue on which are set the five ritualistic objects: two vases, two candlesticks, and an incense burner. The table is a place on which followers can offer flowers, light candles, and burn incense sticks. The furnishing in the Mahavira Hall has more ornamentation, such as streamers, flags, and canopies, as well as percussion instruments such as bells, drums, and wooden fishes (hollow wooden blocks) used by monks when chanting scriptures. All the furnishings are designed to accentuate the solemnity of the religious aura in the temple.

The sacrificial objects in a Buddhist temple fall into six categories: flowers, sandalwood, water, incense sticks, food, and lamps, which represent the six *paramitas* (the six things that ferry one beyond the sea of mortality to nirvana), that is, 1) *dana*, charity, or giving, including the bestowing of the truth on others; 2) *sila*, keeping the commandments; 3) *ksanti*, patience in the face of insults; 4) *virya*, zeal and progress; 5) *dhyana*, meditation or contemplation; and 6) *prajna*, wisdom, the power to discern reality or truth.

The tolling of the bell in a Buddhist monastery may vary in rhythm and tonality, but the number of the tolls is the same, 108. The Buddhist interpretation of this is that there are 108 misgivings in the mundane world, and the 108 bell tolls may help dispel them.

The wooden fish is a ritualistic object peculiar to the Han tradition of Buddhism, and it is a popular percussion instrument among the people. It is said that the fish never closes its eyes, day or night, and a monk may knock on the wooden fish to overcome drowsiness and to concentrate on meditation.

Chapter 5

Four Holy Mountains and Major Halls of Patriarchs

1. Mount Wutai

With a circumference of 250 kilometers, Mount Wutai in the northwest of Wutai County, Shanxi Province, consists of five peaks with flat crests. Hence the term, *wutai*, or "five terraces." They are Wanhai Peak in the east, Guayue Peak in the west,

Wuliang Hall at Mount Wutai

Jinxiu Peak in the south, Yedou Peak in the north, and Cuiyan Peak in the center. The tallest of the cluster, the Yedou Peak at 3,058 meters above sea level, is dubbed the "Rooftop of North China." Because of its cool and refreshing climate, Mount Wutai is also known as Qingliangshan, or Mountain of Coolness.

Mount Wutai is one the four holy mountain sanctuaries of Buddhism, the others being Mount Putuo, Mount Jiuhua and Mount Emei. Wutai is known for its large numbers of monasteries and picture-perfect landscape. Rambling among its green peaks and gurgling streams is a most refreshing experience. The reputation of Mount Wutai as a Buddhist sanctuary probably stems from the mention of the relationship between the Mountain of Coolness and Bodhisattva Manjusri in the *Garland Sutra*, translated into Chinese by the eminent Indian monk Buddhabhadra (359-429) during the Eastern Jin Dynasty (317-420). The Mountain of Coolness referred to in the *Garland Sutra* may be another mountain of the same name, but it is an established fact that Mount Wutai has long been regarded as the domain of Bodhisattva Manjusri.

According to the *Gazetteer of Qingliang Mountain*, temples had already appeared on Mount Wutai as early as the Eastern Han Dynasty (25-220). This, however, may be hearsay because after Buddhism spread to China during the Han Dynasty, the imperial government banned Chinese from abandoning the world and becoming monks. Since there were no monks at all at that time, what was the use of temples? A plausible theory dates the construction of Buddhist monasteries on Mount Wutai back to the Northern Wei (385-534) of the Northern and Southern Dynasties. Today, some 40 such temples remain on the mountain.

Amidst the five peaks of Mount Wutai stands the town of Taihuai, which is home to 39 monasteries. Outside the mountain there are eight other temples. With the splendor of architecture, and the exquisiteness of paintings and sculpture, these temples are regarded as paragons of Chinese culture. The following is a brief introduction to the major ones.

(1) Xiantong Monastery. When this was first built during the 471-499 reign of Emperor Xiaowen of the Northern Wei, it was known variously as the Great Futu (Buddha-stupa) Monastery and the Garden Temple. After Wu Zetian of the Tang Dynasty took the throne and made herself the empress to reign over the nation from 684 to 704, it was renamed Great Huayan Monastery. When it was reconstructed during the Ming Dynasty (1368-1644), the founding emperor Zhu Yuanzhang gave it a horizontal board inscribed with the name, "Great Xiantong Monastery," which is still displayed there today. Reconstruction during the Qing Dynasty expanded the monastery to its present size of approximately 80,000 square meters, with 400 or so halls, chambers, and pavilions laid out in a picturesque fashion. The seven main halls, arranged along the axial line, each assumes a different design, and their flank buildings are of a uniform style. Adding luster to the entire assemblage are three finely cast bronze halls. The pomp of architecture, and the elaborate beauty of sculptured detail in its statues, serve to justify the reputation of the Xiantong Monastery as the largest, most venerated, and foremost Buddhist establishment on Mount Wutai.

(2) Tayuan Temple. In former times, this was a courtyard of the Xiantong Monastery and the site of an imposing stupa that is an emblem of Mount Wutai. It was not until the stupa was rebuilt during the Ming Dynasty that the courtyard became an independent temple. The archway rising in front of the entryway gate was also a product of the Ming Dynasty. The stupa forms the center of the temple and is sandwiched between the Mahavira Hall at the front and the Tripitaka Pavilion at the rear. Its eastern side is lined with a row of auxiliary halls. The Tripitaka

Pavilion differs from its counterparts in that it features a 20-tiered wooden wheel with various scriptures placed on it for the followers to worship. The stupa is a white structure about 50 meters in height. A total of 250 bells hanging on it sway gently in the wind and emit a pleasant tinkling sound.

(3) Shuxiang Temple, another major Buddhist establishment on Mount Wutai about five tenths of a kilometer south of the town of Taihuai. The name of the temple, Shuxiang, means

A Dagoba (also called Dabai Pagoda, meaning Big White Pagoda) on Cuiyan Peak of Mount Wutai

'Statue of Manjusri.' The temple was built during the Tang Dynasty, rebuilt during the Yuan Dynasty, only to be burned down shortly afterwards, and built once again in 1487 (23rd year of the Chenghua reign) during the Ming Dynasty. Sitting behind the front gateway and the Hall of Heavenly Kings is the Hall of Manjusri, behind which is the abbot's residence and the meditation hall. Both sides of the temple are lined with flank halls and corridors. The Hall of Manjusri is a dignified structure five bays in width, and looks unique under a roof that has double-tiered eaves and is graced with colorfully glazed fringes and elaborate painted corbel brackets. In the hall, the image of Manjusri sitting on the back of a lion is cast in a statue about nine meters in height. Behind him are the statues of the Buddhas of the Three

Horizontal Lands, that is, Baisajya-guru-vaidurya-prabhasa, Sakyamuni, and Amitabha. Suspended on the sidewalls of the hall are sculptures of the 500 arhats in graphic imagery and superb craftsmanship.

(4) Pusading, also known as the Zhenrong Temple or Manjusri Temple, was first built during the Northern Wei Dynasty and repeatedly rebuilt in the succeeding dynasties. After the Ming Dynasty the place became a settlement for lamas from Mongolia and Tibet. Both emperors Kangxi and Qianlong of the Qing Dynasty were housed here during their repeated visits to Mount Wutai, and because of this link with the emperors, the temple had the unusual attention of the imperial court. Some of its buildings were constructed in a palatial style. No other temple is in possession of as many horizontal boards and stone tablets inscribed with the handwriting of various emperors as the Pusading Temple. The temple perches on the crest of a mountain, and access to the stone archway in front of it is by a 108-step trapezoidal stairway. The layout of its main buildings — the Hall of Heavenly Kings, the Bell and Drum Towers, the Pusading Hall, and the Mahavira Hall — diffuses a pervading assiduity, and their roofs are covered in a most stately fashion with tri-colored glazed tiles.

(5) Luohou Temple, situated to the east of the Xiantong Monastery, is a lamasery of considerable size. Its construction began during he Tang Dynasty, and it was rebuilt in 1492 (5th year of the Hongzhi reign, Ming Dynasty). The Qing emperors Kangxi, Qianlong, and Yongzheng never missed a visit to this temple during their repeated tours of Mount Wutai. With its Hall of Heavenly Kings, Hall of Manjusri, Mahavira Hall, Tripitaka Pavilion, ancillary halls and anterooms remaining largely intact, Luohou Temple is one of Mount Wutai's best preserved temples. On the 14th of the sixth lunar month, the lamas in this temple

masquerade as ghosts and celebrate the legendary birthday of Manjusri by mounting an entire day of sorcerers' dances, which never fails to attract a large crowds of curious onlookers. A rare hall of the temple houses a strange gadget, a round altar engraved with water-wave patterns and the portraits of 18 arhats. In the center of the altar stands a wood-carved lotus flower, which is fixed on a central axis dovetailed to a cog wheel. If one pulls the string attached to the cog wheel, the petals will open and close repeatedly, first revealing a figurine of the Buddha in the center of the flower and then concealing it. This "open-the-flower-to-see-the-Buddha" contraption serves as an amusement for visitors.

(6) Longquan (Dragon Spring) Temple, also known as the Jiulonggang Temple, stands by the White Dragon Spring nine km to the south of the town of Taihuai. Construction of it began during the Song Dynasty, but it was rebuilt repeatedly during the Ming and late Qing dynasties and during the Republican years. A monumental brick carving of Manjusri riding his trademark lion, inlaid in the screen wall of the temple, is lauded as a masterpiece of sculpture for its ingenious and impeccable chisel work. A 108-step stone stairway conducts the visitor to a stone archway that renders access to the temple's row of three courtyards that are interlinked yet independent of each other. The anterooms of the eastern courtyard, which is a combination of two smaller yards, are known for their colorful paintings. Two pagodas stand in the central and western courtyards that are skirted by zigzagging corridors. Longquan Temple has a different layout from most Buddhist temples, probably for topographical reasons.

(7) Jinge (Golden Pavilion) Temple, 15 kilometers from the town of Taihuai, is another renowned Buddhist establishment on Mount Wutai. It dates back to the Tang Dynasty. Jinge Temple

has all the major elements a Buddhist temple should have, such as the Hall of Vairocana, the Hall of Amitabha, the Hall of Avalokistesvara, the Hall of Ksitigarbha, and the Hall of Bhaisa-jyaguru-vaidurya-prabhasa. But what's unique about this temple is that it has a golden pavilion built to receive envoys sent by Emperor Daizong (reign 762-779) to perform ritual deeds for him there. The pavilion looks golden because its bronze tiles are gilded with gold powder. Enshrined in it is a 17-meter-tall bronze statue of Guanyin sitting in the company of the 24 Deva-statues of Mahayana Buddhism.

(8) Nanshan Temple. Three kilometers to the south of the town of Taihuai are three buildings that originally belonged to three temples — Youguo Temple, Jile Temple and Shande Hall — when they were first built in 1296, the second year of the Yuanzhen reign of the Yuan dynasty, and rebuilt during the Jiaqing reign (1522-1566) of the Ming Dynasty. By the Qing Dynasty more buildings were added, and the entire cluster was combined to form the Nanshan Temple. In an expansion project conducted during the Republican years, the interiors of the three main buildings were linked. The temple today is a colossal congregate of halls, towers, pavilions, and chambers, totaling 300 *jian*, or bays, arranged in distinct rows along the contours of the mountain slope. Access to the front gateway is by a stone stairway of 108 steps. The brick engravings on the temple's screen wall are renowned for their fastidious craftsmanship. The buildings have a variety of architectural styles. The main hall is enshrined with the statues of Sakyamuni, Kasyapa, Ananda, the Attendant Boddhisattva, and the 18 arhats, a legacy of the Ming Dynasty. It is believed that the sculpture of the Nanshan Temple leads Mount Wutai in artistic attainment.

(9) Guangjimaopeng Temple, also known as the Bishan Temple. Situated two kilometers to the northeast of the town of

Taihuai, Guangjimaopeng Temple is said to have been built during the Northern Wei Dynasty (386-534). In its front courtyard there are a Hall of Heavenly Kings, Bell and Drum Towers, a Hall of Vairocana, an altar, and eastern and western flank rooms. The backyard, higher in elevation than the front courtyard, features a floral-pendant gate, a Tripitaka Pavilion, meditation rooms, and monastic dormitories. All the buildings look resplendent with unique and beautiful carvings. Among the temples of Mount Wutai, Guangjimaopeng is an influential temple with an international prestige.

(10) Foguang Temple, 25 kilometers to the northeast of the seat of Wutai County. Foguang Temple, which faces west, was built during the 471-499 reign of Emperor Xiaowen of the Northern Wei Dynasty, but was demolished during the crackdown on Buddhism launched by Emperor Wuzong who reigned during the Tang Dynasty 841-846. It was not rebuilt until 857, or the 11th year of the Dazhong reign of the Tang, when Emperor Xuanzong ascended the throne and resurrected Buddhism. The pagoda of the Foguang Temple of today is a Northern Wei legacy, while the Eastern Hall was built during the Tang. The temple is in possession of a collection of Tang-Dynasty sculptures, murals, stone pillars inscribed with incantations, stupas with remains of monks buried underneath, and marble sculptures. The main hall is a rare and extremely precious example of a Tang-Dynasty wood structure.

(11) Yuanzhao Temple. Also known as Puning Temple, the Yuanzhao Temple north of the town of Taihuai was built during the Yongle reign (1403-1424) of the Ming Dynasty. It is said that at that time the Indian monk Patra Lisha arrived in China and the imperial court honored him as a State Tutor and bestowed a gold seal on him. He later settled on Mount Wutai, and the Xiantong Temple was his residence. He died during the Xuande

reign (1426-1435) of the Ming Dynasty. After his remains were cremated, part of his sariras were sent to Beijing to be enshrined in the Zhenjue (Five-Pagoda) Temple, built specially for this purpose, and part of them were retained for the construction of the Yuanzhao Temple. The front gateway to the temple is guarded by a pair of stone lions, and the Hall of Heavenly Kings, the Hall of the Great Buddha, the courtyard containing a pagoda, and the Tripitaka Pavilion are all arrayed along the axial line. The statue of the Buddha in the Hall of the Great Buddha looks distinctive for his tall stature and calm composure. Behind the temple are a cluster of five pagodas elevated on a square base. With a small pagoda standing on each corner, and a large one in the center, the layout looks like a copy of Beijing's Five-Pagoda Temple.

(12) Zhenhai Temple. The name of the Zhenhai Temple, half way up a mountain and five kilometers south of the town of Taihuai, means the "temple to subdue the son of the Dragon King." The spring running by the front of the temple, known as the "Ocean Bottom Spring," is a legendary "eye of the sea." It is where the ninth son of the Dragon King fell in love with a human woman and created havoc. When word about this reached Manjusri, the bodhisattva subdued him by holding him under a cauldron. The Temple to Subdue the Dragon King's Son was built during the Qing Dynasty. Containing a Hall of Heavenly Kings, a Hall of the Great Buddha, a Hall for Propagating Buddhism, and left and right ancillary rooms, the temple was the residence of Lcan-Skya, a living Buddha of Tibetan Buddhism.

2. Mount Putuo

Putuoluojia is the full name of Mount Putuo, which is actually an islet among the Zhoushan Islands on the East China Sea, off the shore of Ningbo, Zhejiang Province. Covering 12.76 square km, 8.6 km south and north by 3.5 km east and west, and with its highest peak rising at 291.3 meters above sea level, this is one of the four mountain sanctuaries of Chinese Buddhism.

Legend has it that in 858 (12th year of the Dazhong reign, Tang Dynasty), a Japanese monk by the Chinese name of Hui'e was shipping to Japan a statue of Guanyin he had acquired during a pilgrimage to Mount Wutai. Shortly after he began his sea voyage at present-day Ningbo, Zhejiang Province, a windstorm rose, and his boat was stranded among the reefs off an islet. Those on board panicked, and Hui'e made haste to pray, "If the time is not ripe yet for this venerable statue to settle down on the eastern side of the sea, please allow me to leave it on this mountain...." He did not know that the mountain he was referring to was none other than Mount Putuo. His prayer was hardly finished when the boat stirred and began moving towards the islet. The statue was thus moved ashore. The experience deeply saddened the Japanese monk. Giving up his homecoming plan, he had a thatched hut built on the islet to house the statue and he stayed behind to take care of it. A different version of the story dates the event back to 916 (2nd year of the Zhenming reign, Later Liang Dynasty), and asserts that after the statue was moved ashore a man surnamed Zhang evacuated his home to enshrine it, and named it the "Temple of Guanyin Who Is Reluctant to Leave."

The name of Mount Putuo has something to do with a record in a Tang-Dynasty Chinese translation of the *Garland Sutra*, which asserts that Potaraka Mountain in the South Sea of India is the abode of Bodhisattva Avalokitesvara. Because the place where Hui'e went ashore happened to be an isle of the South Sea (East China Sea), a transliteration of the name Potaraka Mountain was borrowed for it.

Despite its tiny size, Mount Putuo is a beautiful island and studded with scenic spots, the better known of these being Pantuo Rock, Chaoyin Cave, and Qianbusha Beach.

As a Buddhist sanctuary, Mount Putuo exerts a great influence on Chinese religious life. Avalokitesvara, also known as Guanyin, or the Goddess of Mercy, is widely worshiped by Chinese Buddhists, who regard her as perhaps the most endearing of all the celestial beings in the Buddhist pantheon. That is why the temples on Mount Putuo have been thriving and have been thronged with pilgrims over the last thousand or so years, earning the place the nickname "Buddhist Kingdom on the Sea." The common saying is that on Mount Putuo, "whoever you see is a monk and whatever house comes in sight is a temple" is something of an exaggeration, but it is somewhat truthful in reflecting the religious prosperity in this Buddhist Kingdom on the Sea. Incomplete statistics show that prior to 1949 there were 218 temples and nunneries and more than 2,000 monks and nuns on the mountain, a fact that renders authenticity to the islet's reputation as a Buddhist kingdom, given its mere size of 12 square kilometers. Mount Putuo is a mecca for pilgrims and visitors from home and abroad all year around, and it is especially crowded during the three festivals in celebration of Guanyin's birthday (19th of the 2nd lunar month), achievement of enlightenment (19th of the 6th lunar month), and entry of nirvana (19th of the 9th lunar month). The following is a brief introduction to the three major temples of Mount Putuo and its scenic spots that have Buddhist associations:

(1) Puji (Universal Relief) Monastery. Also known as the Frontal Temple, this is the largest monastery of Mount Putuo. Perched south of the crest of the Baihua Peak, it was the Baotuo Guanyin Temple when it was first built in 1080 (3rd year of the Yuanfeng reign, Northern Song Dynasty). The monastery has

had its fill of ups and downs through the years, and it was not until its main hall was reconstructed in 1699 (38th year of the Kangxi reign, Qing Dynasty) that it assumed its present name by taking the tone from Emperor Kangxi's four-character inscription "puji qunling" (meaning "For the universal relief of souls"). The size of the temple continued to grow in the intervening years, and by the time another round of major constructions were finished in 1731 (9th year of the Yongzheng reign, Qing Dynasty), it became a 14,000-square-meter structure with more than 200 halls, chambers, pavilions, and towers. Arranged in a majestic fashion along the temple's axial line are the Hall of Heavenly Kings, the Hall of Universality, the Tripitaka Pavilion, and the abbot's residence. In front of the temple is the Haiyin Pond, into which captive fish are released, and in which lotus plants grow. Facing the front gate are an octagonal pavilion and a kiosk that provides a roof for a stone stele inscribed in the emperor's own handwriting.

(2) Situated to the left of the crest of the Baihua Peak is the Fayu Temple, or Posterior Temple, whose predecessor was the "Haichao Convent" built in 1580 (8th year of the Wanli reign, Ming Dynasty). It was renamed the "Haichao Temple" in 1594 (22nd year of the Wanli reign), but was destroyed in war shortly after it was renamed the "Huguo Zhenhai Temple" (Temple for Protection the Country and Guarding the Territorial Sea) in 1606 (34th year of the Wanli reign). When it was rebuilt in 1699 (38th year of the Kangxi reign, Qing Dynasty), it was renamed the Fayu (Reign of the Law) temple, according to Emperor's Kangxi's inscription "tianhua fayu" (heavenly flower and reign of the law) on a lacquered horizontal board bestowed to the temple. More halls were erected or expanded during the reigns of emperors Tongzhi and Guangxu that covered the 1862-1909 period. Today, the Fayu Temple is in possession of 245 buildings, laid

out in rows that snugly hug the rim of the mountain. The main buildings on the temple's axial line are the Hall of Heavenly Kings, the Bell and Drum Towers, the Hall of the Jade Buddha, the Guanyin Hall, the Yupai Hall, the Mahavira Hall, the Tripitaka Pavilion, and the abbot's residence. The Guanyin Hall, known for its "Dome of Nine Coiling Dragons," is also called the "Hall of Nine Dragons." The nine vertical rafters suspended from the ceiling of the hall's dome are each carved with a coiling dragon that rears its head in a scramble for a large ball hanging down from the center of the ceiling.

(3) Huiji Temple. Also known as Fodingshansi (Temple atop the Buddha's Mountain), this temple used to be the site of a stone pavilion enshrined with a statue of the Buddha. During the Ming Dynasty (1368-1644), a monk by the name of Huiyuan had the Huiji Convent built, which was expanded and became a temple in 1793 (58th year of the Qianlong reign, Qing Dynasty). In 1907 (33rd year of the Guangxu reign, Qing Dynasty), the temple acquired a complete collection of the *Tripitaka* (including the *sutra-pitaka*, *vinaya-pitaka*, and *abhidharma-pitaka*). On the premises are four halls, seven palaces, and six chambers that are marked for their breathtaking architecture and impeccable craftsmanship. The scenic surroundings are embellished with ancient trees and exotic flowers.

(4) Luojia Mountain, which is part of Mount Putuo but stands opposite it across a narrow strip of sea, forms an islet 0.34 square km in size and 2 km in circumference on the Lotus Flower Ocean. It is home to a convent. The top of the mountain offers an overview of the sea extending into the distance until it merges with heaven. At the foot of the mountain is the Crystal Palace, which is a mountain cave that can accommodate curious visitors for an inside look as the sea is ebbing. During the time of the year when spring gives way to summer, the islet and the

sea around it are cocooned in mist, which thickens and thins miraculously to conjure up one exotic scene after another.

(5) Purple Bamboo Grove. Legend has it that after the Japanese monk Hui'e had the statue of Guanyin moved ashore, he had a "Temple of Guanyin Who Is Reluctant to Leave" built in the Purple Bamboo Grove. Scattered on the floor of this grove are fragments of broken purplish slates with traces of bamboo leaves visible underneath their surfaces. These are fossils resulting from the movement of the earth's crust. A convent is found tucked away in the heart of the grove, which was planted by local residents during relatively recent years.

(6) Chaoyin (Thundering Wave) Cave, which is deeply recessed in the mountain close by the Purple Bamboo Grove. When the sea surges, water tumbles into the cave and thrusts into the rocks inside it with a thunderous roar. Hence the name of the cave, "Cave of Thundering Waves." A wall in the cave is inscribed with three Chinese characters that say, "Where Bodhisattva Avalokitesvara Was Seen." This may be interpreted either as this was where Guanyin once made her physical presence felt, or that inside the cave someone had once spotted the Goddess of Mercy. Towering over the Chaoyin Cave and overlooking the sea is an overhanging cliff appropriately called the "Suicidal Crag" because quite a few people have committed suicide here by jumping off and plunging into the sea below. Today precautions have been taken to prevent such tragedies from happening again.

(7) Southern Heaven Gateway. This is a mammoth monolith that soars into the sky and extends a solitary arm into the ocean. It is separated from the main island by a narrow strip of water. A stone slab stands astride the water to serve as a bridge. The area around the Southern Heaven gateway is clustered with rocks, whose varied strange forms add a somewhat outlandish touch to

the scene. In the neighborhood are a number of tourist attractions including cliff carvings and the Dragon-eye Well.

(8) One-Thousand-Step Beach. The beach, one hundred meters wide and one thousand seven hundred meters long, lies on the eastern rim of Mount Putuo. The best bathing ground one might hope for, it is covered with a layer of fine sand feeling so soft to the feet that walking on it is like walking on a golden carpet.

(9) Western Heaven Gate. Arranged through the invisible hands of nature, two rocks facing each other soar into the sky with a third one, inscribed with the wording "World of Law of the West Heaven," balanced horizontally atop them to form the lintel of the "gate." A footpath leads beyond the stone gate and reaches the summit of the Damu Peak. North of the "gate" there are a string of tourist attractions, including the Meifu Convent, the Pantuo Rock, the Rock of Two Turtles Listening to a Priest, and the Guanyin Cave. Situated in the sequestered repose of verdant trees to the west of Puji Monastery, it is also the site of a camphor tree (*Cinnamomum camphora*) that has been around for at least eight centuries.

With its caves enshrouded in religious mystery, its rocks assuming forms ranging from the fabulous to the grotesque, its peaks cocooned under luxuriant woods, and its ethereal maritime scenery seemingly changing all the time, Mount Putuo is at once a nice summer resort and a paradise for nature lovers.

3. Mount Jiuhua

Twenty km to the southwest of Qingyang County, Anhui Province, Mount Jiuhua rises, a mountain range that serpentines its way for approximately 90 km from west of Mount Huangshan into Qingyang County. Of its nine peaks, the tallest rises to 1,300 meters above sea level. The entire area is a topographical turmoil of cliffs that overlap and overhang to conjure up numerous scenes of natural beauty. Ten of these have been garnered by Huang Chanhua in his travelogue *Mount Jiuhua*.

(1) Tiantai (Heavenly Terrace) Peak. This is the tallest peak of the entire Mount Jiuhua range, where the purplish forms of numerous razor-sharp cliffs gleam amidst woods and thrust into the heavens like so many swords of colossal dimension.

(2) Green Peach Cliff. Legend has it that a Taoist alchemist by the name of Zhao Zhiwei was trying to make pills of immortality at the foot of Mount Jiuhua. While there he planted a thousand peach trees that bore green flowers. Hence the name of the cliff. A long and massive waterfall can be seen cascading from the head of the cliff. Known as "Overhanging Waterfall," this is dubbed the number one scene of Mount Jiuhua.

(3) Shugu Pools. A cluster of streams converge by the side of the Cuigai (Green Canopy) Peak to form three pools known as Shangxue (Upper Snow), Xiaoxue (Minor Snow), and Yingluo (Necklace of Pearls and Jade). The place looks most enchanting when night falls and the moon is mirrored quivering in the pools.

(4) Jiuzi (Nine-Boy) Cliff. Standing to the northeast of Guangsheng Mountain, this cliff features a crest that looks as if nine boys are huddling and frolicking together. In summer and autumn, water bursts forth with a vengeance from fountains hidden underneath the cliff and breaks into seven sections as it lands at the bottom of the ravine below, emitting a persistent din evocative of a mixture of tolling bells and drum beats.

(5) Lotus Flower Peak. This is yet another jumble of rock prominences clustering together like so many lotus flowers to the east of Cuigai Peak. Mount Jiuhua has made a name for itself because of its abundance of lotus flowers, but none of its peaks deserve this reputation more than the Lotus Flower Peak.

(6) Five-Stream Bridge. From a bird's-eye view, the five streams look as if they were the base of a colossal bridge. Looking east from these streams, one sees an ethereal ocean of mists and clouds that have inundated the mass of mountains so thoroughly that only a few peaks can be seen protruding into the blue sky.

(7) Pingtian (Flatland) Ridge. Mount Jiuhua is a world of perpendicular and soaring mountain peaks with razor-sharp edges. That is why this ridge stands out simply because its crest is as uninterrupted as flat land.

(8) East Cliff. This mountain is so named because it stands to the east of the Huacheng Temple and is 1.5 km taller, but it is better known for having a dwelling-like cave in it that had provided lodging for quite a few famous people. These include Gim Kyokak, Zhou Jing (an eccentric monk during the Zhengde reign of the Ming Dynasty), and Wang Yangming. Hence its nickname, "Dwelling Cliff."

(9) Tianzhu (Heavenly Pillar) Peak. The name of this mountain, situated behind Jingju Temple, stems from its pillar-like form that soars straight into the blue sky.

(10) Huacheng city. This turns out to be a mountain-rimmed tableland several kilometers up the slope of Mount Jiuhua. A river runs across the tableland. It is home to a hundred or so families that make a living tilling the farmland.

Statuesque forms of mountains and a graceful landscape have earned Mount Jiuhua the reputation as "Number One Mountain of Southeast China." The mountain, however, was called Mount Jiuzi until Li Bai, a celebrated Tang-Dynasty poet, composed a poem to eulogize the mountain's nine lotus flower-like peaks. The poem goes like this:

> "Sailing down the Jiujiang River the other day
> I espied nine fabulous peaks (jiuhua) in the distance.

Looking as if they were nine lotus flowers
Embroidered by the Heavenly River using its emerald water as thread."

Drawing inspiration from these lines, people of later generations gave the mountain its present name, Mount Jiuhua. The fame of the mountain stems not so much from its enchanting scenery as from the fact that it is one of the four mountain sanctuaries of Chinese Buddhism and the domain of Ksitigarbha, a bodhisattva belonging to Mahayana Buddhism.

Legend has it that in 741 (last year of the Kaiyuan reign, Tang Dynasty), a man whose religious name was Ksitigarbha Kim and whose secular name was Gim Kyokak, left Silla, a kingdom in present-day Korea, and arrived in Mount Jiuhua to practice Buddhism. One day he was stung by a poisonous insect, but he kept his composure and went on with his meditation as if nothing had happened. In no time a beautiful young woman materialized, bowing to him and offering him a dose of medicine. "This stupid woman is ignorant of who you are, and I'll atone for my misconduct by offering you a spring of water," she said, and then disappeared without a trace. Presently clear water gushed out of a stone crevice, saving Kim the trouble of having to fetch water from a nearby ravine. People of later generations dubbed the woman the "Goddess of Mount Jiuzi," and the spring as the "Spring of the Dragon King's Daughter."

When Kim was cultivating himself through religious austerities, he had the fortune of being provided for by a man named Min Ranhe. (Another version has his name Ming Zhangzhe.) The man's son later became Kim's disciple and he assumed the monastic name "Daoming." Later, Min himself was converted to Buddhism and came under Kim's tutelage.

Kim died in 794 (10th year of the Zhenyuan reign, Tang Dynasty) at the age of 99. It is said that his remains, placed in a sitting position within a stone sarcophagus, were found intact three years after his burial. This struck awe into the hearts of the local people, who regarded Kim as the reincarnation of Bodhisattva Ksitigarbha. They erected a statue in his image. Flanking the statue are the likenesses of his two disciples, Min Ranhe and his son, Daoming.

Because Kim is regarded as the reincarnation of Bodhisattva Ksitigarbha, Mount Jiuhua rose in fame as the domain of Ksitigarbha. It was visited by large numbers of pilgrims from around the country all year around. And this resulted in the construction of more temples on the mountain. By the Song Dynasty there were more than 50 temples there. Construction of such temples reached a peak during the Ming and Qing dynasties. History books show that by 1911, the year that saw the fall the Qing Dynasty, Mount Jiuhua was home to 150 or so Buddhist temples (another version puts the number at more than 300). However, during the Republican years, many of these were ruined as a result of long years of war and turmoil. A little more than 70 such temples now remain there. The major ones:

(1) Huacheng Temple. Situated at the center of Mount Jiuhua, with Lotus Flower Peak to the south, East Cliff to the east, Shenguang Peak to the west, and Baiyun Mountain to the north, Huacheng Temple looks much like a mountain-rimmed town. Its buildings, arranged in four courtyards that ascend a mountainside one atop another, are simple and pithy in style, and methodical in layout. With a history of more than 1,400 years, it is the oldest temple on Mount Jiuhua. Legend has it that during a tour of the mountain, Zhuge Ji and some other squires from Qingyang County were able to see Gim Kyokak, who lived a Spartan life in a cave abode and ate nothing but a mixture of millet and white clay. The sight of the monk's hard lot generated feelings of self-reproach in the visiting gentry for not having

done their bit to provide for him. They immediately pooled money to build the Huacheng Temple, and moved Kim into it with pomp and ceremony. At the request of Zhang Yancheng, commanding governor of Chizhou (present-day Guichi, Anhui Province), Emperor Dezong (reign 780-805) gave the temple a horizontal board inscribed with its two-character name "Huacheng," written in his own handwriting. More Ming and Qing monarchs followed suit. The imperial favor bestowed on the temple, however, failed to save it from repeated destructions in the intervening years. Among the buildings remaining on the premises, only the Tripitaka Pavilion is a Ming-Dynasty legacy. The others were all rebuilt during the Qing Dynasty. Among the temple's collection of artifacts are a Ming-Dynasty version of the *Tripitaka* and edicts issued by some emperors.

(2) Precious Hall of the Holy Body. Popularly known as the Roushen[1] Pagoda, this hall is poised on Shenguang Peak of Mount Jiuhua, a grandiose architectural phenomenon whose double-eaved Chinese hip-and-gable roof is covered with cast-iron tiles and propped up by elaborate corbel brackets. A stone balustrade runs around the hall that looks resplendent with carved rafters and lacquered pillars. Access to the front of the hall is a stone stairway with 81 steps (another version puts it at 84), its iron-chain railing offering a sense of security for those climbing up the steep mountain. Placed in state in the hall is a 17-meter-high wooden pagoda with eight niches for figurines of Ksitigarbha on each of its seven layers. Inside the pagoda, the Guardian of the Earth, whose mission is to deliver suffering beings from the torments of hell, gazes down on the world from a portrait that is flanked by a standing statue of the

---

[1] *Roushen*, meaning "physical body," refers to one who becomes a bodhisattva in the physical body while still in the present world.

ten kings presiding over the ten departments of purgatory[1]. Inscribed in gold on the walls of the pagoda is the full text of the *Ksitigarbha-sutra*. Underneath the pagoda is the chamber where the physical body of Gim Kyokak is preserved. On a platform behind the hall, incense sticks keep burning all day long in an iron tripod. The hall and its pagoda were repeatedly destroyed and reconstructed, and what is seen today was built during the Tongzhi reign (1862-1878) of the Qing Dynasty.

(3) Zhiyuan Temple. The predecessor of this temple, situated to the east of Huacheng Temple, was a convent of the same name built during the Jiaqing reign (1522-1566) of the Ming Dynasty. After repeated reconstructions and expansions it eventually emerged as a three-courtyard affair. Its centerpiece, the Mahavira Hall, stands 13 *zhang* (43 meters) in height and is splendidly graced with a golden-glazed roof. The road and ramp leading up to the front of the hall is paved with stone slabs engraved with lotus and coin patterns. The awesome architecture and breathtaking ornamentation are perhaps reasons why the Zhiyuan Temple is regarded as the foremost Buddhist establishment on Mount Jiuhua.

(4) Tiantai Temple. Tiantai Peak is the venue for this temple which is named after it, but which is officially known as Ksitigarbha Bodhimandala. Its construction began during the Ming Dynasty, and it was rebuilt during the Guangxu reign (1875-1908) of the Qing Dynasty. The buildings, including its Chamber of Ten Thousand Buddhas, Hall of Ksitigarbha, and Hall of Maitreya, are arranged in five rows laid out neatly one above the other along the contours of the mountain slope so that in the

---

[1] The ten kings presiding over the ten departments of purgatory are known popularly as "ten kings of hell," and Yama, the King of Hell, is actually the name of the fifth of these kings.

distance the entire cluster looks like a titanic edifice. Numerous Buddhist figurines are carved into the walls and pillars of the temple. The place is a nice spot for marveling at the sun rising in the morning from underneath an ocean of clouds at the foot of the temple.

(5) Ganlu Temple. Standing at the waist of the Huacheng Mountain, this temple was known as the Ganlu Convent or Ganlu Bodhimandala before it assumed its present name in 1667 (6th year of the Kangxi reign, Qing Dynasty) at the suggestion of Yulin, a monk of Chan Buddhism who visited Mount Jiuhua and was impressed by the auspicious topography of the temple. Shortly afterwards, another monk by the name of Dong'an raised money to expand the temple, but it was razed to the ground in a war during the Xianfeng reign (1851-1861) of the Qing Dynasty. The present building was erected in 1864 (3rd year of the Tongzhi reign, Qing Dynasty). Its large size and august style of architecture rank it among the orthodox temples of Mount Jiuhua.

(6) Wannian Temple. This temple is popularly called "Centenarian's Palace" to honor the venerated age of the monk who built it. Legend has it that during the Wanli reign (1573-1620) of the Ming Dynasty, Haiyu, whose style name was Wuxia, arrived at Mukong Peak of the East Cliff and built a thatched hut just below the Zhaixin Pavilion. He named it the Star Picking Hut. The hut was expanded into a temple in 1630 (3rd year of the Chongzhen reign, Ming Dynasty), burned down in a major fire in 1717 (56th year of the Kangxi reign, Qing Dynasty), reconstructed in 1721 (60th year of the Kangxi reign), repaired on a large scale in 1826 (6th year of the Daoguang reign, Qing Dynasty), and expanded and given its present name in 1839 (19th year of the Daoguan reign, Qing Dynasty). The grandeur and magnitude of the temple are richly imbued with a rare antiquarian quality.

(7) Zhantan (Sandalwood) Temple. There is no historical record about when the predecessor of this temple was built, but it is known that it used to be part of the Huacheng Temple and that it was rebuilt in 1896 (22nd year of the Guangxu reign, Qing Dynasty) by a monk by the name of Chanding. The temple covers an area of about 5,000 square meters, and housed in its halls, which evince the classic sanctity of a religious sanctuary, are horizontal nameboards, stone inscriptions, and many other artifacts.

(8) Huiju Temple. The predecessor of this temple was the Huiju Convent dating back to the Qing Dynasty, and it assumed its present name in 1938. The temple features a complete collection of statues of the Buddha and bodhisattvas in lifelike images. Its posterior hall is a two-floor structure, with the second floor devoted to the Pavilion of Guanyin, and the ground floor occupied by the Hall of Ksitigarbha.

4. Mount Emei

Mount Emei, located in a municipality bearing its name in Sichuan Province, is another one of the four holy mountains of Chinese Buddhism. It is regarded as the domain of Samantabhadra, or Bodhisattva of Universal Benevolence, depicted as riding upon an elephant. Its highest peak is Golden Peak, also known as Wanfo (Ten Thousand Buddha) Peak, which rises 3,077 meters above sea level. A world of rocky eminences cocooned under a green blanket of trees, with a thicket of peaks emerging from the clouds and thrusting into the sky, Mount Emei is quite up to the saying, "No place under heaven is as beautiful as Mount Emei." Only by following a stone-paved path that begins at the foot of the mountain and winds its way around one peak after another for 120 *li* (60 km) can one climb to the summit of the mountain. The amazing topography and this unique mountain path found expression in a poem composed by a man of the Ming Dynasty:

> "High is Mount Emei,
> Which is like a sword thrusting into high heavens.
> A mountain path stretches for one hundred and twenty *li*,
> Only to disappear in an abyss of clouds and mists.
> High above, birds nose their way along a course full of twists
>   and turns,
> Yet still find it hard to make the rounds of the mountains.
> Each mountain is in a strange form,
> But all of them bear a resemblance to a green lotus plant."

The unusual height and dimensions of the place result in a temperature difference of 15°C between the foot of the mountain and its summit.

Stories differ as to when Mount Emei became the domain of Samantabhadra. One version dates this back to the Yongping reign (58-75) of the Eastern Han Dynasty, when an old man surnamed Pu, who was picking medicinal herbs on the mountain, happened to spy the auspicious signs of the Bodhisattva of Universal Benevolence. The *Gazetteer of Mount Emei*, citing Volume 45 of the *Garland Sutra*, has this to say, "In the southwest there is a place called the Mountain of Brightness, where many bodhisattvas have resided since ancient times. The current bodhisattva living there is someone by the name of 'Xiansheng,' who has 3,000 companions including his own family and some bodhisattvas. He often preaches there." However, to associate this quotation with the origin of Mount Emei is farfetched, and has been justifiably repudiated by Shi Yinguang in his amended version of *Gazetteer of Mount Emei* for the simple reason that Mount Emei is not situated to the southwest of Buddhagaya, where the Buddha preached his doctrines, and that Samantabhadra was never called

"Xiansheng." Buddhism found its way to Mount Emei probably during the Western and Eastern Jin dynasties (265-420), but at that time the place was dominated by Taoism. Buddhism did not begin to thrive there until after the Tang and Song dynasties. It was during the Song dynasty that Mount Emei was formally declared as the domain of Samantabhadra.

According to historical records, in 968 (6th year of the Jiande reign of Emperor Taizu, Song Dynasty), the imperial court, after receiving repeated reports from Jiazhou Prefecture (present-day Jiading, Sichuan Province) about the discovery of auspicious signs of Samantabhadra, dispatched Zhang Chongjin, a palace attendant, to investigate. In 980 (6th year of the Taipingxingguo reign, Song Dynasty), the imperial court cast a bronze statue of Samantabhadra mounted on an elephant, and built a hall to enshrine this colossal sculpture with a height of more than two *zhang* (approximately 7 meters), thereby establishing Mount Emei's history as the domain of Samantabhadra. Buddhism reached its zenith during the Ming and Qing dynasties, when more than 100 temples of various sizes were built there, but it went into decline during the Republican years, when many of those temples fell into disrepair. The damp weather took its toll as well. So many temples crumbled and became dilapidated, and not more than half of them still looked like temples. It was not until the founding of the People's Republic in 1949 that some of the major temples were repaired and restored. The following is a brief introduction to some of the better known ones.

(1) Wannian Temple. A relatively old Buddhist establishment on Mount Emei, it was originally the Puxian (Samantabhadra) Temple that became the Baishui Temple during the Tang Dynasty and the Baishui Puxian Temple during the Song Dynasty, assuming the name of Shengshou Wannian Temple, or Temple of Ten-Thousand-Year Sacred Longevity, during the Wanli reign

Wannian Temple on Mount Emei

(1573-1620) of the Ming Dynasty. It used to be a colossal affair with seven courtyards, but it has had its fill of destructions. A major fire in 1946 reduced all the wooden structures to ashes, and only the brick halls built during the Ming Dynasty survived. The present temple, reconstructed in 1953, has two courtyards, with the main hall enshrined with statues of Vairocana, Sakyamuni, and Amitabha. What is special about this temple is the Ming-Dynasty legacy, a square brick hall 16 meters high and 15.7 meters in circumference that is the shrine for the Song-Dynasty bronze sculpture of Samantabhadra and his trademark elephant, which looks imposing at a height of 7.3 meters and has a weight of 62 tons. A total of 24 niches are scooped into the lower parts of the four walls of the hall, and each of them is enshrined with a cast-iron figurine of the Buddha. There are 307 tiny bronze Buddhist figurines that have been placed in horizontal niches dug into the upper parts of these walls. The front gate of the temple opens onto a forest whose rich piles of foliage obliterate the sun, and a limpid stream that flows with a rich whispering sound. When night falls on a summer day, the place is taken over by a contingent of frogs whose croaks are evocative of the notes of many zithers. Such frogs are native to Mount Emei.

(2) Baoguo Temple. When it was first built at the foot of Mount Emei during the Wanli reign (1573-1620) of the Ming Dynasty, it was known as "Huizong Chamber." It assumed its present name during a major refurbishment during the Kangxi reign (1662-1722) of the Qing Dynasty. The horizontal name-board hanging above its front gate is inscribed in the handwriting of Emperor Kangxi. The temple contains four main buildings with anterooms — the Maitreya Hall, the Mahavira Hall, the Seven-Buddha Hall, and the Tripitaka Pavilion — which are laid out in a descending order following the contours of the terrain. Baoguo Temple is situated where people start climbing the mountain, and has quite a few fine artifacts on display. These

The main Gate of Baoguo Temple at Mount Emei

include the cast-copper Huayan Pagoda, a masterpiece of foun-
dry art that is a 14-layer, 7-metre-tall structure with 4,700-odd
Buddhist likenesses and the unabridged text of the *Garland Sutra*
engraved in its walls. There is also an invaluable 2.4-meter-high
color-glazed porcelain sculpture of the Buddha dating back to
1415 (13th year of the Yongle reign, Ming Dynasty). The big
bronze bell hanging in front of the temple weighs 12,500 kg.

(3) Fuhu Temple. Nestling at the foot of Mount Emei and
one km from the Baoguo Temple, the Fuhu Temple, meaning
"Temple to Subdue Tigers," was first built during the Tang Dynasty, and renamed the Shenlong Chamber during the Song Dynasty. At the time the place was terrorized by man-killing tigers,
and the monks of the temple erected a victory-honoring dhvaju
(a pillar with a silk stream fluttering atop it) to subdue them.
(Another version asserts that the name "Fuhu" stems from the
mountain's tiger-like form.) This temple also had its fill of ups
and downs throughout its history, and its last major repairs took
place in 1651 (8th year of the Shunzhi reign, Qing Dynasty). The
temple is one of the largest Buddhist centers of Mount Emei,
with its 13 halls and chambers tucked away in the shade of a forest. What is special about the Fuhu Temple is that although all its
buildings are under an overhead canopy of trees, withered leaves
seldom settle on its rooftops. This prompted Emperor Kangxi
to name it a "Dust-Free Garden," and he inscribed this on a
horizontal board for the temple. During the War of Resistance
against Japan (1937-1945), the temple became the school buildings of Sichuan University. In recent years, it has gradually been
restored to its former scale and glory, with Buddhist statues
being re-erected in its various halls.

(4) Qingyin Pavilion. Situated at the foot of the Niuxin
Mountain, Qingyin Pavilion used to be the Niuxin Temple during the Tang Dynasty. This is where two rivers converge, the

Bailong River in the east and the Heilong River in the west. In its vicinity there is the Niuxin Rock, several meters in height, and two bridges, one on the Bailong River and the other on the Heilong River, that are known as the "twin flying bridges." Water tumbles down the two rivers from a height and plunges into the depth of a ravine, and in the process produces a peculiarly ringing sound. Hence the designation, "Twin Bridge Reverberating with a Ringing Sound." This is one of the ten major scenic sights on Mount Emei. About one km west of the Qingyin Pavilion is the place known as "Strip of Sky" — two vertical cliffs standing facing each other, squeezing the blue sky into a narrow strip.

(5) Hongchunping (Toon Tree) Terrace. This is also the name of the temple on this terrace, with Chinese toon trees growing in front of it. The predecessor of this temple was the Thousand-Buddha Temple built during the Ming Dynasty. It was rebuilt in 1790 (55th year of the Qianlong reign, Qing Dynasty), and its main hall is graced with a couplet in Emperor Qianlong's own handwriting. The treasure of the temple, however, is a lotus flower lantern two meters in height and one meter in diameter. Wrought towards the end of the Qing Dynasty, the lantern is carved with seven dragons and several hundred Buddhist statues in admirable craftsmanship.

(6) Xianfeng Temple, also known as Cave of Nine Old Men. Legend has it that this was where during a visit to Mount Emei the Yellow Emperor came across an old man and asked him how many companions were with him. The old man answered that he had nine. Such is the origin of the name of the Cave of Nine Old Men, which is known more popularly as Celestial Mansion of Nine Old Men. The cave is situated a few hundred meters to the right of the temple. When the temple itself was erected during the Wanli reign (1573-1620) of the Ming Dynasty, it had four halls whose roofs were paved with cast-iron tiles. The Ming court

bestowed it with a collection of the *Tripitaka*. The buildings as they stand today were mostly repaired or rebuilt during the Qing Dynasty. The temple is frequented by monkeys who come to beg for food. Visitors to this place make it a point to bring some food with them. Otherwise, a disappointed monkey may grab one's bag, hang it high in the tree, and stalk away, leaving the visitor exasperated.

(7) Xixiang (Elephant Bathing) Pool. This is a small affair known as the Chuxi Convent when it was first built in 1368, the year the Ming dynasty was founded. In 1699 (38th year of the Kangxi reign, Qing Dynasty) it was expanded and became a temple. The tiny pool in front of the temple was said to be where Bodhisattva Samantabhadra bathed his elephant. The main hall, which is enshrined with the statues of three bodhisattvas — Guanyin, Ksitigarbha, and Mahasthamaprapt, stands atop a peak that is surrounded by firs. In the quiet of a moonlit night, the place gives rise to a feeling that one is alone in the boundless firmament. The place also teems with delightful monkeys.

(8) Golden Peak, which is the summit of Mount Emei at an altitude of 3,077 metres above sea level. Because of its sheer height, the temple halls were often hit in the past by lightening and burned down. New halls were built there a few years ago to accommodate those who come to marvel at the Buddha's auspicious halo and the holy fire. It is said that when a person stands at the top of the Golden Peak and looks down over the cliff side, the reflected sunshine often conjures up a huge multihued halo with the silhouette of the person in the middle of it. This is evocative of the light behind a Buddhist statue, but the phenomenon does not happen on a daily basis. The "holy fire" stems from Mount Emei's rich phosphorus ores. Looking down from atop the Golden Peak on the night of a fine day, one can see numerous lights that look like electric lamps on the mountain.

This phenomenon, popularly known as "ten thousand bright lamps paying homage to Mount Emei," is actually a congregate of flickering lights that appear only at night. The backside of the Golden Peak is a perpendicular cliff that rises high above a bottomless ravine where many desperate people have come to commit suicide. The Golden Peak also allows visitors to extend their vision to see the snow-clad mountains many miles away, and to be astonished to see how vast a globe one inhabits.

5. Ancestral Halls of Buddhist Sects

There are eight sects of Chinese Buddhism and each has at least one place of origin, or "Ancestral Hall." The following is an introduction to one such cradle for each sect.

(1) Guoqing Temple. This is the cradle of the Tiantai sect on Mount Tiantai, 3.5 km north of Tiantai County, Zhejiang Province. Zhiyi (538-597), an eminent Sui-Dynasty monk who was the father of the Tiantai sect, practiced austerities in self-cultivation here for many years. After his death in 597 (17th year of the Kaihuang reign, Sui Dynasty), his disciple Yang Guang, or the Prince of Jin, carried forward his wish and built the Guoqing Temple. During the Tang Dynasty, this became one of the four major Buddhist temples in the country. The buildings as they stand today, including 14 halls, pavilions, chambers, and 600 rooms were reconstructions from the Qing Dynasty. Along the temple's axial line are the main halls — the Maitreya Hall, the Yuhua Hall, and the Mahavira Hall. The Maitreya Hall is flanked east and west by Bell and Drum towers. In the Mahavira Hall, a 6.8-meter-high, 13-ton bronze statue of Sakyamuni sits in the company of 18 arhats carved out of *nanmu* wood. Along the eastern line are the canteen, the abbot's abode, the Yingta

(Greeting the Pagoda) Chamber, the Xiuzhu Studio, the Meditation Chamber, and the Jingguan Hall. Along the west line are an array of ancillary rooms, including the Anyang Chamber, the Guanyin Hall, the Artifact Display Room, and the Miaofa Chamber that has a *Tripitaka* library on the second floor and a preaching room downstairs. The Guoqing Temple is sequestered in the rural repose and scenic beauty of Mount Tiantai. A plum tree in the compound, reportedly planted during the Sui Dynasty by Guanding (who was a disciple of Zhiyi), is more than 1,400 years old. Standing in front of the temple is a nine-tiered hexagonal stupa, 59.3 metres in height. Seng Yixing, a Tang-Dynasty astronomer, once paid a visit to the Guoqing Temple to learn arithmetic from a hermit who had become a monk there. Legend has it that the hermit, who had an inkling of the impending visit, told his disciple that Seng would arrive by the time the stream in front of the temple began to flow west. A stele at the site is inscribed with the line, "The arrival of Yixing caused this stream to flow westward." Visitors are also impressed by a host of other scenic spots in the vicinity.

(2) Xixia Temple, which was the domain of the patriarch of the Sanlun (Three Sastras) sect, is in the suburbs of Nanjing, Jiangsu Province. When it was completed during the Jianyuan reign (479-482) of the Southern Qi Dynasty of the Southern and Northern Dynasties, it became the hermitage of Ming Sengshao. After Ming became a close friend of the monk Fadu, he evacuated his hermitage, converted it into a temple, and moved Fadu into it. The temple was first named Xixia Jetavanavihara, or Xixia Mountain Temple. Later, Senglang, a monk from north China, became the abbot and vigorously disseminated the doctrines of the Three Sastras sect. Xiao Yan, or Emperor Wudi of the Liang Dynasty of the Southern and Northern Dynasties, dispatched ten monks to the Xixia Temple to learn from Senglang,

of whom Sengquan emerged as the best student. After several generations' hard work, the Xixia Temple became the central bodhimandala of the Three Sastras School for the region south of the Yangtze River. Falang, who was the teacher of Jizang (549-623), the founder of the Three Sastras sect, was a major figure in the religious tradition of the Xixia Temple. It is because of this relationship that even though Jizang had never been to Xixia Temple, his renovated theory on the three sastras is of the same origin as the theory advocated at the Xixia Temple.

A dagoba in Xixia Temple

During the Tang Dynasty, Xixia Temple was expanded and renamed the Gongde Temple for a time. With 49 halls, chambers, and pavilions on the premises, it was one of the four major Buddhist temples of the time. It became the Xixia Temple once again in 1392 (25th year of the Hongwu reign, Ming Dynasty). In 1855 (5th year of the Xianfeng reign, Qing Dynasty), the temple was razed to ground during war and turmoil. The existing buildings of the temple today, including the gate hall, the Hall of Heavenly Kings, the Vairocana Hall, the Tripitaka Pavilion, and the Shicui Pavilion, were mostly reconstructed in 1908 (34th year of the Guangxu reign, Qing Dynasty). More additions were made during the Republican years.

Xixia Temple is marked for its unique architecture and layout. When one enters the gate hall and passes the Maitreya Hall, one finds oneself in a spacious enclosed courtyard whose four sides are lined with other halls and anterooms. This courtyard is lower in elevation than the Vairocana Hall, which perches imposingly high on the mountain. The artifacts in the collection of this temple include stone sculptures of the Southern Dynasties and stone inscriptions of the Five Dynasties.

A stupa standing 15 meters tall beside Xixia Temple was built in 601 (1st year of the Renshou reign, Sui Dynasty). It is a four-layered octagonal structure built of white stone and richly engraved with exquisite designs. The grottoes and cliff carvings up Xixia Mountain abound in works of consummate art, earning the mountain a widespread reputation.

(3) Huayan Temple. Built in 803 (19th year of the Zhenyuan reign, Tang Dynasty), Huayan Temple used to command a vantage point on the tableland of Chang'an County, Shaanxi Province, 15 kilometers from the city of Xi'an. As its name suggests, this was the cradle of the Huayan sect of Chinese Buddhism. During the Qianlong reign (1736-1795) of the Qing Dynasty, the foundation of the temple collapsed, destroying all the halls, chambers, and pavilions. Only two pagodas survived. One is dedicated to Du Shun (also Fashun), the father of the Huayan School. Popularly known as the Huayan Pagoda, it is a 17-meter square structure of seven layers, with two Chinese characters that mean "Patriarch of the Huayan Sect" inscribed on the top layer and six Chinese characters meaning "Dust-free Precious Pagoda of Pure Light" on the third layer. The other is a five-layered hexagonal structure seven meters in height, dedicated to Chengguan, the fourth-generation patriarch of the Yuayan sect. There are also some stone inscriptions that offer valuable information on the men and deeds of this sect.

(4) Xuanzhong Temple on Shibi Mountain in Jiaocheng County, Shanxi Province. This cradle of the Pure Land sect was built in 472 (2nd year of the Yanzhong reign, Northern Wei Dynasty) and rebuilt and renamed the "Shibi Yongning Temple"

during the Zhenguan reign (627-649) of the Tang Dynasty. During the Northern Wei Dynasty (386-534), Tanluan (476-542) lived in this temple and earned the nickname "Divine Luan" for his devotion to the study of the Pure Land sect. During the Tang Dynasty, Monk Daochuo (562-645) settled in this temple and advocated chanting incantations, but his disciple, Shandao (613-681), moved to Chang'an to preach the Pure Land doctrine and became the *de facto* founder of the Pure Land sect of Chinese Buddhism. Xuanzhong Temple nestles at the foot of a mountain. Its Hall of Ten Thousand Buddhas, Kusala (Mental Virtue) Hall, and East and West Ancillary Rooms were destroyed in a major fire during the Guangxu reign (1875-1908) of the Qing Dynasty. Only the Pavilion of a Thousand Buddhas survived. In 1956, the temple was rebuilt and restored to its old size. This is a temple of international influence, as both the Jodo Shinshu (True Pure Land sect) and the Jodo sect of Japan regard it as their cradle and often dispatch pilgrims to pay respect to it. The peace and quiet of the environment around the Xuanzhong Temple make it an ideal place for those dedicated to cultivating themselves and searching for enlightenment.

(5) Ci'en Temple, the cradle of the Ci'en (Vinnanavada) sect. During the Tang Dynasty, Xuanzang was the abbot who translated Buddhist scriptures in this temple, which was the largest of its kind in Chang'an (present-day Xi'an) and had at that time a dozen or so courtyards. After Xuanzang died, his disciple Kuiji (632-682) became the abbot. More than 1,000 years later the size of the temple has shrunk considerably, with less than one tenth of its original buildings remaining today. To the north stands a square structure, the Greater Wild Goose Pagoda, that was built to store the Sanskrit versions of Buddhist scriptures brought back to China from India by Xuanzang. Here is a story that explains why the pagoda was named after a wild goose.

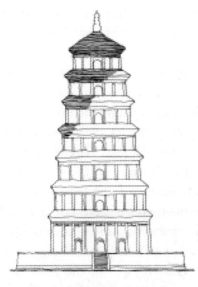

Greater Wild Goose Pagoda in
Ci'en Temple

Once upon a time there was a temple in India in which the monks followed Hinayana Buddhism and ate only three kinds of "clean" meat.[1] One day, when a monk was taking a stroll during a meditation session,[2] he saw a flock of wild geese flying overhead. He murmured jokingly, "Our temple has run out of supply of the three kinds of clean meat, and we monks are on the verge of starvation...." He had hardly finished his sentence when one of the geese crashed to the ground dead. The monk lost no time in relating to his fellow monks what he had seen, and a gloomy mood settled among the monks. Drawing inspiration from the death of the wild goose, they converted to Mahayana Buddhism, built a pagoda and named it the "wild goose pagoda." Xuanzang borrowed this name for the pagoda that was built to store his scriptures. The Greater Wild Goose Pagoda, which underwent major repairs during the Ming Dynasty, stands at 64.1 meters tall (its pedestal included), and is an emblem of Xi'an.

---

[1] Three kinds of "clean meat" — the meat is deemed clean when a monk has not seen the creature killed, has not heard of its being killed for him, and has no doubt thereon.

[2] This is a form of self-cultivation in Buddhism. When a monk feels drowsy while sitting and contemplating the creeds, he can rise to take a walk to and fro in a cloister, a corridor, etc. to prevent sleepiness. It is also an exercise to promote digestion of food and stay healthy.

(6) Nanhua Temple, the cradle of the Chan sect. Situated in Qujiang County, Guangdong Province, the Nanhua Temple was the Baolin Temple built in 504 (3rd year of the Tianjian reign, Liang Dynasty). In 677 (2nd year of the Yifeng reign, Tang Dynasty), Huineng arrived at the Baolin Temple and stayed there for more than three decades while disseminating the doctrine of the Chan sect. During the Tang Dynasty the temple was renamed the "Zhongxing Temple," and later, the "Faquan Temple." It was not until the early Song Dynasty that it assumed the name that remains to this day. The original buildings of the temple are no more. The buildings as we see them today were constructed during the 1930s under the supervision of Monk Xuyun. The temple today covers 12,000 square meters in area. Arranged on its axial line are the Hall of the Heavenly Kings, the Mahavira Hall, the Tripitaka Pavilion, the Lingxing Pagoda, the Hall of Six Patriarchs, and the Abbot's Mansion. There are also bell and drum towers and other ancillary buildings. The awesome scale and architectural grandeur of this structure are well matched by this temple's prestige as the foremost establishment of the Chinese Chan sect. Among the temple's host of valuable artifacts is the physical body of Huineng. The temple nestles in a place whose scenic beauty is accentuated by the rich verdure of towering trees

A bird's eye view of Nanhua Temple

that have been around since times unknown.

(7) Longchang Temple. The predecessor of this major establishment of the Vinaya sect on Baohua Mountain in Jurong County, Jiangsu Province, was the Public Baozhi Temple dating back to 502 (1st year of the Tianjian reign, Liang Dynasty). During its heyday, the temple boasted 999 *jian* of buildings and a population of more than 300 monks. Its main buildings, including the Altar, Dining Room, Beamless Hall, Bronze Hall, Manjusri Hall (Institute of Wisdom), and Cigu Chamber nestled snugly against the contours of the mountain. The quadrangular courtyard containing the Mahavira Hall and the Mahakaruna (Great Mercy) Hall alone occupies an area of 72,000 square meters. Few Buddhist monasteries in south China can match the Longchang Temple in size. The Fengde Temple in the Zhongnan Mountain, where the Vinaya sect originated, is no more. The Longchang Temple rose in fame to become the center of this sect beginning in the late Ming Dynasty. When Jiguang, a master in *samathi* (intent contemplation) had an alter built there to introduce the commandments during the late Ming Dynasty, the temple's fame rose to an all-time high. His disciple, Jianyue (1602-1679) went out of his way to expand the temple and enforce strict discipline; his *Standard Instructions on Commandments and Rules* spread all over the country and was acted upon in all the temples of the Vinaya sect, thus turning Longchang Temple into the *de facto* ancestral hall of the Viyana sect.

(8) Great Xingshan Temple, the cradle of the Esoteric sect of Chinese Buddhism in Xi'an, Shaanxi Province. This temple was a scripture translation workshop when it was built in 582 (2nd year of the Kaihuang reign, Sui Dynasty). In 720 (8th year of the Kaiyuan reign, Tang Dynasty), the celebrated esoteric master Vajrabodhi (669-741) settled in the Great Xingshan Temple to disseminate Tantrism in a big way, and built an altar to

preside over the *abhiseka*, a ritual to consecrate novices by pouring water on their heads. Through his work he laid down the foundation for the establishment of the Esoteric sect in China. Vajrabodhi's disciple, Amoghavajra (705-774), followed his master's instruction and led a delegation to Sinhala to study the doctrines of Esoteric Buddhism and returned to China to establish this sect of Chinese Buddhism. The Great Xingshan Temple has had its ups and downs in the intervening years. In 1955, the government provided a huge sum of money and rebuilt the temple. The main buildings, such as the Hall of Heavenly Kings, the Drum and Bell Towers, the Mahavira Hall, the Guanyin Hall, and the Dharma Preaching Hall, as well as the anterooms, are all imposing structures arranged on a methodical plan. They never fail to strike awe into the beholder. It is one of the major Buddhist temples in Xi'an.

Chapter 6

Organization and Life in the Cloisters

1. Principles and Positions

The existence of an organization is predicated on well-defined rules and regulations. Otherwise its members are like sheep without a shepherd, and the organization itself has no hope of long-term survival. This is true of the monks' organization in a temple. The Buddhist term *sangha* means the assembly of at least three monks, one of whom is the leader empowered to hear confessions, grant absolution, and ordain. The principles for the *sangha* are known as the "Six Points of Reverent Harmony" that demand strict observation and tolerate no violation. These six points are: 1) bodily unity in the form of worship, without fighting; 2) oral unity in chanting, mental unity in faith, and refraining from quarrels; 3) mental unity in faith, and the sharing of happiness; 4) moral unity in observing the commandments and self-cultivation; 5) doctrinal unity in views and explanations; 6) and economic unity in community of goods, deeds, studies, or charity.

The Six Points of Reverent Harmony were laid down during the time of Sakyamuni some 2,500 years ago, and they have been in force since Buddhism spread to China during the Han Dynasty. But, given China's different conditions and customs and habits, these six points are not enough to keep a monastery in order, and that is why in a Chinese monastery specific positions are instituted to supervise every aspect of life in the cloisters.

The abbot is the master of a Chinese monastery. Under him there are four supervisors and eight executives who preside over the practice of self-cultivation and conduct of the monks and take care of daily life according to a division of labor. The four supervisors are the *sthavira* (the superintendent), the supervisor of the western chamber, the supervisor of the rear chamber, and the supervisor at large, and their task is to provide leadership over the search for Buddhist truth and the chanting of incantations in the prayer hall. These four positions are filled by monks of high accomplishment and are appointed by the abbot.

The eight executives are professional managers of various affairs in the monastery. They are:

1) Jianyuan: popularly known as the homemaker, who handles general affairs, and controls the financial affairs in particular;

2) Zhike: in charge of the reception room and receiving visiting monks and laity.

3) Sengzhi: supervising the enforcement of monastic rules and regulations, and the deportment of monks.

4) Weina: supervising the meditation hall, and providing leadership over daily religious rituals.

5) Dianzuo: managing the kitchen and the canteen, and taking care of meals for the entire monastery.

6) Liaoyuan: taking care of the Hall for Roaming Monks, and receiving wandering monks who stay in it.

7) Yibo: taking care of the abbot's mansion, assisting the abbot in running the mansion and handling personnel affairs.

8) Shuji: secretary in charge of drafting and writing documents concerning public relations.

These eight executives are appointed by the abbot for a term of one year. Where and when necessary, assistants are appointed to serve as accountants, warehouse managers, alms collectors, doormen, vegetable garden managers, water fetching foremen, bell tolling managers, drum beaters, men who burn incense sticks and light lamps, managers of wandering monks, meal dispensers, etc. Thus life in a monastery progresses smoothly with the coordination of supervisors, executives, and their assistants. In some monasteries there is also the position of a general executive, but this is actually an honorary title, and the holder of it is not required to do anything.

For a time different sects had different hierarchies in Chinese Buddhism, but after the Song Dynasty, the influence of the Chan sect became so dominant that its arrangement was copied by the other sects.

2. Commandments and Prohibitions

The Commandments were prescribed by the Buddha, and followers are required to obey them unconditionally. According to historical records, there were no such commandments during the first 12 years after Sakyamuni achieved Buddhahood, and members of the *sangha* followed no rules of conduct. Some monks were thus carried away by their impulses and scandalized society by doing things that were improper to their status. To safeguard the honor of the *sangha* and appease public feelings, the Buddha began to formulate the commandments. But he did not finish the task in one stage. Rather, he laid down each commandment whenever a misdeed was committed. The commandments accumulated in this fashion until they formed a complete body. Each commandment had a reason behind it.

For details, refer to the "complete collection of monastic rules" in the *Tripitaka*.

The commandments fall into two categories: commandments for those who have renounced the world and commandments for those who have not. Lay Buddhists are required to abide by the Five Commandments[1] or Eight Commandments[2], while a mendicant is required observe 250 commandments and a nun, 500 commandments. The commandments are the rules of conduct governing the body, language, and will of a Buddhist. Accordingly, monks in a monastery are required to congregate on the 15th and 13th of each lunar month to chant the commandments. Such congregations serve two purposes. One is to remind the monks of the commandments, and the other gives an opportunity for malfeasants to make confessions. A monk who refuses to confess is held guilty, and if his misconduct has been exposed, he will be given a good talking to or, if the case is serious, expelled. The fortnightly recitation of the commandments is known as *upavasatha* (retreat for spiritual refreshment). Today, *upavasatha* is not held in the monasteries of most sects, but remains a compulsory formality in the Vinaya sect.

Commandments hold an important position in Buddhism. They are the foremost of the *trisiksa*,[3] or three studies. A monk who refuses to abide by them can accomplish nothing no matter

---

[1] The Five Commandments, or *Pancasila* in Sanskrit: no killing, no stealing, no adultery, telling no lies, and abstention from liquors.

[2] The Eight Commandments: Not to kill; not to take things other than given; abstention from ignoble sexual conduct; not to speak falsely; not to indulge in cosmetics; not to indulge in personal adornments, dancing or music; not to sleep in fine beds; and not to eat out of right hours.

[3] *Trisiksa*, meaning "three studies": learning by the commandments, or prohibitions, so as to guard against the evil consequences of error by mouth, body, or mind, in other words, word, deed, or thought; by *dhyana*, or quietist meditation; and by philosophy, i.e., study of principles and solving of doubts.

how hard he tries self-cultivation. Only by strictly observing them can a monk proceed to study by *dhyana* and by philosophy. The Buddha's purpose in laying down the commandments was to prevent misconduct and ward off evil, and to promote the accumulation of morality.

Apart from the commandments laid down by Sakyamuni, monks in China are also subject to a series of prohibitions set forth by the eminent monk Huaihai of the Tang Dynasty in light of Chinese customs and habits and on the basis of the 800 year practice of Chinese Buddhism after it spread to China during the Han Dynasty.

Huaihai (720-814) was a native of Changle in present-day Fuzhou. Surnamed Wang, he was tonsured and became a disciple of Huizhao at Xishan in Chaoyang and was ordained with the commandments by the monk Falang on Mount Hengshan. One day, while studying the *Tripitaka* in the Fucha Temple in Lujiang, Anhui Province, he got word that Mazu (also known as Daoyi, 709-788) was preaching Chan Buddhism in Jiangxi. He went all the way there to seek Mazu's advice. After Mazu died, Huaihai settled on Baizhang Mountain in Fengxing, Jiangxi Province, where he built a temple to recruit followers and receive wandering monks. He did this because at the time, monks of the Chan sect did not have fixed residences and most of them were put up in temples belonging to the Vinaya sect. Though they were put up in separate courtyards in these temples, there were still many inconveniences to their practicing meditation on the Chan philosophy and preaching it. When the population in his temple grew to a considerable size, this gave rise to the need to enforce certain rules and regulations to maintain peace and order. Huaihai created the *Rules of Conduct for the Chan Sect,* known to posterity as the "Monastic Prohibitions." The original version of the book is not extant, but judging from an introduction in Volume

Six of the *Quotations of Buddhists in the Jingde Reign of the Dynasty* by Daoyuan, they were rather simple rules and regulations. A similar book appeared by the Song Dynasty, which confused monasteries across the land as to which version was the correct one. In 1335 (3rd year of the Yuantong reign, Yuan Dynasty), the court of Emperor Yuanshun ordered Dehui, the abbot of a monastery in the Baizhang Mountain in Jiangxi, to compile a new version. The book he compiled was none other than the *Imperial-Mandated Monastic Prohibitions of the Baizhang Monastery*, which was distributed among monks nationwide and has been in use ever since. The new version was far more comprehensive than Huaihai's original, and reflected the progress society had made with the passage of time, but its spirit remained the same, that is, how to run the *sangha* and the monasteries well.

The emergence of the "Monastic Prohibitions" was, to a certain extent, a transformation of the commandments that were necessary to prevent the *sangha* from being detached from a society that provided the lifeblood for the existence of monasteries.

3. Economic Sources for Monasteries

Except for the *tricivara*, begging bowl and bedding,[1] a monk is not supposed to have other private possessions. The monastery, however, is allowed to own property to be shared by all the monks. "Egalitarianism in property and interests" is an organizational principle for the *sangha*.

In the past, land was a major source of revenue for the

---

[1] *Tricivara*, or three habits, include *sanghati* 九至二十五条衣, *uttarasanga* 七条衣, and *antaravasaka* 五条衣. The bowl 钵 is used for begging for food while on the road. The bedding 具 is made of cloth about 80 cm in width, to be spread out to sit or lie on, and serves as a cushion for prostration during important religious rituals.

Buddhist monasteries. Monasteries lent their land to local farmers in return for annual rents to be used as upkeep and to provide for the monks. After the Land Reform in New China, the monasteries lost the land in their possession, and monks in rural areas were allotted the same amount of land as local farmers. As a matter of fact, monks had not tilled their own land for many centuries. During the Tang Dynasty, when the famed Chan monk Huaihai built the first Chan monastery, he attached equal importance to farming and Chan meditation, and his "Monastic Prohibitions" contained rules for monks to participate in farm labor. The rules, known as "Rules for Collective Labor," required monks to share all the chores in the monastery. In his old age, Huaihai insisted on taking part in collective labor. One day, the monk in charge of collective labor, wanting Huaihai to take a rest on account of his advanced age, hid his farm tool. Huaihai could not find it, but he refused to take a rest. "I am an immoral man only if I shift my end of physical labor onto other people," he said, adding that he would refuse to eat if he was not allowed to work. This story later evolved into the famed adage: "I'll eat nothing the day I haven't done any work."

The financial sources for a monastery in China today are mainly as follows:

(1) Visitor tickets. Monasteries, no matter where they are, are always regarded as cultural facilities with much to see, and tickets are sold to visitors to earn the upkeep. As a matter of fact, tickets have become a major source of revenue for the monasteries. The earnings can be very impressive if a monastery is a big one or situated on a famous mountain.

(2) Almsgiving (*dana*). Since the advent of Buddhism, monks who renounced the world have lived on alms contributed by lay followers. Even today, lay Buddhists are in the habit of contributing money and materials to monasteries in the belief that

this helps them accumulate virtue and attain the Buddha's blessings.

(3) Morality-accumulation Box. In the Mahavira Hall of virtually all the monasteries there is a box that looks like a piggy bank, but much bigger. This is the morality-accumulation box, into which pilgrims and visitors toss whatever amount of money they wish as a token of their piety. The box can yield a substantial amount of earnings every year. In some monasteries the morality-accumulation box can be found in every hall.

(4) The "Circulation Department." The "circulation department" turns out to be a small store selling Buddhist scriptures, statues, and other religious objects, as well as souvenirs. If run well, such a store can provide a good income.

(5) Vegetarian's restaurant. For the convenience of pilgrims, patrons, and visitors, some temples run restaurants in which only vegetarian food is served. A well-run restaurant can earn a lot of money.

(6) Religious services. The Chinese who believe in Buddhism are in the habit of sending for monks to recite scriptures in order to seek the Buddha's blessings. When someone has died in a family, they invite monks to come home to perform rituals to expiate the sins of the dead. These services are another major source of income for a monastery.

(7) Farming. In temples situated in rural areas, most monks earn a living by farming. The monks of the Guoqing Temple on Mount Tiantai, for instance, till the land while cultivating themselves in search of enlightenment. They run their farm so well that the crops yield a surplus on a yearly basis. Another source of income for this monastery are the woods on its premises.

(8) Government subsidy. Temples with a rich historical and cultural tradition are duly protected by the government, which finances major repairs and expansion projects.

With the above mentioned sources for collective income, each monastery is able to offer allowances to its monks according to their responsibilities and contributions. Even those who do not shoulder any responsibilities are entitled to an allowance.

4. Everyday Life in the Cloisters

Everyday life in a monastery is both physical and spiritual. As to the physical aspect, a monk needs to be fed and clothed. As to the spiritual aspect, he practices austerities in searching for the Buddhist truth, attending sutra-chanting sessions in the halls and studying the creeds. His daily routine in the cloisters consists of the following four aspects:

(1) Incantation-chanting sessions. The first thing a monk does after he gets up in the morning and washes his face and brushes his teeth is to go to the hall to chant incantations. Under normal conditions, he arises at five in the morning. After he has finished tidying himself up and putting on his habit, he will queue up with fellow monks, and then the *karmadana* (deacon) chaperons them all into the Mahavira Hall where the monks who live in the meditation rooms stand along the eastern wall and those who live in other dormitories stand along the western wall. With the deacon taking the lead, they sing hymns and chant incantations. All the while bells, drums, wooden-fish, and chimes are struck to mark the beats of the hymns and the rhythm of the chanting. Among these concussion instruments, the wooden fish has a special function to play: it serves to admonish those who have renounced the mundane world to follow the example of the fish, which never sleeps, and to be assiduous in seeking self-cultivation through meditation. The morning session in the Mahavira Hall finishes in about an hour's time. The afternoon session, which begins at four,

is the same as the morning session in terms of duration and rituals, but the incantations to be chanted are different.

(2) Mealtime ritual. A religious ritual is performed before a meal is served in the monastery. After the morning incantation-chanting session is dismissed, the monks who live in the meditation rooms are the first to evacuate the Mahavira Hall and return to their rooms. When a bell is tolled, they queue up again and file into the dining room to be seated in a prescribed order. The dining room is furnished with long tables and benches. Those whose task is to dispense the meals lay out the bowls and chopsticks and fill the bowls with food. After everybody is ready, the monks collectively say the prayer before setting their chopsticks to their bowl. Under the watchful eyes of those on duty, monks are not supposed to talk while they eat. After the meal is over, they chant a meal-ending invocation, file out of the dining room and return to their dormitories. The lunchtime ritual is more or less the same, but the food served is more generous. No rituals are held for supper. This practice has something to do with the commandment that monks should not eat anything after noontime, and because supper is not offered, there is no need for such rituals. However, in China monks are mostly followers of Mahayana Buddhism and generally do not observe this commandment. There being no such taboo for them, it is customary, therefore, for them to have supper. The commandment against eating after noontime is carried out strictly in Buddhist countries in southeast Asia, where a monk is in for disgrace if he is found eating in the afternoon or at night. But why does the commandment forbid monks from eating supper? This is because monks are asked to curb greed, and to give up supper is one way to keep greed from rising in their hearts. It is thus advocated that "monks should often look three percent sick."

(3) Self-cultivation. Self-cultivation in a monastery falls into

two categories. In the Chan sect, monks meditate, while in the Pure Land sect they chant the Buddha's name. The meditation room is where monks of the Chan sect attend such sessions. Each session begins by the clockwise circumambulation of a shrine in the room, and in this process the monks' steps are gradually accelerated until they find themselves running at a fast pace. Incense sticks are burned to mark the time to be taken for the procession. While the monks are circumambulating the shrine, they are spurred on by a supervisor who stands by holding a wooden bar[1] in his hand. After awhile, the run around the shrine is slowed down to a walk, and then the monks will stop and sit down on crossed legs to begin the next part of the session: meditation. In each meditation session the monks are asked to mull over a single question, such as "What was I like before my parents were born?" The supervisor holding the wooden-bar continues his patrol, and will pat the back of someone who's found to be dozing off. After sitting there and meditating for some time, the monks are asked to relax and flex their muscles. The self-cultivation session is repeated three times a day in a monastery where order is strictly maintained.

In the Pure Land sect, self-cultivation in a monastery takes the form of chanting the Buddha's name, but the rituals and time arrangement are more or less the same as in the Chan sect. The monks are also required to circumambulate the Buddha's shrine in the hall in a clockwise fashion while chanting *"Namah Amitabha"*[2]

---

[1] The wooden bar is used to maintain order when monks of the Chan school are circumambulating the Buddha's shrine or meditate in the meditation room. It is also an instrument of torture, used to spank those monks who have violated the commandments and prohibitions in a monastery.

[2] *Namah Amitabha* 南无阿弥陀佛: Used constantly in liturgy, incantations, etc, as the formula of faith of the Pure Land sect, representing the believing mind of all beings and Amitabha's power and will to save; repeated in the hour of death, it opens the entrance to the Pure Land.

in a smooth liturgy. After chanting the Buddha's name for some time, the monks will sit down with crossed legs to meditate and ask themselves the question, "Who is the one who chants the Buddha's name?" This ritual, which came into vogue when different sects of Chinese Buddhism began to mingle after the Song Dynasty, is known as "self-cultivation by meditation in the fashion of Chan and chanting the name of the Buddha in the fashion of the Pure Land." But in some temples of the Pure Land sect the monks only chant the Buddha's name and do not sit down to meditate.

(4) Sanitation work. Monks in China are fastidious about environmental sanitation and personal hygiene. As a temple covers a wide area, the workload to keep it clean and tidy is so heavy that it calls for the coordinated efforts of all the monks. The sanitation work in a monastery is routine, with no one to organize it, and nobody doing it out of someone else's pressure.

Apart from these aspects of daily life in the cloisters, monks also arrange their own self-cultivation and study. In rural areas, they are required to till the land. Generally speaking, life in a temple is marked by serenity and regularity. Free from the worries of lay persons and busy traffic, and free of the mundane world, the monks are resigned to the leisure, peace, and quiet of monastic life, to the great envy of those who have had their fill of worldly trepidations.

Chapter 7

The *Tripitaka* of Buddhism

1. Origin of *Sutra-Pitaka*, *Vinaya-Pitaka* and *Sastra-Pitaka*

The *Tripitaka* are the canonical writings of Buddhism that include *sutra-pitaka*, *vinaya-pitaka*, and *abhidharma-pitaka*. These books
emerged in different ages, and here we begin our introduction
with the *sutra-pitaka* and *vinaya-pitaka*.

After Sakyamuni achieved Buddhahood more than 2,500
years ago, he and his disciples roamed the valley of the Ganges
and preached for 45 years before he entered nirvana at Kusinara
at the age of 80, but he left no written records of his lectures.
After his death, his disciples thought that his words would fall
into oblivion if they were not collected in time. In the same year
of Sakyamuni's nirvana, 500 disciples, headed by Mahakasyapa,
held the First Samgiti (Council) in Rajagrha. During the meeting,
Ananda recited the *sutra-pitaka* and Upali recited the *vinaya-pitaka*
before the audience. Ananda recalled what, where, and to whom
the Buddha had said this, and the audience discussed Ananda's
recollections, made up for what Ananda had forgotten and col-
lectted his errors, until consensus was reached on the final version.
To indicate that each sutra had been verified after Sakyamuni's
death, it was preceded by the wording, "The following is what I

heard…" In very much the same fashion Upali's recollections of each and every commandment the Buddha had set, the reason why he set it, and where he set it were subjected to the audience's perusal before they were accepted as the official version of *vinaya* or commandments.

As no written records were kept of the *sutra-pitaka* and *vinaya-pitaka*, they were thus collected and verified. The consensus reached on them during the First Council contributed to peace and unity in the ranks of the followers for a whole century, which historians have dubbed the "primitive period of Buddhism." However, disagreement gradually flared up in the understanding of these holy words, causing the *sangha* to come apart into two groups, Theravada and Maha-samghika, which further broke up into 18 or 20 sects. Personal and geographical reasons also contributed to the split. The major sects have each followed their own sutras and commandments for nearly five centuries, a period known in history as the Nikayas Schism or Sectarian Buddhism.

In the first century BC, Buddhists became keenly aware of the inconvenience and lack of cohesion in the oral versions of the sutras and commandments, and so they began to write them down one after another. The first to come out in a written form was the *Samyuktagama*, the miscellaneous treatise on abstract contemplation and one of the *Four Agamas.*[1] Written versions of the commandments emerged later. Thus for a time it became something of a fashion among the various sects of Buddhism to write down their respective sutras and commandments.

While the Buddhist sects were busy producing written ver-

---

[1] *Four Agamas* 阿含经, including *Dirghagama* 长阿含经, the long treatises on cosmogony; *Madhyamagama* 中阿含经, the middle treatises on metaphysics; *Samyuktagama* 杂阿含经, the miscellaneous treatises on abstract contemplation; *Ekottaragama* 增益阿含经, the numerical treatises.

sions of the Buddha's creeds, classics of Mahayana Buddhism emerged. The major tenets of Mahayana Buddhism originated in the teachings of the Buddha. But just as the development of any ideological school calls for absorption of new things and adapting to society, the same is true of the development of Buddhism. Mahayana Buddhism emerged with such a vengeance that it soon superseded Sectarian Buddhism. The result was that the compilation of Mahayana scriptures and commandments flourished.

However, even to this day, followers of Theravada Buddhism refuse to accept the Mahayana classics. In their opinion, only the *Four Agamas* are records of the Buddha's genuine words, and what is contained in the Mahayana scriptures are not. Though this controversy remains unresolved today, it does not prevent the Buddhists of different sects from keeping in touch with one another and coexisting in a friendly manner while preserving their differences.

The differences of opinion among Buddhists stem from different outlooks of the Buddha. Followers of Theravada Buddhism regard the Buddha as a man instead of a god, and a man with high moral values and superb wisdom at that. Mahayana Buddhists believe that he is a god with unfathomable virtue and resourcefulness. This major difference gave rise to tremendous differences in the preachings contained in the Buddhist classics. In China, Mahayana Buddhism is widely followed.

So much about the origin and formation of the scriptures and commandments. The belief that the Buddha himself had personally recounted the *Abhidharma-pitaka* does not seem plausible, because these treatises are actually his disciples' work on studies of his words. Historical records are unavailable as to the dates of the emergence of the various books in the *Abhidharma-pitaka*. It is estimated that they first appeared during the period of Sectarian Buddhism (3rd century-1st century BC). The

Adhidharma of Mahayana Buddhism, however, did not begin to thrive until the emergence of such major theoreticians as Asvaghosa, Nagarjuna, Deva, Asanga, and Vasubandhu after the first century.

2. Translation of Scriptures

The translation of the scriptures into Chinese was a monumental undertaking that began in the first century and continued for about 1,000 years through the 11th century. During this period large numbers of sutras and commandments and the theories about them were rendered in Chinese and became a major part of Chinese cultural heritage.

According to a traditional theory, the first Buddhist scripture translated into Chinese was the *Forty-two-Chapter Sutra* and it was done by the Indian monks Kasyapa-matanga and Gobharana, who arrived in China during the Yongping reign (58-75) of Emperor Mingdi of the Eastern Han Dynasty (25-220). But this theory remains controversial to this day, and some have gone so far as to allege that the *Forty-two-Chapter Sutra* is a bogus version that was not translated into Chinese from Hindi but concocted by some Chinese. An Shigao, who arrived in China in the mid-second century from Parthia, is unanimously regarded by academicians as the first translator of Buddhist scriptures in China. Arriving shortly afterwards was Lokasema from Indo-Scythae. It is said that An Shigao translated classics of Hinayana Buddhism, while Lokasema worked on Mahayana Buddhism. Even more monks arrived from the Western Territories and India during the Three Kingdoms Period (220-280), the Eastern and Western Jin dynasties (265-420), the Southern and Northern Dynasties (420-589), and the Sui (581-618) and Tang (618-907) Dynasties. In the meanwhile, many Chinese monks made pilgrimages westward and brought scriptures back to China to be translated.

According to the *Biographies of Eminent Monks* by Huijiao of the Liang Dynasty (502-557), the *Sequence to Biographies of Eminent Monks* by Daoxuan of the Tang Dynasty, and the *Biographies of Eminent Monks during the Song Dynasty* by Zanning, a total of 82 monks from home and abroad were engaged in the translation of Buddhist scriptures during the Han-Tang period. Many lay Buddhists also took part in the translation work, such as Anxuan of the Han Dynasty, Zhiqian of the Three Kingdoms Period, Nie Chengyuan and his son during the Western Jin Dynasty, and Juqu Jingsheng of the 16 Kingdoms Period. According to the *Kaiyuan Records on Mahayana Buddhism* by Zhisheng, by 730 (18th year of the Kaiyuan reign, Tang Dynasty), more than 150 lay Buddhists had participated in translating large numbers of sutras, *vinayas*, and *abhidharmas*. The following table, compiled according to the Zhisheng's findings, gives a rough idea in this regard:

Dynasty	Year	Number of translators	Number of classics translated	Number of volumes translated	Notes
Late Han	67-220	12	292	395	Translators unknown for 141 classics in 158 volumes
Wei	220-265	5	12	18	
Wu	222-280	5	189	417	Translators unknown for 87 classics in 261 volumes
Western Jin	265-317	12	333	590	Translators unknown for 58 classics in 59 volumes
Eastern Jin	317-420	16	168	468	Translators unknown for 40 classics in 48 volumes
Former Qin	351-394	6	15	197	

Later Qin	384-418	5	94	624	
Western Qin	385-431	1	56	110	Translators unknown for 41 classics in 86 volumes translated during the 351-431 period
Former Liang	317-376	1	4	6	
Northern Liang	401-439	9	82	311	Translators unknown for 53 classics in 75 volumes
Song	420-479	22	465	717	Translators unknown for 307 classics in 340 volumes
Qi	479-502	7	12	33	
Liang	502-557	4	39	93	
Chen	557-589	3	40	133	
Northern Wei	396-550	12	83	274	
Northern Qi	550-577	2	8	52	
Northern Zhou	557-581	4	14	29	
Sui	581-618	9	64	301	
Tang	618-907	21	263	1962	Up to 731 (18th year of the Kaiyuan reign)
Total		156	2,233	6,730	

As the above table indicates, more Buddhist literature was translated into Chinese during the Tang Dynasty than any other dynasty, even though the translators and classics done after 730 are not included. However, towards the end of the Tang Dynasty, translation of Buddhist works came to a basic standstill. Though the endeavor was somewhat revived during the early Song Dynasty, the works done during this period were mostly esoteric books that failed to gain popularity because they ran counter to prevailing Chinese ethics. Since then no more Buddhist translation work has been done in China.

For their voluminous numbers and quality of contributions, Kumarajiva (344-413), Tipitakacariya Paramattha (498-569), Xuanzang (600-664), and Amoghavajra (705-774) are regarded as the four major translators in Chinese Buddhist history. To this day, the scriptures translated by Kumarajiva and Xuanzang remain the favorites among Chinese Buddhists.

3. Composition and Versions

It took nearly 1,000 years for the *Tripitaka* to grow from almost nothingness to the magnum opus we know it to be today. The *Tripitaka* is the mammoth combination of *sutra-pitaka* (holy words of the Buddha), *vinaya-pitaka* (discipline the Buddha laid down for his followers), and *abhidharma-pitaka* (treatises written by disciples of different generations in their research into the Buddha's doctrines). Translation of the *sutra-pitaka* and *vinaya-pitaka* started sporadically in the early days. Only after a period of time did some people begin to register the books they had translated, and because many of the translations were not signed, the names of the translators remain unknown to this day. By the Eastern Jin Dynasty, Dao'an (314-385) began collecting catalogs and books, and after many years of effort, he came up with the Catalog *of Miscellaneous Scriptures* that provides a general record of the scriptures translated, but he failed to classify them. By the Southern and Northern Dynasties, something akin to the *sutra-pitaka* appeared. This is the catalog titled *All the Scriptures Available*, but it fell short of a streamlined classification. At that time, printing was yet to be invented, and all the translated sutras and commandments were hand-copied and bound in separate volumes. Those who specialized in copying were known as "sutra copiers," and the job became fashionable. For example,

Emperor Wudi (reign 557-559) of the Chen of the Southern Dynasties once issued an order for making 12 copies of the *All the Scriptures Available*; and his successor, Emperor Wendi, ordered that 50 copies be made. The same happened during the Northern Dynasties as well. Emperor Daowu (reign 386-408) of the Northern Wei Dynasty once issued an instruction to copy the *All the Scriptures Available*. In 560, Emperor Xiaoshao of the Northern Qi Dynasty personally copied 12 collections of scriptures for his father; and his court officials followed suit, picking up a writing brush one after another to copy the sutras. Copying became even more popular during the Sui and Tang dynasties.

The emergence of Dao'an's Catalog *of Miscellaneous Scriptures* was followed by a series of other sutra catalogs. Among the better known are the *Collected Records of the Tripitaka* by Sengyou of the Liang Dynasty, Catalog *of Scriptures during the Wei Dynasty* by Li Kuo of the Northern Wei Dynasty, Catalog *of Scriptures of the Qi Dynasty* by Sha Menfa of the Northern Qi Dynasty, *Records of the Three Treasures (Triratna) of Various Dynasties* by Fei Changfang of the Sui Dynasty, *Records of Internal Classics of the Tang Dynasty* by Daoxuan of the Tang Dynasty, and *Kaiyuan Records of Mahayana Buddhism* by Zhisheng of the Tang Dynasty. Among these, the *Kaiyuan Records of Mahayana Buddhism* is the best in classification. The author divided the translated sutras and commandments into two sections: Mahayana Buddhism and Hinayana Buddhism. In the section for Mahayana Buddhism there are 515 titles of sutras in 2,173 volumes that were contained in 203 cloth slip-cases; 26 titles of commandments in 54 volumes put in five cloth slip-cases; and 97 treatises in 518 volumes in 50 cloth slip-cases. In the Hinayana section there are 240 sutras in 618 volumes in 48 cloth slip-cases, 54 titles of commandments in 1,446 volumes in 45 cloth slip-cases, and 36 treatises in 689 volumes in 72 cloth slip-cases. These, in addition to a collection of works by sages and wise men and writings by eminent monks of various dynasties, add up to 1,076 titles in 5,048 volumes. And a 1,000-word rhyme was compiled to facilitate reference. With its scientific classification, the *Kaiyuan Records* became the standard for all versions of *Tripitaka* since the Tang and Song dynasties.

The invention of printing during the Song Dynasty rendered hand-copying of Buddhist canons obsolete. Woodblock printed and movable-type printed versions of the *Tripitaka* began to appear. Following is a list of the printed versions during various dynastic periods:

Song Dynasty:

The Shu Version of *Tripitaka* of the Kaibao Reign, abbreviated as *Kaibao Tripitaka* or *Shu-Version Tripitaka*.

1) *Tripitaka* of the Kauyuan Temple of Wuzhou (present-day Jinhua, Zhejiang Province), which is not extant today.

2) Khitan version of *Tripitaka*, printed in the Liao Dynasty, and abbreviated as *Khitan Tripitaka* or Liao-version of the *Great Tripitaka*.

3) *Tripitaka* of the Eastern Temple of Fuzhou of the Song Dynasty, abbreviated as Chongning Wenshou Grand *Tripitaka*, or Eastern Temple version of *Tripitaka* of Fuzhou.

4) *Tripitaka* of the Kaiyuan Temple of Fuzhou of the Song Dynasty, abbreviated as *Vairocana Tripitaka* or *Fuzhou Tripitaka*.

5) *Tripitaka* of the Zifu Temple of Sixi in Anji Prefecture of the Song Dynasty, abbreviated as *Sixi Tripitaka* or *Huzhou Tripitaka*.

6) Tianning Temple *Tripitaka* of Xiezhou (present-day Xiaozhou, Shanxi Province) of the Song Dynasty, generally known as the *Jin Tripitaka*[1] or *Zhaocheng Tripitaka*.

---

[1] At the time the Southern Song Dynasty was in the south while Xiezhou (present-day Xiexian County Shanxi Province) was in the north and under the rule of the Jin Dynasty. Hence the term, *Jin Tripitaka*.

7) Qisha Yansheng Temple *Tripitaka* of Pingjiang Prefecture (Present-day Wuxian County, Jiangsu Province) of the Song Dynasty, abbreviated as *Qisha Tripitaka* or *Yanshengsi Tripitaka*.

Yuan Dynasty:

1) Great Puning Temple *Tripitaka* of Yuhang County, Hangzhou Circuit of the Yuan Dynasty, abbreviated as *Puning Tripitaka* or *Yuan Tripitaka*.

2) Hongfa Temple *Tripitaka* of Yandu of the Yuan Dynasty, which is probably the *Golden Tripitaka*, but needs to be verified.

3) Yuan-Dynasty copper-block printed *Tripitaka*. Historical records have mentioned this version, but it remains to be seen if this was really done.

Ming Dynasty:

1) *Tripitaka* of the Hongwu Version of the Ming Dynasty, i.e., the original version for the *Nanbeng Tripitaka* of the Ming Dynasty, abbreviated as *Chukenan Tripitaka*.

2) Southern version of *Tripitaka* of the Ming, known popularly as *Southern Tripitaka*.

3) Northern version of *Tripitaka* of the Ming, known as *Northern Tripitaka*.

4) Fangche Classical *Tripitaka* of the Wulin Reign of the Ming, which has fallen into oblivion but is recorded in historical books.

5) Classical version of *Tripitaka* of the Lengyan Temple of Jiaxing of the Ming, which is missing but recorded in historical books[1].

What is widely preserved in Buddhist temples today is a Qing-Dynasty version of *Tripitaka*, known for short as the *Dragon Tripitaka*. Few versions of *Tripitaka* prior to the Ming

---

[1] For details about the various versions of the *Tripitaka* in China, please refer to *Random Talks on Buddhism* written by Zhou Shujia.

Dynasty are extant today. The available scriptures belonging to these versions are so rare they have become invaluable cultural artifacts.

Chinese versions of *Tripitaka* found their way into Korea and Japan in the early days, and were converted into local versions. These include the *Koryo Tripitaka* of Korea and the *Taisho Shin-shiu Taisokyo* (*Revised Taisho Edition of the Tripitaka*) in Japan, both of which are printed in Chinese characters, and stand as testimony to the influence of the Chinese-version of *Tripitaka* throughout the world.

In minority-inhabited regions in China there are versions of the *Tripitaka* in Tibetan and Pali languages.

Chapter 8

Grotto Art in Buddhism

1. General Introduction

Grottos, referring to tremendous caves bored into the cliff-faces of mountains far removed from cities, are major structures of Buddhist architecture. In ancient India, they were already in existence as monks' dwellings during the time of the Buddha, who himself lived and preached in such a cave. In the same year after his death, his 500 disciples headed by Mahakasyapa gathered in the Saptaparna (Seven-Leaf Tree) Cave in the suburbs of Rajagrha to recall and summarize the sermons the Buddha had preached and the commandments he had set for his followers. The size of the Saptaparna Cave was indeed astonishing, for it was big enough to accommodate such a large audience. Today, quite a few grottoes are still there in southwest of India. One of these is the Ajanta Caves, built during the period from first century BC to fifth century AD.

The grottoes at the Ajanta Caves were diverse in shape — oblong, square, horseshoe shaped, and so on. Doors and windows were built at the entrance to each cave, which had an assembly hall in the middle, with small rooms scooped into the side walls as the monks' dormitories or meditation rooms and shrines dug into the back wall. A horseshoe-shaped grotto features a huge square pillar that stands in the center of it and is carved with Buddhist statues and pagodas for pilgrims to worship as they circumambulate it clockwise. The walls and ceilings are carved with picture stories about the life of the Buddha, the Eight Aspects of Buddha's Life, and so on. These grottoes started as simple cave dwellings for monks, but they gradually grew in size, and their carvings and murals became more and more exquisitely done. Eventually they emerged as veritable treasure houses of art. The murals in them reflect the styles of art in different historical periods and the themes were closely associated with the life and society of the time.

The construction of grottoes in China began with the introduction of Buddhism during the Han Dynasty. In due time they appeared everywhere — in Kuqa and Qoco in Xinjiang area; Dunhuang, Tianshui, and Yongqing in Gansu Province; Yungang at Datong and the Tianlong Mountain in Taiyuan, Shanxi Province; the 10,000-Buddha Chamber in Yixian County; Longmen in Luoyang, Henan Province; the South and Northern Xiangtang Mountains in Handan, Hebei Province; the Qianfo Mountain in Jinan, Shandong Province; the Xixia Mountain in Nanjing, Jiangsu Province; the Feilai Mountain in Hangzhou, Zhejiang Province; Guanyuan, Sichuan Province; Dazu in Chongqing, and Jianchuan in Yunnan Province. The quick speed at which these grottoes were constructed in this country was as unexpected as their colossal sizes and wide geographical distribution.

In the early days, the grottoes were large or small abodes for monks; later the dwellers were evacuated, and the grottoes gradually evolved into art projects and favorite destinations for travelers. There are so many of them in this country that a comprehensive introduction is out of the question in this book. The following is a terse introduction to some of them.

2. Dunhuang Grottoes

The Dunhuang Grottoes are so named because these cave-temples were found in Dunhuang County, Gansu Province. The name "Dunhuang" has become so popular that few people remember the real name: Mogao Grottoes. In fact "Dunhuang" is so well-known that it has become a synonymous word for cultural artifacts of immeasurable value. For example, Shijing Mountain in Beijing's Fangshan District, known for its nine caves and one cellar stored with a collection of 10,000 or so stone slabs carved with full texts of Buddhist Sutras has been dubbed the "Dunhuang of Beijing."

But why are the Dunhuang Grottoes really called the "Mogao Grottoes"? The term *mugao* means "highland in the desert," and these grottoes are exactly tunneled into the cliff face of one such highland in the Gobi Desert known as Mingsha (Humming Sand) Mountain, some 25 kilometers from the seat of Dunhuang County.

Construction of the Mogao Grottoes was started in the Western Jin Dynasty (265-316), but they were not completed until more than a millennium later, a period that saw the rise and fall of the Sixteen Kingdoms, the Northern Dynasties, the Sui and the Tang dynasties, the

Mogao Grottoes at Dunhuang in Gansu Province

Five Dynasties, the Song Dynasty, the Western Xia Dynasty, and the Yuan Dynasty. According to historical records, this mammoth project was started by a monk by the name of "Lezun," who dug a cave into the Mingsha Mountain for his dwelling. Shortly afterwards, another monk, Faliang, dug another cave, and moved into it to become Lezun's neighbor. Suo Jing, a native of Dunhuang and a famed calligrapher of the Western Jin Dynasty, presented the two monks with a horizontal board inscribed with the name, "Xianyan (Celestial Rock) Temple." The two monks hung the name board on the cliff above their cave dwellings, and before long the name spread far and wide. More and more cave-temples were dug at the site, until the mountain was turned into a beehive-like cluster of more than 500 grottoes. Today, 480 of them are still there. Basing themselves on the different styles of art housed in these grottoes, Chinese archaeologists have drawn up the following list:

Time of construction	Number of temple-caves built
Western Jin, Sixteen Kingdoms, and Northern Dynasties	32
Sui	100
Tang	232
Five Dynasties	40
Song and Western Xia	59
Yuan	9
Time unknown	8

These statistics indicate that no more cave-temples were built at the Dunhuang Grottoes during a period of about 270 years that covered the Eastern Jin Dynasty and Southern Dynasties. The reason is simple: both the Eastern Jin and the Southern Dynasties were situated south of the Yangtze River, whereas Dunhuang is located in the northwest. Construction resumed after the Sui dynasty unified China, and this is shown clearly in the above table.

A salient feature of the Dunhuang Grottoes is the fact that the soft and loose texture of the rocks of Mingsha Mountain makes stone carving impossible. The artists had to erect clay statues inside the grottoes, and mortar the walls before painting on them. The soft texture of the rocks of Mingsha Mountain made tunneling so easy that this was the probable reason why people chose to carve out grottoes here.

Apart from a wealth of sculptures and murals, more than 20,000 Buddhist sutras were found in Cave No. 17 of the Dunhuang Grottoes. Most of these were hand-copied volumes, but there were also some of the earliest woodblock printed versions. During the Guangxu reign (1875-1908) of the Qing dynasty, Cave No. 17 came under the care of a Taoist priest surnamed Wang. Explorers from Europe greased the palms of Wang and made away with more than 10,000 of the sutras, which are now in museums in Britain and France.

The host of sculptures and murals in the Dunhuang Grottoes are rare and valuable treasures. The sculptures are cast in such Buddhist images as buddhas, bodhisattvas, dvarapalas, lokapalas, patrons, and attendants. The murals are mostly picture stories depicting the life of the Buddha and the Eight Aspects of Buddha's Life, and there are also a rich variety of ornamental patterns in designs such as apsaras. These superb works of art never fail to draw exclamations of amazement from whoever happens to be visiting one of these grottoes.

3. Maijishan Grottoes

Maijishan, or Wheat-straw Stack Mountain, stands in the midst

Maijishan Grottoes, Gansu Province

of a jumble of mountains about 30 kilometers southeast of Tianshui County, Gansu Province. In the distance this mountain looks like a stack of wheat-straw with an oversize top. A 9.4-metre-high pagoda perches atop the mountain, but what makes Maijishan famous are the row upon row of grottoes dug into its side that look like a beehive in the distance. These grottoes, or cave-shrines to be exact, provide shelters to 6,200 stone and clay figures and 1,300 square meters of murals, forming a major gallery of Chinese art, second only to Dunhuang and a Buddhist sanctuary on the celebrated Silk Road.

The place fell into oblivion for more than a century after the last cave-temple was dug there. It was rediscovered during an archaeological survey organized by the country's cultural authorities in 1953. A research institute was established to put the grottoes under protection and refurbishment.

Construction of the Maijishan Grottoes began during the

reign of the Western Qin Kingdom (384-431) and slightly later than the Mogao Grottoes at Dunhuang. The number of caves kept growing in the ensuing years — the Northern Wei, Western Wei, Northern Zhou, Sui, Tang, Northern Song, Yuan, Ming, and Qing dynasties. During this course of some 1,500 years, Maijishan enjoyed its heyday during the Western Wei, Northern Zhou, and Sui dynasties, but construction of new caves slowed down considerably after the Tang Dynasty. Today, 174 cave-temples are left. (Another theory puts it at more than 190). The archaeologists' work to number, date, and classify them has resulted in the following table:

Period	Number of caves dug
Western Qin-Northern Dynasties, the first stage	15
Northern Dynasties, the second stage	17
Northern Dynasties, the Third Stage	51
Northern Zhou-Sui	47
Tang	5
Song	9
Ming	4
Qing	1
Dates unknown	25

Each of these grottoes is enshrined with statues and murals. Fastidiously crafted to the minute detail, and mingling lifelike imagery with spiritual resonance, they are paragons of Chinese art of times utterly gone by. Repeated earthquakes during the intervening years have caused the Maijishan Grottoes to split into eastern and western sections. Access to both sections are provided by plank ways built into the cliffs.

The major grottoes in the eastern section are

(1) Nirvana Cave-temple (Cave No. 1). Built in the late Wei Dynasty in about the sixth century, with six stone pillars standing

in front of it. The sculptures inside it were repaired during the Ming Dynasty, but their original style of the Wei Dynasty is palpable.

(2) Thousand-Buddha Corridor (Cave No. 3). Another product of the Wei Dynasty, this is actually a corridor 32.74 meters long, with its two floors crowded with a total of 258 clay figures of rough stone.

(3) Seven-Buddha Tower atop the Shanhua Pavilion (Cave No. 4). This is the largest group of cave-temples of the Maijishan Grottoes, where eight pillars divide a huge cave into seven shrines. The murals on the ceiling are probably works of the Western Wei or Northern Zhou dynasties. The partitioning walls between the shrines are also covered with murals depicting celestial beings playing traditional Chinese musical instruments, burning incense sticks, or tossing flowers. There are a total of 75 sculptures here, some of them are works of a later age.

(4) Buffalo Chamber. This cave-temple is named after its sculpture of a buffalo being tramped under the heels of a heavenly king. Four pillars divide it into three shrines, and each shrine used to be occupied by a set of sculptures. Today, only the heavenly king and the buffalo are still here.

The three major cave-temples of the western section are:

(1) 10,000-Buddha Chamber (Cave No. 133). Also known as "Stele Cave," it stands four 4 meters high, 14.91 meters wide and 11.58 meters deep. A legion of Buddhist figurines are carved into all its walls. On its lintel stand the likenesses of many patrons against a field of relief landscape. Inside the cave stands a 3.5-meter-high statue of the Receptionist Buddha — Amitabha. Probably built during the Tang Dynasty and also repaired during the Song, this work is marked for its high artistic attainment. The ceiling was painted with murals of flying *devarsis*, but most of them have peeled off. A number of stone tablets carved with

portraits on them are found inside the cave, which are treasured for the valuable historical information contained in the portraits and inscriptions.

(2) Tiantang (Paradise) Cave-temple. Paintings of soldiers at war, their colors fading and some of them already peeling off, are found on the walls of this cave which is five meters high, 8.88 meters wide, and 4.29 meters deep. In its center stands a 1.95-meter-high statue of the Buddha flanked on either side by the representation of a bodhisattva 1.28 meters in height. The trio is believed to have been made during the Northern Wei Dynasty.

(3) Cave No. 127. The central floor of this cave-temple, 4.42 meters high, 8.63 meters wide and 4.85 meters deep, is occupied by a Buddhist statue made during the Western Wei Dynasty. The nimbus behind the statue is surrounded by the likenesses of ten deva-dancers each holding a musical instrument in hand. Despite the ravages of age, the murals on the ceiling and walls of this cave are still of a highly ornamental value.

All the caves of the Maijishan Grottoes were dug more than 70 meters up the vertical cliff of a mountain. This begs the question: How did the ancients make the impossible possible at a time when science and technology were not well developed? Historical information indicates that they did it the hard way. They stacked up firewood at the foot of the cliff to a height that allowed them to tunnel, sculpt, and paint. Obviously, the plank ways that provide access to the cave-temples were built in the same fashion.

At the foot of the cliff stands the Ruiying Temple, whose predecessor was the Maijishan Temple, also known as the Shiyan (Rock) Temple, in ancient times. As a shelter for monks, it was renamed the Jingnian Temple during the Sui Dynasty, Yingqian Temple or Ling'an Temple during the Tang Dynasty, and the

Ruiying Temple during the Northern Song Dynasty. In days of yore, the temple was always thronged with pilgrims because the Maijishan Grottoes were a holy place of Buddhism. The Ruiying Temple is still there as property of the local archaeological department.

The prestige of the Maijishan Grottoes lies first of all in its religious sculpture, which shows what superb artistic conception and lifelike imagery can do to please the eye of the most exacting appreciator of art.

4. Yungang Grottoes

The third group of grottoes behind the leading Dunhuang and Maijishan is found on a mountain 16 kilometers west of Datong, Shanxi Province. The Yungang Grottoes extend east and west in a row about one kilometer in length along the side of a mountain which was known as Wuzhou in ancient times and assumed its present name, Yungang, during the Ming Dynasty. Fifty-three caves remain today, and 51,000 statues — ranging in height from 17 meters to several centimeters — are housed in them. The Yungang Grottoes is unquestionably another rich repository of Chinese culture associated with Buddhism.

A Buddhist statue at Yungang Grottoes in Datong, Shanxi Province

Construction of the Yungang Grottoes began in 453, or the second year of the Xing'an reign of the Northern Wei Dynasty, at the suggestion of Tanyao, a prominent monk of that day. Tanyao, whose dates of birth and death and birthplace are known, was tonsured and became a monk at Zhongshan (present-day Dingxian County, Hebei Province) while still a teenager. During the (424-451) reign of the Northern Wei Dynasty, Emperor Taiwu cracked down on Buddhism and persecuted the monks and lay followers. When his son, Toba Jun, ascended the throne as Emperor Wencheng (reign 452-465), he changed his father's policy and began to rejuvenate Buddhism. In 453, the emperor summoned Tanyao from Zhongshan to Juping (present-day Datong, Shanxi Province), the capital city of the Northern Wei Dynasty, and appointed him as an official in charge of *sramanas* (monks and nuns). Upon assuming this office, Tanyao submitted a proposal to build Buddhist grottoes on Wuzhou Mountain. With the approval of the emperor, five major grottoes were constructed under Tanyao's supervision, and posterity calls them "Tanyao's Five Cave-temples." They immediately became the most splendid of all the grottoes in China at that time. The leading Buddhist statue of the cluster stands 13 meters in height, and legend has it that the Buddhist statues enshrined in these grottoes are images of the five emperors of the Northern Wei Dynasty — Daowu, Mingyuan, Taiwu, Jingmu, and Wencheng. The authenticity of this legend, however, is questionable, because strict Buddhist requirements on the sculpture of deities made it impossible for a Buddhist statue to assume the looks of an emperor. It is therefore more appropriate to say these Buddhist statues were erected in honor of the five emperors. In each of Tanyao's Five Cave-temples, which are none other than Cave Nos. 16-20, there is a major statue surrounded by tiny niches of Buddhist figurines. As the front of Cave No. 20 has collapsed, its statue of the Buddha looks as if sitting in state in the open, and this has become the emblem of the Yungang Grottoes.

The second-stage of construction of the Yungang Grottoes began probably during the period from 465, the year Emperor Wencheng died, to 493, when Emperor Xiaowen moved the capital city of the Northern Wei Dynasty to Luoyang. More grottoes were dug during this stage than during the previous stage to form the major body of the entire Yungang complex. There are 12 of them, that is, in a numerical order, Cave Nos. 1-3 and 5-13. The sculptures contained in them feature richly varied images. Apart from different likenesses of the Buddha, there are also bodhisattvas, Vajra-viras (guardian deities) and patrons, as well as pagodas and pillars. Some of the murals are depictions of flying devatas (apsaras), and some tell stories about the life of the Buddha and events in Buddhist history. At a height of 17 meters, the statue of the Buddha in Cave No. 5 is the largest of all the stone Buddhas of Yungang.

What was built during the third-stage construction that began after Emperor Xiaowen moved the Northern Wei capital to Luoyang, were mostly small grottoes and shrines that are scattered at both ends of the original row and in the vicinity, but the forms and themes were even more diversified. Historical records indicate that the Northern Wei Dynasty later split into the Eastern Wei (534-550) and the Western Wei (535-557), and that after the downfall of both Weis, construction of the Yungang Grottoes came to a standstill. During its heyday the Yungang Grottoes were the site of ten temples and a monastic population of several thousand, and for a time it was the Buddhist center of north China. The Yungang Grottoes underwent repeated refurbishments and major repairs during the periods after the Sui and Tang dynasties, and restoration work reached its climax during the Liao and Jin dynasties.

The Yungang Grottoes were built in ways different from its counterparts. At Dunhuang and Maijishan, the builders had to dig the caves first and then erect statues. At Yungang, the tunneling of the caves and the chiseling of Buddhist statues took place simultaneously.

5. Longmen Grottoes

The Longmen Grottoes are named after a mountain 13 kilometers south of Luoyang, Henan Province. Two lofty peaks stand facing each other, and in the ravine down below the Yishui River tumbles away. The vertical cliffs on both banks of the river have been converted into beehives of grottoes that are divided into five zones — four on the eastern bank and one on the western bank. A total of 1,021 cave-temples have been counted by the local archaeological department, and these do not include the

Longmen Grottoes in Luoyang, Henan Province

the ones that are too small or have become too dilapidated and contain nothing valuable.

Specifically, there are 61 caves in Zone One, 97 in Zone Two, 386 in Zone Three, 399 in Zone Four, and 78 in Zone Five.

By sheer numbers, Longmen stands out as the largest of all the grottoes in China.

Construction of the Longmen Grottoes began during the Northern Wei dynasty when local bureaucrats opened a number of small grottoes or shrines on Longmen Mountain. In 493 (17th year of the Taihe reign, Northern Wei Dynasty), Emperor Xiaowen moved the capital from Pingcheng (present-day Datong, Shanxi Province) to Luoyang. In 500 (1st year of the Jingming reign, Northern Wei Dynasty), Emperor Xuanwu followed the example of the Yungang Grottoes on Wuzhou Mountain near Pingcheng, and had three grottoes tunneled into the Longmen Mountain. This ushered in a period of large-scale construction. According to historical records, construction of the Longmen Grottoes reached a peak during the 500-528 period, which encompassed the Xuanwu and Xiaoming reigns of the Northern Wei Dynasty, but this came to a stop due to war and turmoil arising from brutal infighting within the ruling class. Construction went off and on during the period that saw the rise and fall of the Northern Qi, Sui, Tang and Northern Song dynasties, but none of these dynasties beat the Tang in the number of grottoes built and the scale of construction at the site. The colophons on the stone sculptures indicate that joining the ruling class in the construction of the Longmen Grottoes and the erection of Buddhist statues and shrines during the Tang were lay Buddhists, monks, and nuns as well. A salient feature at Longmen is the fact that all the Buddhist statues were carved into rocks at the same time as their cave shrines were being chiseled into the mountainsides. Even the ornamental patterns are fine examples of stone carving in the Chinese tradition. Not a single mural, however, has been found in these grottoes. The following is a brief introduction to some of the representative works at Longmen:

(1) Guyang Cave. One of the earliest built at Longmen, the Guyang Cave was completed around the time when the Northern Wei Dynasty capital was moved to Luoyang. A rich collection of Buddhist images were arranged in three rows of Buddhist shrines inside it. The Buddhist deities were all graced with elegant and exquisitely crafted nimbuses and their drapery comes in a rich variety as well. The images of patrons look so real that they seem ready to step out at one's beckoning. The inscriptions are fine examples of Chinese calligraphy in unadorned simplistic elegance, and they furnish valuable materials for the study of classical Chinese calligraphy.

(2) Binyang Cave that is actually three caves. Construction of the cave began in 500, but it took 802,366 workdays in a 24-year span to bring it to completion. Sitting in the center of this cave is a sculpture of Sakyamuni with Kasyapa and Ananda in attendance. The sharp touches of the chisel are still highly visible in the rich piles of tracery on these three images, as befitting the artistic style of Northern Wei Dynasty sculpture. The southern and northern walls of this cave are each carved with statues of the Buddha and two bodhisattvas. The ceiling is richly embellished with lotus flower patterns and gracious forms of deva-dancers and musical players. The walls are covered with large relief sculptures of picture stories about the life of Sakyamuni. Construction of the two flank caves began during the Northern Wei Dynasty but the sculptural work inside them was not finished until the early Tang Dynasty.

(4) Yaofang (Prescriptions) Cave. This cave came under construction during the late Northern Wei, and interior sculpture

was finished more than 200 years later during the 684-704 reign of Empress Wu Zetian of the Tang. This is the only cave at Longmen in which works of the Northern Qi (550-577) mingle with Northern Wei creations. The walls at the entrance of the cave are inscribed with 140-odd medical prescriptions for various diseases. Hence the name of the cave: Prescriptions Cave.

(3) Lotus Cave, also known as Yique Cave. Construction of this cave also began during the late Northern Wei Dynasty. The statue of Sakyamuni inside it stands 6.1 meters high, but, alas, damage of different degrees has been inflicted on the Buddha's face and hands. The statue of Kasyapa standing by the Buddha holds a Buddhist staff in his hand. The figurines in the many shrines come in a good variety of forms. Over sized lotus flowers are carved in the center of the ceiling and are surrounded by flying devatas.

(5) Qianxi Temple. This turns out to be an immense cave-temple that came under construction during the early Tang Dynasty. It is dedicated to Maitreya, the Buddha of the Future, who sits in the company of his two disciples, two bodhisattvas, and two lokapalas (heavenly kings). All the figures inside the Qianxi Temple have fleshy-looking faces in a style representative of Tang-Dynasty sculpture.

(6) 10,000-Buddha Cave. Construction of this cave started in 680, or the founding year of the Yonglong reign of the Tang Dynasty. In the center of it is a statue of Sakyamuni sitting on his lotus throne. The wall behind him is carved with 54 lotus flowers, with the representation of a bodhisattva or patron sitting on each of them, a design unseen elsewhere in the Longmen Grottoes. Fifteen thousand statues of the Buddha are hewn into the southern and northern walls. Hence the name: 10,000-Buddha Cave. At the foot of this awesome array of Buddhist statues are deva-musicians and dancing devatas in graphic images and figures.

Standing outside the cave is a rendition of Guanyin, holding a duster in her right hand and a holy-water vase in her left hand. The pity is that her face has been marred by vandalism.

(7) Fengxian Temple. Built in 672 (3rd year of the Xianheng reign, Tang Dynasty), this is the largest Buddhist shrine among all the grottoes of Longmen, considering the fact that the statue inside it, a likeness of Locana (the First Dhyani Buddha), is 17.14 metres in height and that there are also ten huge sculptures of disciples, bodhisattvas, heavenly kings, and guardians. Locana assumes the image of a man with a plump face and long and narrow eyes under slender brows, and the corner of his mouth tilts slightly upward to show his concern for the human world. The other sculptures inside the cave are also works of impeccable craftsmanship. Legend has it that Empress Wu Zetian donated 12,000 strings of coins for the construction of this cave-temple. When the temple was completed, she personally attended the consecration ceremony.

(8) Kanjing Temple, built during the reign (684-704) of Empress Wu Zetian. The caisson ceiling of this cave-temple is ornamented with lotus flower carvings flanked by the buxom forms of chubby-faced apsaras dancing in the heavens. The temple is dedicated to 29 arhats — the legendary patriarchs of the Western Heaven for 29 generations — evidence that it was a sanctuary of the Chan sect of Chinese Buddhism. For the elaborate beauty of their sculptured detail, these renditions of arhats are lauded as masterpieces of Chinese sculpture.

6. Dazu Grottoes

The Dazu Grottoes encompass a number of groups of stone caves and cliff carvings in Dazu County in Chongqing. They

A statue of Guanyin, the Goddess of Mercy, in the Dazu Grottoes, Chongqing

were latecomers in the history of Chinese Buddhist grotto art. The individual cave-temples may have been in existence during the late Tang Dynasty in the ninth century, but large-scale development did not happen until the Song Dynasty (960-1279). One of the creators of the Dazu Grottoes was Zhao Zhifeng, a monk of the Esoteric sect. Thus the sculptures in the grottoes that he developed are dedicated to this school of Chinese Buddhism.

The grotto art of Dazu County incorporates elements of the three major religions of Confucianism, Buddhism, and Taoism that happened to be developing hand in hand at that time, but Buddhism holds the lion's share of the art.

(1) Shimenshan Grottoes. Situated 12 kilometers east of the county seat, this is a group of a dozen cave-shrines that provide shelter for more than 1,000 large and small statues belonging to Confucianism, Buddhism, and Taoism. These include Emperor Wuxian (a god in Chinese folklore), Prince Bingling (the God of Fire in Taoism), and the Three Emperors. In the center of Cave No. 6 is a statue of Amitayus, the Buddha of Boundless Life, flanked on either side by a statue of Avalokitesvara in a different image. The two side rock walls of the cave are carved with five Buddhist deities holding ritual objects in their hands. According to the colophons, these statues

date back to the Southern Song Dynasty (1127-1279).

(2) Shizhuanshan Grottoes. Confucianism, Buddhism, and Taoism coexisted in the Zimu Hall and on the Thousand-Buddha Cliff to form the Shizhuanshan Grottoes, 27 kilometers southwest of the county seat. The nine shrines in the Zimu Hall contain a mixture of Vairocana, Manjusri, Samantabhadra, and Ksitigarbha of Buddhism; Confucius, the father of Confucianism; and the Supreme Master Lao and Holy Mother of Taoism. All these sculptural renditions date back to the Northern Song Dynasty (960-1127) and are of high artistic value. The Thousand-Buddha Cliff, as the name suggests, is a domain for Buddhist statues done during the Ming Dynasty (1368-1644).

(3) Baodingshan Grottoes. Situated 15 kilometers to the northeast of the county seat, Baodingshan is known for its awesome collection of over 10,000 Buddhist sculptures and cliff carvings in three sections: 1) Shengshou Temple, which was first built during the Song Dynasty, but the halls as they are today are legacies of the Ming and Qing dynasties. The main structures are the Hall of Heavenly Kings, the Hall of the Jade Emperor, the Mahavira Hall, the Incantation Hall, the Hall of Dipamkara, and the Hall of Vimalakirti. Among the major statues is one of Vimalakirti. Scooped into the sides of the platform in this temple are 77 shrines each housing a Buddhist figurine. True to the Chinese tradition that a group of grottoes invariably contains a temple, the Shengshou Temple is an essential part of the Baodingshan grottoes and cliff carvings. 2) The Lesser Bay of the Buddha, also known as Dabao Chamber, is by Shengshou Temple. It is said that this was where Zhao Zhifeng conducted experiments before he began his large-scale construction of grottoes and cliff carvings at Baodingshan. The Lesser Bay of the Buddha used to cover a wide area, but only 600 or so statues and four sculptures carved into the cliff walls remain today.

There is also a three-tiered square stone pagoda, whose walls are engraved with Buddhist portraits and titles of Buddhist scriptures — these titles are believed to be the titles of the 12 volumes of the *Tripitaka*, but a close perusal of them shows that they are not. 3) Greater Bay of the Buddha is where the largest cluster of the Baodingshan Grottoes and Cliff Carvings is situated. It is a deep ravine six meters below the ground and 140 meters in length. Its rock walls are carved with picture stories of Buddhism and the texts of certain scriptures. A rendition of the Thousand-Hand Guanyin covers 88 square meters of the eastern wall of the bay. The statue, three meters in height, portrays the Goddess of Mercy as a study of serenity as she sits on her lotus throne wearing a crown and cupping the palms of one pair of her many hands together before her chest. Her other 10,000 hands are chiseled into the cliff wall behind her and arrayed in neat lines in the shape of a fan that is evocative of a peacock fanning out its tail in a splash of color. Each hand holds a different ritual object. The fineness of the carving is indeed a feast for one's eyes. The Greater Bay of Buddha is perhaps named after the monumental sculpture of the Buddha sleeping in nirvana in a gigantic cave. The Sleeping Buddha's reclining body extends for 41 meters, with part of his legs extending into the depth of the cliff. He has the company of his ten major disciples, all carved as busts. The entire group of sculpture is a superb piece of traditional Chinese art.

(4) Northern Mountain Buddhist Sculpture. Two kilometers to the northwest of the county seat is Northern Mountain, known in ancient times as Longgang Mountain, where the first group of Buddhist statues appeared in this place in 892 (1st year of the Jingfu reign, Tang Dynasty). Dubbed the "Bay of the Buddha," this is where 264 cave-shrines were tunneled into the seven-meter-high, 500-meter wide surface of a cliff. The statues

inside them belong to both the Five Dynasties Period (907-960) and the Song Dynasty. Of all the grottoes of Dazu County, the Northern Mountain is second only to Baodingshan in artistic value. Apart from stone sculptures, the place abounds in stone inscriptions, and it is the site of a multiple-treasure pagoda.

(5) Yuanjue (Perfect Enlightenment) Cave. Sitting in this cave, 12 meters deep, eight meters wide and five and a half meters high, are three statues of the Buddha with a number of disciples kneeling in front of him and kowtowing, and 12 other disciples sitting beside him on lotus thrones in different postures. This group of stone carvings is regarded as quintessential of the art of the Greater Bay of the Buddha.

Chapter 9

Festivals and Major Occasions

1. Festivals

Sakyamuni's birthday, his achievement of enlightenment, and his entry into nirvana are the occasions for the three foremost festivals for Buddhists the world over. However, they are marked on different dates in China than they are in the various countries of southeast Asia. The Chinese Buddhists celebrate Sakyamuni's birthday on the eighth day of the fourth lunar month and his achievement of Enlightenment on the eighth day of the 12th lunar month, and commemorate his entering nirvana on the 15th day of the second lunar month. For followers of Theravada Buddhism in southeastern Asian countries, these festivals fall on the same day, the 15th day of the fourth lunar month (the day of the full moon in May). There is no ready explanation for this difference. My surmise is that because history was not accurately chronicled in ancient India, the local people were often confused about issues concerning time. The margin of error in dating the Buddha's birthday is likely the result of different understandings of the concept "fortnight." As a month contains 30 days, the period from the first to the 15th is a fortnight; whereas it takes exactly a fortnight for the full moon to appear. Thus Buddhists of southeast Asia count the Buddha's birthday by the number of days in a fortnight, while Chinese Buddhists calculate the date by the fortnight cycle of the full moon. It is hard to say which method is wrong, and as long-time traditions, they are hard to change. In the 1950s, the World Fellowship of Buddhists (WFB) passed a resolution to designate the day of the full moon in May, that is, the 15th day of the fourth lunar month, as the birthday of the Buddha. Buddhists in various countries, however, stick to the old ways, rendering the WFB resolution as a mere scrap of paper.

The birthday of the Buddha is a major red-letter day for Buddhists around the world. In monasteries, the "Bathing the Buddha" Ceremony is held in pomp and pageantry, and lay Buddhists congregate at a local temple for the occasion. During the ceremony, a clean basin filled to near capacity with sandalwood-soaked water is placed in front of the statue of Sakyamuni in the Mahavira Hall. Placed in state in the basin is a figurine of Sakyamuni several inches in height and appearing as a newborn infant, the Prince Siddhartha, pointing one hand upward to the sky and the other hand downward to the ground. In this posture he declares, as the legend has it, "Both in heaven and on earth, I'm the one and only respected one."

When the followers have queued up in the Mahavira Hall, a monk will lead the crowd in singing hymns and chanting incantations. Then they all begin circumambulating the basin, and take turns bathing the baby prince by using a tiny ladle to pour water over him while the smooth litany of "Namah Sakyamuni Our Lord" rises from every corner of the building. The duration of the ceremony may differ with the size of the congregation, but generally it lasts for two hours. The Birthday of the Buddha is an occasion for joy, and so the followers all celebrate it in a jubilant spirit.

The festivals marking Sakyamuni's achievement of Enlightenment and nirvana are based on legend instead of history. In

Buddhist temples in China, no ceremony is observed on either occasion. They are, however, generally marked by adding certain passages to the incantations to be chanted in the hall. However, on the eighth day of the 12th lunar month, Chinese Buddhist temples are in the habit of dispensing *laba* porridge prepared of cereal, beans, nuts, and dried fruit among patrons to mark Sakyamuni's achievement of Enlightenment.

The pantheon of Chinese Buddhism in the Mahayana tradition includes quite a few Buddhas and bodhisattvas apart from Sakyamuni. A series of festivals are dedicated to them. For example:

1st day of 1st lunar month: Birthday of Maitreya, the Buddha of the Future

19th day of 2nd lunar month: Birthday of Avalokitesvara, the Goddess of Mercy

21st day of 2nd lunar month: Birthday of Samantabhadra, the Bodhisattva of Universal Benevolence

4th day of 4th lunar month: Birthday of Manjusri, the Bodhisattva of Wisdom

19th day of 6th lunar month: Festival of Avalokitesvara's achievement of Enlightenment

13th day of 7th lunar month: Birthday of Mahasthamaprapta, the bodhisattva representing the Buddha-wisdom of Amitabha

30th day of 7th lunar month: Birthday of Kshitigarbha, the bodhisattva who protects children and travelers and intervenes in Hell for those suffering there

19th day of 9th lunar month: Anniversary of the Tonsuring of Avalokitesvara as a monk

30th day of 9th lunar month: Birthday of Bhaisajyaguru, the Buddha of Healing and Medicine

17th day of 11th lunar month: Birthday of Amitabha, the Buddha of Immeasurable Splendor

These festivals are generally observed with simple ceremonies in Chinese monasteries, and are not taken seriously because they are based mostly on legends rather than historical facts. Among them, however, the festivals associated with Avalokitesvara, that is, the Goddess of Mercy (Guanyin), are more popular because worship of the goddess is widespread in this country, especially among women.

2. Major Functions

Morning and evening recitations of incantations are daily activities in a Chinese temple. Activities are also organized on special occasions, generally for two purposes: to intensify self-discipline and cultivation, and to pray for other people or expiate the sins of the dead. These include:

(1) Water-and-Land Service. A major religious activity among Chinese monks, the Water-and-Land Service was initiated by Xiao Yan (502-548), Emperor Wudi of the Liang during the Southern and Northern Dynasties. Legend has it that Xiao Yan dreamed of a celestial monk saying to him, "To go through the six cycles of transmigrations[1] and the four forms of birth[2] involves untold sufferings. Why don't you perform the water-and-land service[3]

---

[1] Six cycle of transmigrations 六道, or six-way samsara: *deva-gati* 天, of deva existence; *manusya-gati* 人, of human existence; *asura-gati* 阿修罗, of malevolent nature spirits; *naraka-gati* 地狱, or that of the hells; *preta-gati* 饿鬼, of hungry ghosts; *tiryagyoni-gati* 畜生, of animals — which represent the six directions of reincarnations in a cycle that has no beginning and can be ended only by Enlightenment.

[2] The four forms of birth 四生, or *catur-yoni: jarayuja* 胎生, viviparous, as with mammalia; 四生 and *aja* 卵生, oviparous, as with birds; *samsvedaja* 湿生, moisture, or water-born, as with worms and fishes; *aupapaduka* 化生, metaphorphic, as with moths from the chrysalis, or with devas, or in the hells, or the first being in a newly evolved world.

[3] Water-and-land service 水陆大斋: Large-scale alms-giving activity in Buddhism.

to deliver the souls of the dead from misery?" After he woke up from the dream he consulted Baozhi, a famous monk of the day, who suggested that he consult the sutras for an answer. After three years of intensive reading of the Buddhist scriptures, Xiao Yan composed the "Water-and-Land Rhapsody," had an altar built in the Jinshan Temple at Runzhou (present-day Zhenjiang, Jiangsu Province), and invited monks of the temple to perform the Water-and-land Service to redeem the souls inhabiting the waters and the land. This religious ritual was rather simple in the beginning. During the Xianheng reign (670-672) of the Tang Dynasty, it was combined with the esoteric Buddhist service to offer sacrifices to ghosts, and became very fashionable during the Song Dynasty. Xiao Yan's "Water-and-Land Rhapsody" has been repeatedly revised and added to until it has become the version we see today. The Water-and-Land Service is an elaborate and grand occasion that takes place on the internal altar and external altars in a temple, but most of the rituals are performed on the internal altar, which is therefore more solemnly decorated for this purpose. Altogether there are six external altars: the Primary Altar, manned by 24 monks who recite the *Confession of the Emperors of the Liang*; the Sutra-recitation Altar, where seven monks read aloud all kinds of Buddhist scriptures; the Fahua Altar, where seven monks chant the *Saddharmapundarika-sutra* (*Lotus Sutra*); and the Yogacara Altar, manned by a team of monks whose task is to appease fire-spitting hungry ghosts once a night. The entire Water-and-Land Service lasts for seven days and nights, and it is generally funded by affluent patrons. Today, it has evolved into a Water-Land-Air Service because of the fact that air crashes have become common disasters throughout the globe.

(2)The ritual to offer alms to fire-spitting hungry ghosts. This service to redeem the souls of the deceased is closely related to

Tantrism. The Esoteric sect of Chinese Buddhism all but disappeared towards the end of the Tang Dynasty, but the ritual to appease the hungry spirits by offering them alms has survived. The ritual is derived from a scripture translated into Chinese by Amoghavajra（705-775）, an Indian monk residing in China. According to this scripture, when Ananda was cultivating himself in his meditation room, the king of fire-spitting hungry ghosts said to him, "You will die and find yourself living among hungry ghosts in three days. If you do not want to suffer, you had better give me a serving of food today and tomorrow." Ananda reported this to the Buddha, who taught him what incantations he should chant when handing out the alms. These incantations thus became part of a Buddhist's daily meditation ritual. After the Song Dynasty, different versions of alms-giving incantations appeared, and only in the recent past was a unified version adopted to be routinely performed at the end of any major religious ceremony.

(3) Seven-day Period of Self-Cultivation. This period is divided into two seven-day phases in which a monk is required to intensify his meditation or chanting the Buddha's name. It is said that some monks have achieved Enlightenment through intensive self-cultivation during these seven-day phases in which a monk is supposed to keep meditating or chanting except when he is eating or sleeping. There will be no absence, no going outdoors, and no contact whatsoever with the outside world.

(4) Liturgy for Confession. This is yet another form of self-cultivation. There are a number of texts to be chanted for this ritual, including the *Thousand-Buddha Confession*, *Ten-Thousand-Buddha Confession*, *Confessions of Emperors of the Liang Dynasty*, *The Confession of Great Mercy*, and the *Water Confession*. These confessions vary in length and are selected to meet specific requirements. Each confession consists of a text to be read aloud, as well as

the names and titles of the Buddhas and bodhisattvas, which are to be worshiped during the ritual. Through the Liturgy for Confession, a monk hopes to own up to his misdeeds, repent for them, and ask the Buddha and bodhisattvas for forgiveness.

(5) Ullambana, the Festival in Memory of Ancestry. This is a routine ceremony held in a monastery on the 15th day of the seventh lunar month every year to redeem the souls of ancestors. According to the *Ullambana Sutra*, Mahamaudgalyayana, one of the ten major disciples of Sakyamuni, acquired *divyacaksus* (instantaneous view of anything anywhere) and found that his deceased mother was suffering among hungry ghosts. Wanting to come to his mother's rescue, he asked the Buddha for instruction. The Buddha told him to perform the Ullambana Service, at which he was supposed to offer generous delicacies to fete the hungry ghosts. By this virtuous deed he could deliver his mother from the misery. "Ullam" is a Sanskrit term that means "hang something upside down," and "bana" denotes utensils for holding alms. Using the "bana" to offer alms can immediately deliver the hungry ghosts from the pain of being hung upside down. The Ullambana Service is performed in Chinese monasteries for monks to show great mercy for those in misery.

(6) Home service to recite sutras and worship. This ritual, which has been mentioned in Chapter 6, involves monks of a monastery going to a lay follower's home to chant sutras or confessional texts for him or her. It is rather popular in south China and is a major source of income for many monasteries. Whenever someone has died in the family, a lay Buddhist is obliged to send for monks to perform religious rituals to redeem the soul of the deceased. By paying a certain amount of money, a patron has the right to decide how many monks to hire, for how long the ritual should last, what sutras or confessional texts are to be chanted, and where this ritual should be performed. After a

monastery has received such an assignment, the monks go out of their way to meet the patron's requirements. Every monastery has set prices for this service, and the monks assigned the job are also paid. However, many temples refuse to offer this service in the belief that offering this service is tantamount to selling the Law of the Buddha for money and therefore blasphemous to the good name of Buddhism.

(7) Worshipping Service. Followers of Buddhism believe that to chant sutras and make confessions not only helps redeem the souls of the deceased but also is conducive to warding themselves off from disasters and prolonging their lives. The monks of a monastery are often asked to render a hand in such services. A patron may request the monastery to hold a special service for him. He may also ask the monastery to chant and pray for him in passing during a routine session in the Sutra Chanting Hall. In the process, the patron is obliged to hand out red envelopes containing a certain amount of cash among the monks as his donation. This service is offered even in monasteries that refuse to offer compensated home services.

Chapter 10

Organizations and Undertakings

1. Organizations

Apart from the *sangha* in various temples in which monks live a communal life, there are also social organizations for Buddhist followers. These include Buddhist associations at various levels and layman's institutes.

Since the founding of the People's Republic in 1949, the religious policy of the People's Government has guaranteed complete freedom of religious belief for monks and lay followers across the land. In autumn 1952, famous personages of the Chinese Buddhist circles convened in Beijing and established a Preparatory Committee for the Establishment of the Chinese Buddhist Association. After about six month's of preliminary work, the First National Buddhist Congress was held during the festival to celebrate the birthday of the Buddha in May (8th day, 4th lunar month) 1953, and the Chinese Buddhist Association was officially established. A total of 140 delegates attended the congress, and elected Dharmacarya (Master of the Law) Yuanying (1878-1953) president. When Yuanying died in autumn of that year, he was succeeded by Shes-rab-rhya-mtsho (1884-1968), a famed Tibetan Buddhist scholar. In 1980 Zhao Puchu (1907-2000) began to serve as president, and the present president is Ven. Yicheng. The association has convened the National Buddhist Congress seven times so far, with the number of delegates to each congress increasing steadily. During its early days, the goal of the association was to "unite with all the Buddhists of the country under the leadership of the People's Government to participate in the movement to love and to protect the motherland and world peace, assist the People's Government in carrying out the policy of freedom of religious belief, and rally the efforts of Buddhists across the land to carry forward the fine traditions of Buddhism."[1] The Constitution of the Chinese Buddhist Association has been revised according to the actual situation at various periods of time. For instance, the Constitution adopted at the Sixth National Congress added new tasks to the association's original goal, saying, "The goal of this association is to assist the People's Government in carrying out the policy of freedom of religious belief and safeguard the lawful rights and interests of the Buddhists; disseminate the doctrines of Buddhism, carry forward the fine traditions of Buddhism, step up the building of Buddhism itself, and develop Buddhist undertakings; unite Buddhists of various ethnic backgrounds to participate in economic development and promoting socialist culture and ethics, and contribute to the reform and opening up to the outside world, economic growth, the reunification of the motherland, and world peace."[2]

As the national organization representing Buddhists of all ethnic backgrounds across the land, the Chinese Buddhist Association has done a great deal of beneficial work at home and abroad over the last five decades. At home, it assists the government in carrying out its policy of freedom of religious belief and serves as a bridge between Buddhists and the government.

---

[1] See the Constitution of the Chinese Buddhist Association, *Modern Buddhist Studies*, Issue No. 6, 1953.

[2] See the revised version of the Constitution of the Chinese Buddhist Association, *Fayin*, Issue No. 12, 1993.

Abroad, it carries out friendly cultural exchanges with Buddhists of foreign countries on behalf of the Chinese Buddhists. On both fronts the association has made outstanding contributions.

The association has also done much to promote Buddhism by repairing temples and monasteries, training monks, and publishing books and periodicals. Today, it is leading Buddhists across the land to join the Chinese people in building socialism in the Chinese way.

Local Buddhist associations have been established in various provinces, municipalities, and autonomous regions. There are also Buddhist associations in many counties as well. These local associations are not affiliated with the Chinese Buddhist Association, but they are connected in religious work. Leaders of local associations are almost without exception council members or standing council members of the Chinese Buddhist Association. And the local associations have basically the same goals and tasks as the national association.

In some large cities there are also layman's associations that provide venues for lay Buddhists to hold meetings or meditation sessions at regular intervals. Leaders of such organizations are elected at layman's congresses. These people meditate the sutras and chant incantations on a regular basis, but they also invite well-accomplished monks to preach for them. The thriving Buddhist activities among the lay followers are evidence that China's policy of freedom of religious belief has been implemented down to the grass-roots level.

2. Undertakings

Buddhists are duty-bound to promote Buddhist undertakings. In order to disseminate the Buddhist creeds and carry forward the fine traditions of Buddhism, Buddhists in China have developed diverse forms of undertakings.

1. Establishing Buddhist Seminaries. In 1956, the Chinese Buddhist Association set up its first Buddhist Academy in Beijing. Situated in the Fayuan Temple, this institution of higher learning has over the last few decades cultivated a vast contingent of senior scholars in Buddhist studies. The principle of the academy is to "integrate self-cultivation with study, and to follow a monastic lifestyle." That is to say, to cultivate oneself without learning new things can lead one astray, and to be immersed in studies without self-cultivation can turn a student into an armchair strategist. That is why the academy advocates integration of self-cultivation and study. Monk students in the academy have prerogatives, and they live the same communal life as do monks in a large monastery. They devote two times for Prayer and spend the rest of the day chanting the name of Buddha or meditating, and are obliged to maintain the decorum and etiquette of a monk. The students are asked to foster a monastic lifestyle so that they can become role models in observing Buddhist discipline and set a good example in their conduct. If they are divorced from the regular monastic life and the *sangha*, it would be a great disservice to the dissemination of Buddhism.

Students study for a term of four years in the academy, which enrolls students once every two years. Only senior middle school graduates and those with the same level of education are eligible for enrollment. Outstanding undergraduates have the opportunity to apply for postgraduate courses. Buddhist studies comprise 70 percent of the curricula, while literature, history, philosophy, and foreign languages (English and Japanese) account for 30 percent. The Chinese Buddhist Academy has two branches — one on Xixia Mountain at Nanjing and the other on Lingyan Mountain at Suzhou.

There are 20 or so elementary and secondary seminaries in various provinces, municipalities, and autonomous regions in which thousands of monks and nuns receive training to become a staunch force in disseminating Buddhism and developing Buddhist undertakings.

2. Restoring Sutras Engraving Centers. These centers employ the traditional technology of engraving the texts of Buddhist scriptures on wood blocks so that printed copies can be obtained for circulation. Towards the end of the Qing Dynasty, a lay Buddhist by the name of Yang Renshan founded the Jinling Sutra Engraving Center at Nanjing, Jiangsu Province, and soon the center made a name for itself at home and abroad. Even the great man of letters Lu Xun donated money to it for the engraving of the *Sutra of One Hundred Parables*. After Yang died, his student, Ouyang Jian, took over. After a period of thriving business, the center gradually went downhill during the 1937-1945 War of Resistance against Japanese Aggression. It was all but closed on the eve of liberation in 1949. In the early post-liberation years, with the support of the People's Government, farsighted personages in the Chinese Buddhist circles restored the center, and shipped woodblocks engraved with texts of Buddhist scriptures from across the country to it, in an effort to preserve the heritage of Chinese Buddhism. In 1957, the sutra engraving center came under the direct leadership of the Chinese Buddhist Association. However, during the catastrophe of the ten-year "cultural revolution" of 1966-1976, the center fell prey to cultural vandalism. Its houses were put to other uses, and its engraved wood blocks were messed up and became piles of waste material. It was only after Premier Zhou Enlai intervened in the 1970s that things returned to normal. Today, the center is in possession of a hundred thousand wood blocks, and supplies Buddhist circles at home and abroad with close to 200 titles of scriptures. The value

of this only Buddhist woodblock printing center in China speaks for itself.

3. Publishing periodicals to disseminate knowledge of Buddhism. After the founding of New China, some personages in the Buddhist circles began to put together a monthly journal to publicize cultural knowledge associated with Buddhism. With the approval of the People's Government, the *Modern Buddhist Studies* journal was created in September 1950. When the Chinese Buddhist Association was established in 1953, it became the association's mouthpiece. In 1964, after 15 years of circulation, *Modern Buddhist Studies* went out of operation. In 1981, the Chinese Buddhist Association launched another journal, *Fayin* (*Voice of the Dharma*). In recent years, the Chinese Buddhist Culture Research Institute affiliated with the Chinese Buddhist Association created the periodical *Buddhist Culture*. Today, more than 20 Buddhist periodicals are being published in China, which is undoubtedly a result of the policy of reform and opening up to the outside world.

4. Helping the distressed, succoring those in peril, and curing diseases to save lives. Buddhism lays stress on benevolence. Acting on the Buddha's teachings of having mercy at one's heart, the Chinese followers of Mahayana Buddhism are ready to come to the rescue of those in distress and trauma. Whenever a major natural calamity hits the country, they are always among the first to come to the relief of the victims by donating money and materials. In 1998, when the worst floods in 100 years struck some regions, Buddhists all over the country vied with one another to donate money and materials. The Chinese Buddhist Association alone donated one million yuan. The Charity Society of the Southern Putuo Monastery of Xiamen, Fujian Province, has been a staunch force in helping people in distress and danger; in 1998 alone, the society donated 4.5 million

yuan and built ten "Project Hope" primary schools in disaster stricken areas. Some rich monasteries operate hospitals or clinics to treat low-income patients or those having financial difficulties for free or at a minimum rate. In 1997 alone, the Puji Hospital of the Putuo Mountain, Zhejiang Province, registered more than 200,000 yuan in exemptions and reductions of medical bills for poor patients. The fine work ethics and good services of the medical staff of this hospital are highly acclaimed by a grateful public.

Appendices: Major Buddhist Temples

Beijing

Fayuan Temple

Situated in the Xuanwu District, the Fayuan Temple, or Temple of the Source of the Dharma, is the oldest temple in Beijing, having been established more than 1,300 years ago. Its predecessor was the "Temple to Mourn the Loyal War Dead" founded in 645 (19th year of the Zhenguan reign, Tang Dynasty) by Emperor Taizong (Li Shimin) in memory of his generals and soldiers who had fallen in an east expedition to Liaoning. It was repaired and renamed "Chongfu Temple" in 1437 (2nd year of the Zhentong reign, Ming Dynasty), and assumed its present name, "Fayuan Temple," during the Yongzheng reign (1723-1735) of the Qing Dynasty. In 1780 (45th year of the Qianlong reign, Qing Dynasty) Emperor Qianlong personally bestowed a name board on this temple. The horizontal board is still hanging there, inscribed with four Chinese characters in the emperor's own handwriting that read: "Genuine Source of the Sea of Dharma."

After the birth of New China, the dilapidated Fayuan Temple was repaired and restored to its former grandeur with the support of the People's Government. In 1956 it became the venue of the Chinese Buddhist Academy, established by the Chinese Buddhist Association to train top-notch personnel for Buddhism. During the "cultural revolution" the temple had its fill of destruction, and the academy was closed down. But in 1979, the temple was repaired, the academy was reopened, and the Chinese Buddhist Books and Artifacts Museum was set up in the temple, whose display of an immense collection of precious artifacts and original versions of classical books is indeed a dazzling feast for the eyes. One of these is a three-layered Ming bronze sculpture of the Buddhas of Five Directions that rises to a height just below the ceiling of the hall. The bottom layer of this sculpture is in the shape of a huge lotus flower throne, with a Buddhist figurine standing on each of its 1,000 petals; sitting on the middle-layer are the Buddhas of Four Directions; and sitting in the center of the upper layer is a likeness of the Buddha Vairocana. This bronze sculpture, titled "Vairocana Amidst a Thousand Buddhas," is marked for its fine casting and craftsmanship, and there is nothing like it anywhere in the world. The temple also houses a 5.4-meter-long Ming-Dynasty wood carving of the Buddha sleeping sideways in serenity.

Guangji Temple

The Guangji (Vast Succor) Temple, whose full name is "Hongci Guangjisi" (Temple of Wide Mercy and Vast Succor), is a renowned old establishment of Buddhism that stands at Fuchengmen in the West District of Beijing.

The predecessor of the Guangji Temple was the Temple of West Liu Village during the Jin Dynasty (1115-1234) before it was reduced to ruins. During the Jingtai reign (1450-1456) of the Ming Dynasty, someone digging at the site found Buddhist statues and other relics under the earth, and it thus became known

Guangji Temple

that the place used to be a temple. During the Chenghua reign (1465-1487) of the Ming Dynasty, Monk Puhui and his disciple Yuan Hong began building a new temple on the site with money donated by a eunuch by the name of Liao Ping. When the temple was completed two years later, Emperor Xiangzong, in response to Liao Ping's petition for a name, issued an edict naming it the Hongci Guangji Temple. Since then resident monks have kept expanding the temple, and more than 500 years later, the Guangji Temple has today earned prestige for its immense size, imposing buildings, and vast trove of treasures that include copper structure of the four deva-kings, a richly engraved tripod, a stele inscribed with a poem by Emperor Qianlong, and a huge scroll painted by the artist's fingers rather than a brush. The centerpieces of the temple are the Hall of the Deva-kings, the Mahavira Hall, the Universality Hall, and the Hall of Multiple Treasures.

The statues of saints enshrined in these halls look serene in varied expressions. The Hall of Multiple Treasures offers a public display of the valuable gifts that the Chinese Buddhist Association has received from various countries in the last few decades. Some of the halls on the premises have been converted to non-religious purposes for the headquarters of the Chinese Buddhist Association. For example, the Meditation Hall has become a reception room, and the dining hall is now used as a library. But the layout of the entire temple remains unchanged.

Yunju Temple

The Yunju Temple, or the Temple of Cloudy Residence, is found on Zhuolu Mountain in the Fangshan District about 75 kilometers from downtown Beijing. It was built during the Sui Dynasty by Shi Jingwan, the monk who started a monumental project of engraving the full texts of the voluminous *Tripitaka*

A bird-view of Guangji Temple

on stone slabs to the benefit of posterity. The temple used to be an immense architectural phenomenon in itself, consisting of five compounds and six rows of major halls flanked with monks' dormitories and guest rooms. However, during the 1930s, the Yunju Temple was razed to the ground by Japanese invaders intent on ferreting out local resistance forces.

The Yunju Temple owes its prestige to nine caves in the nearby Shijing Mountain, and the cellars at the foot of it. Enshrined in them is a gargantuan trove of Buddhist scriptures-on-stone dating back to the Sui and Tang dynasties. In 1956, to commemorate the 2,500th anniversary of the nirvana of Sakyamuni, the Chinese Buddhist Association spent three years producing rubbings from the inscriptions of all the 14,000 stone slabs stored in the mountain. After this project was finished, all the stone slabs housed in the nine caves were returned to where they were from, and a warehouse was erected to house those from the cellars. A few years ago, when the stone slabs stored in the warehouse were found to be deteriorating from the weather, and the inscriptions on them blurring, they were immediately returned to the cellars. A decision was then made to build a modern underground hall, and to take proper measures to preserve these slabs. The underground hall was completed in 1999, and more than 10,000 people arrived from around the world to take part in a ceremony held on September 9 in 1999 to celebrate the move. All told, 1,122 titles of sutras in 3,572 volumes are inscribed on these slabs, which is a rare legacy of Chinese culture. And this is the reason why the Yunju Temple and Shijing Mountain are billed as Beijing's answer to the Dunhuang Grottoes.

A few years ago the temple underwent a major reconstruction with the unstinting support of the Municipal Government of Beijing. The reconstruction was so immense in scale and so thorough in refurbishment, that the ancient temple took on a completely new look and became a favorite destiny for travelers and pilgrims alike.

Lingguang Temple

According records, after Sakyamuni entered nirvana, two of his teeth were missing. One found its way to Sinhala, the other ended up in Khotan, Xiangjiang. In the 5th century, the eminent Chinese monk Faxian paid a visit to Khotan and brought the Buddha's teeth with him back to the capital city of the Southern Qi (present-day Nanjing, Jiangsu Province), where he kept it for himself. After the Sui unified China, the tooth somehow found its way to Chang'an, the national capital, and ended up in Yandu (present-day Beijing), capital of the Liao Dynasty. In 1071 (7th year of the Xianyong reign, Liao Dynasty), it was enshrined at the Zhaoxian Pagoda, according to the *History of the Liao Dynasty · Records of Emperor Daozong*, but it was never heard of again until the pagoda crumbled some 800 years later.

The Lingguang (Divine Light) Temple, the second of the Eight Great Sites in the Western Hills of Beijing, was known as "Dragon Spring Temple" when it was first built during the Dali reign

A dagoba in Lingguang Temple

(766-779) of the Tang Dynasty. It was renamed the "Jueshan Temple" after being rebuilt during the Jin Dynasty (1115-1234). It was not until 1478 (14th year of the Chenghua reign, Ming Dynasty) that it assumed its present name. At the side of this temple there used to be a Liao-Dynasty pagoda of ten layers and a Zhaoxian (Beckoning at Celestial Beings) Temple, which were both destroyed by the cannon fire of the Eight-Power Allied Forces that invaded Beijing in 1900. When sorting through the debris of the foundation of the pagoda, the monks accidentally hit upon the sarira of the Buddha's tooth, and the discovery shook the entire Buddhist world. After the birth of New China, the Chinese Buddhist Association had a new pagoda built at the old site to provide a permanent shrine for the sarira.

When the new pagoda was constructed in 1964, many foreign friends attended a grand consecration ceremony for it. It is a 13-layered octagonal structure 51 meters in height, built in the architectural style of the Liao Dynasty. The pagoda is surrounded by a number of ancillary buildings, which, though comparing unfavorably with the Lingguang Temple of yore in scale and grandeur, still attracts a constant stream of visitors because this place is part of a famed scenic belt.

Wofo Temple

The Wofo (Sleeping Buddha) Temple, whose true name is "Shifang Pujuesi," or Temple of Universal Enlightenment in Ten Directions, nestles at the foot of Fragrance Hill in west Beijing. Its predecessor was the Tusita Temple established during the Zhenguan reign (627-649) of the Tang Dynasty, which was renamed "Shou'an Temple" when it was expanded in 1320 (7th year of the Yanyou reign, Yuan Dynasty). It was renamed repeatedly as "Shaoxiaosi," "Hongqingsi," and something else before it assumed its present name following a major reconstruction during the Zhengtong reign (1436-1449) of the Ming Dynasty.

Standing in front of the Wofo Temple in sublime solemnity is an archway roofed with tiles glazed in multiple colors. Behind the front gate hall is a semi-circular pond crossed by a tiny bridge and flanked by a Bell Tower and a Drum Tower. The major halls are spaced neatly along the axial line, with the Hall of the Sleeping Buddha at the end of it. The sleeping Buddha turns out to be a bronze sculpture some five meters in length cast in 1321 (1st year of the Zhizhi reign, Yuan Dynasty). The eastern flank of the Hall of the Sleeping Buddha is where the monks reside and religious activities are conducted, and the western flank was the visiting emperor's temporary residence. When spring sets in, the Beijing Botanical Garden that surrounds the Wofo Temple becomes a tapestry of blossoming peach trees that attract legions of visitors.

Biyun Temple

The Biyun Temple, or Temple of Azure Clouds, is a compound of six courtyards that cover a scenic area of four hectares in the Xiangshan (Fragrance Hills) Park of the Haidian District. Here old pines and cypresses soar to unbelievable heights, heaping up rich piles of foliage that blot out the sun and provide soothing shelter to the temple's various buildings.

The temple was first built in 1289 (26th year of the Zhiyuan reign, Yuan Dynasty) and known as the Biyun Convent. During the Zhengde reign (1506-1521) of the Ming Dynasty, a eunuch by the name of Yu Jing expanded it into a temple, and because of this it was known as Lord Yu's Temple at the time. In 1748 (13th year of the Qianlong reign, Qing Dynasty), new buildings were added following a large-scale refurbishment. These include a Diamond Throne Pagoda on the rear hill of the temple, a Hall of 500 Arhats to the right, and temporary palaces to the left for emperors and concubines on excursions, but little was done to altar the place's Ming architectural style.

A major tourist destination in Beijing, the Biyuan Temple today holds forth the fascination of three sites of unique cultural and historical interest. First, the Arhats' Hall enshrined with 508 gilded statues, and Statue No. 444, the Devine One Who Subdues Evils, is actually a likeness of Emperor Qianlong made on the order of the emperor. Second, the Diamond Throne Pagoda, a 34.7-metre-high square white-marble terrace built on the site of graves prepared by two Ming-Dynasty eunuchs, Yu Jing and Wei Zhongxian, was constructed for themselves. A taller pagoda stands in the center and is surrounded by four shorter ones at the four corners of the terrace. The front of the Diamond Throne Pagoda is flanked by a pair of Tibetan-style pagodas. Third, the Sun Yat-sen Memorial Hall, where the coffin containing Sun's remains temporarily rested in state after his death in 1925. The hall has since been dedicated to the memory of the father of the democratic revolution of China, and some of his clothes were buried under the Diamond Throne Pagoda as well. As the most beautiful temple in Beijing's Western Hills, few visitors leave the capital city without paying a visit to it.

Jietai Temple

The Jietai Temple, or Temple of the Ordination Altar, lies at Ma'anshan Hill in the suburban district of Mentougou, some 35 kilometers west of downtown Beijing. The Jietai Temple's venerated history goes back to its days as the Huiju Temple, which was built in 622 (5th year of the Wude reign, Tang Dynasty) as the hermitage of Zhizhou, a Chan master well-versed in the study and practice of Buddhist commandments. During the Qingning reign (1055-1064) of the Liao Dynasty, a world-renowned monk by the name of Fajun settled there as a hermit. In 1069

Jietai Temple

(5th year of the Xianyong reign, Liao Dynasty) he erected an ordination altar to the left of the temple and soon acquired a following of several thousand disciples. The fame of the Jietai Temple spread far and wide as a result. During the Yuan Dynasty, the temple came under the care of another eminent monk, Yuequan, who rebuilt the halls, but towards the end of that dynasty, war and turmoil reduced both the temple and the altar to debris. The temple was rebuilt in 1434 (9th year of the Xuande reign, Ming Dynasty) and renamed the "Wanshou Temple." More halls were added to the temple during the Qing Dynasty, but it gradually fell into oblivion during the Republican years. It was not until a large-scale refurbishment was done after the founding of New China that this thousand-year-old temple came into its own once again.

The Jietai Temple stands facing east on a gentle mountain slope, and its halls are laid out along two parallel axial lines that run east and west. The southern line includes a Hall of Deva-kings, a Mahavira Hall, a Hall of One Thousand Buddhas, and a Hall of Guanyin. The northern line consists of a Fayun

Pagoda, a Mingwang (Rajas) Hall, an Ordination Altar, and a Mahakaruna (Great Pity) Hall. The Ordination Altar (jietai) is the namesake for the temple. Between these two clusters of halls lies a Peony Garden, a place that speaks for the captivating loveliness of southern Chinese landscaping style.

The Jietai Temple is known for its five ancient pine trees, each striking a unique pose that taxes the wisdom of the Creator. One of them is the rare and fantastic "Mobile Pine" — a gentle tug at one branch sets its entire luxuriant foliage shaking incessantly as if it had just been caught by a high wind.

Tanzhe Monastery

The Tanzhe Monastery sprawls on Oak Pool Mountain (so named because of the Dragon Pool and a kind of oak tree, *Cudrania tricuspidata,* growing there) and is therefore known as the

Tanzhe Temple

Oak Pool Temple. The oldest of its kind in Beijing, the temple was first built during the Western Jin Dynasty (265-316) and then known as the "Jiafu Temple." The venerated age of the Tanzhe Monastery is reflected in the saying, "The city of Beijing was nowhere before the Tanzhe Monastery was built."

The man who founded the monastery was Huayan, a Chan master of the Western Jin Dynasty (265-316). It was not until the Tang Dynasty (618-907) that the monastery came upon a flourishing age. During the Five Dynasties Period (907-960), Congshi, another master of Chan Buddhism, arrived with more than a thousand disciples. After the Jin Dynasty (1115-1234) unified north China and established its capital in Beijing, a monk by the name of Tongli expanded it and renamed it the "Great Wanshou Monastery." The monastery was destroyed towards the end of the Yuan Dynasty (1279-1368), was rebuilt during the Ming Dynasty (1368-1644), and renamed "Youyun Monastery" in 1692 (31st year of the Kangxi reign, Qing Dynasty).

A typical establishment in the tradition of Chinese Buddhism, the gigantic complex of the Tanzhe Monastery is laid out providently along three lines of a well-conceived plan. Among its cluster of old buildings is the Floating Winecup Kiosk, a marble structure whose double-eaved, hipped square roof is paved with a mixture of tiles glazed green and gold. Its marble floor is carved with a water channel in the fashion of a gyrating dragon so that when a wine cup is placed in the channel it will drift along with the water flow. The rule of the game played here is that wherever the cup stops the man who happens to be sitting in front of it is obliged to drink the wine to ward off bad luck. This "floating winecup" tradition dates back to the Han and Wei dynasties: on the third day of the third lunar month, people would gather at a zigzagging stream, put wine cups into it and allow them to flow downstream. People of later generations added something entertaining to the ritual: the man who is obliged to drink the wine is also asked to improvise a poem.

The Tanzhe Monastery is also known for its ordination altar, a three-terraced structure built entirely with white marble blocks engraved with elaborate ornamental patterns. It is said that Princess Miaoyan, the daughter of Kublai Khan, was a nun in this monastery and a pious worshipper of the Bodhisattva Guanyin. She is said to have trodden the floor of the Hall of Guanyin so many times that she left a pair of footprints 30 centimeters deep. The monastery's other legacies include what is reputedly the nation's largest grove of stupas, a wok large enough to prepare porridge for 1,000 monks, and the "King of Trees."

Heilongjiang

Jile Temple

The Jile Temple in Harbin is a large affair founded in the 1920s by Tanxu (1875-1963), a famous monk and a native of Ninghe

Jile Temple

County, Hebei Province, who was tonsured at the age of 43. During his lifetime he had the building of a number of temples to his credit, and the Jile Temple was one of them. The Jile Temple occupies an area of 57,500 square meters, and its architecture is marked by an elegance that reveals no traces of ostentation. Four major halls form the centerpiece of the complex. Behind the gate hall stands the Hall of Deva-kings dedicated to a 2.7-metre-tall bronze statue of Maitreya, who is habitually in the company of the lokapalas of four directions that stand on both sides with Skanda behind him. Behind the Hall of Deva-kings are the Drum Tower and the Bell Tower. The center of the complex is occupied by the Mahavira Hall, and the sculpture of Sakyamuni enshrined in it is also cast of bronze at a height of 3.34 meters. Sitting in attendance on the Buddha are his disciples, Kasyapa and Ananda, while behind him is Guanyin with 1,000 hands and 1,000 eyes. All these statues are remarkable for their graceful images and flawless craftsmanship. The Trinity Hall behind the Mahavira Hall is the domain of Amitabha, Guanyin, and Mahasthamaprapta portrayed in bronze statues 2.84 meters in height. Bringing up the rear of the complex is the Tripitaka Pavilion known for its three treasures on its second floor: the Qianlong edition of *Tripitaka* printed during the 1735-1738 period, an edition of *Tripitaka* engraved and printed in Qisha (present-day Wuxian County, Jiangsu Province) in 1322, and the Kalavinka edition of *Tripitaka* of 1913. The monks' meditation rooms, incantation chanting rooms, and residential quarters are found in the ancillary compounds and anterooms on both sides of the temple. The pagoda outside the compound stands more than 30 meters tall. Built in 1941, it is dedicated to a number of 1.6-meter-high bronze statues of the Buddha and bodhisattvas in stately images, and its walls are covered with murals. The Jile Temple is a major site of religious life in Harbin, and a popular tourist spot as well.

Jilin

Banruo Temple

Built in the 1920s, the Banruo (Prajna) Temple covers an area of 10,000 square meters in the city of Changchun. The gate hall of the temple opens onto a compound which is flanked by bell and drum towers in a unique architectural style. Arrayed on the axial line are the Hall of Deva-kings, the Mahavira Hall, and the Tripitaka Pavilion. A salient feature of this temple is that all its presentations of Buddhas, bodhisattvas, and 18 arhats are cast in bronze statues of massive sizes. An exception is the likeness of Guanyin, which is made of porcelain. The statue of Sakyamuni in the Mahavira Hall stands more than three meters tall, and the 18 arhats sitting beside him are one-meter-tall figures. The ground floor of the two-storied Tripitaka Pavilion is occupied by 1.51-meter-high statues of the Trinity of the West (Amitabha, Guanyin, and Mahasthamaprapta), and against its side walls

Banruo Temple, a tranquil place for self-cultivation and
self-meditation among the boisterous city

stand an array of cabinets that contain Buddhist scriptures. The second floor is devoted to a 1.5-metre-high silver stupa. The main halls along the axial line are flanked by ancillary halls and monks' residential quarters. Gazing down at the square of the Banruo Temple is a gigantic milk-white statue of Guanyin in the form of a serene-looking beauty.

Liaoning

Ci'en Temple

Situated in the Shenhe District of Shenyang, the Ci'en Temple is a relatively old Buddhist establishment in northeast China. It is said to have been first built in the Tang Dynasty, rebuilt in 1628 (1st year of the Chongzhen reign) of the Ming Dynasty, and repaired and expanded on a large scale in 1644 (1st year of the Shunzhi reign) of the Qing Dynasty. Then the temple fell into disrepair and was eventually deserted. It took eight years beginning from 1912 (the founding year of the Republic) to rebuild the Ci'en Temple and restore it to a size of 12,693 square

Abstinence Altar in Ci'en Temple, Shenyang City

meters. Among its 135 bays of buildings with a total floor space of 2,995 square meters are the gate hall, the bell and drum towers, the Hall of Deva-kings, the Mahavira Hall, the Bhiksu Altar, the Incantation Hall, and the Meditation Hall, as well as dormitories and halls for miscellaneous purposes. The temple houses a 6,500-volume version of *Tripitaka,* as well as a host of cultural relics dating back to the years before the influence of the Manchus crossed the Shanhai Pass and spread into north China. The Ci'en Temple today is the headquarters of the Shenyang Municipal Buddhist Association.

Tianjin

Dabei Temple

The Dabei (Mahakaruna) Temple on Tianwei Road in the Hebei District is the only Buddhist temple of good size in Tianjin. It differs from its counterparts in that it is composed of two parts, the Old Temple and the New Temple, that are linked by a moon-shaped gate. Because Tianjin is a relatively young city, the Dabei Temple has had a relatively short history. The Old Temple was built in 1661 (18th year of the Shunzhi reign, Qing Dynasty) and rebuilt in 1669 (8th year of the Kangxi reign, Qing Dynasty), and went through major repairs in 1875 (1st year, Guangxu reign of the Qing Dynasty) to assume its present shape as a tripartite compound comprised of a gate hall, a Mahavira Hall, and a Posterior Hall. Consisting of a Hall of Deva-kings, a Mahavira Hall, a Mahakaruna Hall, and ancillary halls and anterooms, the New Temple was built in the 1940s and is larger than the Old Temple. All the halls are linked by corridors. The major earthquake that hit Tangshan in 1976, and the 1966-1976 "cultural revolution" rendered great damage to the Dabei Temple, and it was not until the 1980s that the temple was repaired and given a new look with municipal support. The temple today operates two memorial halls, one of which is dedicated to the celebrated monk of the Tang Dynasty, Xuanzang (part of his skull was enshrined here prior to 1956), and the other is in memory of Hongyi, an eminent monk who happened to be a Tianjin native. The Tianjin Municipal Buddhist Association is also headquartered here.

Dule Temple

The Dule Temple was named after the gurgling spring behind it. Also known as the "Temple of the Great Buddha," it is situated near the Western Gate of Jixian County, Tianjin Municipality. Most of the buildings of this temple were ruined during the 841-846 reign of Emperor Wuzong of the Tang Dynasty, who pursued a policy of cracking down on Buddhism. Some of the buildings were restored in 984 (2nd year of the Tonghe reign, Liao Dynasty), and more buildings were added during the Ming and Qing dynasties. The centerpieces of the temple — from the gate hall at the front to the Guanyin Pavilion at the rear — are aligned along a central line, with monks' dormitories and the Qing emperors' temporary palaces on both sides. A major attraction of the Dule Temple is a 16-meter-tall statue of the Goddess

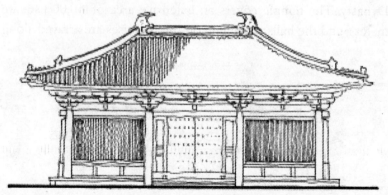

Main gate of Dule Temple

of Mercy in the finely crafted image of a lady who looks graceful and composed despite her awesome stature. This is reputedly representative of the best of sculpture in the Liao tradition. The pavilion that shelters this statue is a stately 23-meter-high building under a roof with three-layered eaves, and its four walls are graced with murals three meters high and 45 meters in total length in the portrayal of the 16 arhats in lifelike images of two meters height. These murals were done during the Liao Dynasty but were later covered up with mortar, and it was not until 1971 that they were brought to light and their invaluable artistic attainment began to be fully appreciated.

Hebei

Longxing Temple

Popularly known as the "Temple of the Great Buddha" because of its giant bronze statue of the Buddha, the Longxing Temple in Zhengding County originated as the Longzang Temple established in 586 (6th year of the Kaihuang reign, Sui Dynasty). It was expanded during the early Song Dynasty, and expanded again and assumed its present name during the Qing Dynasty. The temple covers an extensive area of 50,000 square meters, and the halls remaining on the premises are arrayed along

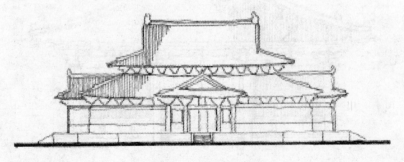

Moni Hall in Longxing Temple

the axial line. A horizontal board bearing the name "Emperor-Mandated Longxing Temple" in the handwriting of Emperor Kangxi of the Qing Dynasty hangs on the lintel of the arched gate of the gate hall. The Moni Hall, that is, the Mahavira Hall, stands on a unique plan in the shape of a cross. Inside this hall is a statue of Sakyamuni in the company of his two major disciples, Manjusri and Samantabhadra. Standing on the sculpture of a mountain behind the statue of Sakyamuni is a likeness of the Goddess of Mercy portrayed in an unaffectedly fabulous posture. The 33-meter-high Mahakaruna (Great Mercy) Pavilion houses a 22-meter-high Song-Dynasty bronze sculpture of Guanyin having 1,000 hands and 1,000 eyes; for its sheer size the bronze sculpture is a rarity in China.

Bailin Temple

The Bailin Temple in Zhaoxian County was known as the Convent of Guanyin when it was founded during the Eastern Han Dynasty. It was the Yong'an Temple during the Song Dynasty, and assumed its present name during the Ming Dynasty. The temple used to be the domain of Congnian, a Chan master who was revered as the "Venerable Buddha of Zhaozhou" for his high moral accomplishments and prestige. Congnian was forced to live a hermit's life in the Culai Mountain when Buddhists were persecuted by Emperor Wuzong of the Tang Dynasty during his 841-846 reign. Congnian returned to the temple after Emperor Xuanzong took the throne and he set about restoring Buddhism, staying there until the ripe age of 120 years. The Bailin Temple he presided over was destroyed in war during the Five Dynasties Period (907-960). It was rebuilt during the early Song Dynasty, but it was razed to the ground during the Republican years (1912-1949), with only a solitary pagoda left. In recent years, under the auspices of the Hebei

Provincial Buddhist Association, the temple has been gradually restored to its former glory. It is emerging as a major Buddhist sanctuary in north China.

Henan

Baima Temple

The Baima (White Horse) Temple was the first temple built in the history of Chinese Buddhism. Legend has it that in 64 AD, or the seventh year of the Yongping reign of the Han, Emperor Mingdi dreamed of seeing a golden man with light emitting from his neck flying past the palace. The following day the emperor related what he saw in his dream to his court ministers and asked them to interpret what this was all about. One minister answered that what His Majesty had seen was actually the god of the West whose name was Buddha. The emperor immediately dispatched an 18-member mission, headed by Cai Yin, to travel west in

Front gate of Baima Temple

search of the truth of the Buddha. In 67 AD (10th year of the Yongping reign, Han Dynasty), the Indian monks Kasyapama-tanga and Gobharana arrived in China, and while they settled down in the Temple of Grand Celebrations, the White Horse Temple was built for them as a studio for translating Buddhist scriptures into Chinese. The White Horse Temple was thronged with scriptural translators during the period from the Han to the Three Kingdoms Period, and reached its heyday during the Tang Dynasty as its halls looked resplendent in pomp and pageantry and there was a large population of 3,000 monks. The temple was so large that, or so it is believed, the doorman had to "ride on horseback to cover the distance required to close down the gate hall." The White Horse Temple as we see it today has probably retained its Ming-Dynasty size and layout as a 40,000-square-meter compound. As befitting its time-honored history, the temple is a veritable treasure house of cultural relics and sites of historical interest.

A view of Baima Temple — Pilu Pavilion

Xiangguo Temple

The predecessor of the Xiangguo Temple in Kaifeng was the Jianguo Temple that was established in 555, or the sixth year of the Tianbao reign of the Northern Qi Dynasty (550-577), and destroyed in war. When it was rebuilt during the Tang Dynasty, it was renamed the "Great Xiangguo Temple." In 804, or the first year of the Zhenyuan reign of the Tang Dynasty, the famous Japanese monk Kukai (774-835) settled for a while in the Xiangguo Temple during a tour of China to study Buddhism. During the early Song Dynasty, the Xiangguo Temple was expanded to become a complex of eight court-yards that covered an area of 545 *mu* (36.33 hectares). During the Chenghua reign (1465-1487) of the Ming dynasty, the temple became the Chongfa Temple, but shortly afterwards, it was inundated along with the city of Kaifeng when the Yellow River

A memorial arch in Xiangguo Temple

Octagonal glazed Hall of Arhats in Xiangguo Temple

overflowed its banks. The temple resumed its present name when it was rebuilt in 1661 (18th year of the Shunzhi reign, Qing Dynasty), but it took another major reconstruction project during the Qianlong reign (1736-1795) of the Qing Dynasty to become what it is today. Most of the structures of this temple, including the Hall of Deva-kings, the Mahavira Hall, the Octagonal Glazed Hall, and the Tripitaka Pavilion, are therefore a legacy of the last feudal dynasty of China. Outstanding among the Buddhist sculptures of this temple is one carved out of a huge gingko tree trunk. It is carved with four images of Guanyin with 1,000 hands and 1,000 eyes, each facing one of the four directions. This sculpture is marked for its unsurpassed ingenuity in chisel work and its immeasurable artistic value.

Hubei

Guiyuan Temple

The Guiyuan Temple on Cuiwei Road in the Hanyang District is one of the famed Buddhist sanctuaries in the tripartite city of Wuhan. Built in the 17th century, it has a relatively short history. In 1658 (15th year of the Shunzhi reign, Qing Dynasty), two brothers from Zhejiang renounced the mundane world and became Buddhist novices. Devoted to the cause of providing the remains of dead people left in the wilderness with proper burials, they donated money to build a bodhimandala that they named the "Guiyuan (Returning to Where You Belong) Temple" to redeem these lost souls. At the beginning the temple was crudely furnished, but after more than two centuries of steady expansion and development, it eventually grew into a big monastery. However, it was destroyed when the Taiping Heavenly Kingdom uprising troops attacked Wuchang

Main Gate of Guiyuan Temple

in 1852. It was not restored until the period from the Tongzhi reign to the Guangxu reign of the Qing Dynasty, only to be razed to the ground once again by the gunfire of the Qing army during the Revolution of 1911. After the war ended, it was repaired and restored once again. The Guiyuan Temple is a 50,000-square-meter affair with an impeccable layout and an original style in which architecture blends almost imperceptibly with landscaping. What is most attractive about this temple, however, is its Hall of 500 Arhats, in which the sculptures are richly variegated in imagery and facial expression but imbued with the same lifelike quality. On display in this temple are a good assortment of precious cultural artifacts that have been collected over the last three centuries.

Baotong Monastery

The Baotong Monastery, situated on the southern side of the Hongshan Mountain outside the Dadong Gate of Wuchang, was originally known as the "Eastern Rock Pavilion" when it was built during the Zhenguan reign (627-649) of the Tang Dynasty. It was expanded and renamed the "Chongning Wan-shou Monastery" during the Song Dynasty (960-1279), only to be reduced to a pile of ruins during war in 1356, or the 16th year of the Zhizheng reign of the Yuan Dynasty. It was rebuilt during the Ming Dynasty (1368-1644) and then assumed its present name, Baotong Monastery. The Hall of 500 Arhats was added to it during repairs done to the temple in 1638 (11th year of the Chongzhen reign, Ming Dynasty). Its heyday came during the Yongzheng reign (1723-1735) of the Qing Dynasty, when the temple had a total population of 1,500 monks, its territory covered an area five kilometers in circumference, and emerged as a gigantic complex of six major halls, a hundred other buildings, and 12 meditation chambers. But all these were

A bird-view of Baotong Monastery

no more following an attack on Wuchang by the army of the Taiping Heavenly Kingdom. In the ensuing years the temple was rebuilt and gradually grew in size. Though it has never attained the apex of its former grandeur, the temple eventually reestablished itself as a major Buddhist center and became the site of the Wuchang Buddhist Seminary. The buildings on the premises today are a legacy of the Guangxu reign (1875-1908) of the Qing Dynasty. Standing on the mountain behind the monastery is the Baotong Pagoda, also known as the "Hongshan Precious Pagoda." A 45.6-metre-high seven-tiered octagonal structure with a masonry interior and an exterior built of stone and brick, it was built in 1270 (7th year of the Zhiyuan reign, Yuan Dynasty), and rebuilt in 1332 (3rd year of the Zhishun reign, Yuan Dynasty). Access to the top of the pagoda is by a staircase built inside, which commands an all-encapsulating view of the tripartite city of Wuhan.

Hunan

Kaifu Temple

Kaifu Temple outside of the Northern City Gate of Changsha was first built in 927, or the second year of the Tiancheng reign of Emperor Mingzong of the Later Tang Dynasty. It was rebuilt during the Jiayou reign (1059-1063) of the Song Dynasty, and rebuilt twice during the Ming Dynasty, only to be destroyed in war towards the end of that dynasty. Reconstruction was done twice more in the Qing Dynasty, in 1660 (17th year of the Shunzhi reign) and 1669 (8th year of the Kangxi reign), but the temple was burned down in a major fire and rebuilt again in 1772 (37th year of the Qianlong reign, Qing Dynasty). Major repairs and restoration were done in 1887 (13th year of the Guangxu reign, Qing Dynasty), but it was burned down once again in 1920, or the ninth year of the Republic, and was restored later with donations from two monks Huixiu and Baosheng. The buildings of the temple, constructed in the 1920s, look rather imposing today. A stone archway rises in front of the gate hall, and along the axial line are the three major halls — the Maitreya Hall, the Mahavira Hall, and the Vairocana Hall — which are flanked to the east by guest rooms, the dining hall, the monks' dormitories, and the abbot's residence, and to the west by the preaching hall, the meditation hall, and the incantation chamber. The entire layout is neat and well conceived, with the courtyards linked by corridors and fronted by porticos. In front of the temple is a pond, known in old times as "Blue Wave Lake," into which captive aquatic animals are released to freedom. The surroundings used to be a beautiful garden, now under reconstruction.

Lushan Temple

The Lushan Temple, which stands on the Yuelu Mountain on

the western bank of the Xiangjiang River of Changsha, was built in 269, or the fourth year of the Taishi reign of the Western Jin Dynasty (265-316). In its early years, the temple covered a vast field with its gate hall standing right by the river at the foot of the mountain and its main buildings extending from the foot to the top of the mountain. This magnificent complex, however, was demolished during the Tang Emperor Wuzong's crackdown on Buddhism. When it was rebuilt towards the end of the Tang Dynasty, the temple lost much of its former size and many of its old halls were never rebuilt. The temple suffered repeated destruction during the Song, Yuan, and Ming dynasties but was restored after each major destruction. In 1944, most of the buildings of the temple were razed to the ground during a Japanese air raid. It was not until recent years that the Changsha Municipal Buddhist Association pooled money to restore the temple and turn it into a new scenic attraction on the Yuelu Mountain Tourist Resort. Quite a few men of past times have filled this temple's 1,700-year history with their deeds and renown. One of these was the monk Dacheng, who successfully disseminated the doctrines of Chan Buddhism from south China into Tibet after he had debated with the famed Indian monk Kamalasila (莲花戒 730-800) for three years, an event that has come down in Buddhist history as the "Lhasa Debate on the Dharma." The temple, situated in a scenic area, is thronged with pilgrims and travelers all day long. The vicinity is strewn with scenes and sights associated with Buddhist culture.

Guangdong

Guangxiao Temple

The Guangxiao Temple on Hongshu Road North, Guangzhou, was known first as the "Zhizhi Temple" and then as the

"Faxing Temple" after it was built during the Three Kingdoms Period (220-265). After the Eastern Jin Dynasty (317-420), this was where some Indian monks lived and translated Buddhist scriptures, including the eminent Gunabhadra (求那跋陀罗 394-468) and Paramartha (真谛 499-569). It was in this temple that Huineng (499-569), the sixth-generation patriarch of Chan Buddhism, became a novice and received his ordination. After the Southern Song Dynasty (1127-1279), the temple was re-named repeatedly, until it finally assumed the name that has re-mained to this day in 1151 (21st year of the Shaoxing reign, Southern Song Dynasty). The Guangxiao Temple used to be a 30,000-square-meter affair with 12 major halls, six chambers as well as the bell and drum towers, and a Sleeping Buddha Pavilion. Some of these buildings, however, gradually crumbled and fell into disrepair. Only the Mahavira Hall, the Hall of the Sixth Pa-triarch, the Samgharama Hall, and the Hall of Deva-kings are still there today. These combine with a vast collection of cultural relics and quite a few sites of historical interest to justify the temple's fame as the oldest Buddhist sanctuary in Guangzhou. On holidays the temple is always crowded with visitors.

Liurong Temple

The predecessor of the Liurong (Six Banyan Tree) Temple, situated on the road that bears its name in Guangzhou, was the Precious Zhuangyan Temple built more than 1,400 years ago during the Liang Dynasty (502-557). It burned down in the early years of the Northern Song and was rebuilt in 989 (2nd year of the Duangong reign, Song Dynasty). In 1100 (3rd year of the Yuanfu reign, Song Dynasty), the celebrated man of letters, Su Dongpo, was delighted to see the six banyan trees growing in the compound during a visit to the temple. He wrote down the two Chinese characters, *liu rong,* meaning "Six Banyan Trees," and presented this inscription as a gift to the temple. The monks thus renamed their temple the "Liurong Temple." In the center of the complex there used to be a pagoda built during the Liang Dynasty, but it was destroyed later. During the Song Dynasty, a 57-meter-high and nine-layered octagonal pagoda was erected, the Flower Pagoda, which is still there today. The temple used to cover a large area, but the remaining halls were built in recent years. The three six-meter-tall bronze Buddhist statues enshrined in the Mahavira Hall are of a high cultural value. A bronze sculpture of Huineng, the sixth-generation patriarch of the Chan sect of Chinese Buddhism, is revered for its graphic image. One of the temple's walls is imbedded with some stone tablets with ancient inscriptions.

Shanghai

Longhua Temple

The Longhua Temple in Longhua Town in the southern suburbs of Shanghai, is a large Buddhist sanctuary with a long history in Shanghai. Its compounds cover a vast area, and its halls are breathtaking in architectural style. The Longhua Pagoda in front of the temple has been there for more than 1,700 years. A 40-meter-tall, seven-storied octagonal structure with a wooden stairway inside it provides access to the top floor. Legend has it that the pagoda was built in 274 (10th year of the Chiwu reign, Three Kingdoms Period) allegedly in association with the Sogdian monk Sanghavarman (? -280). As historical records indicate, Empress Wu Zetian of the Tang Dynasty was the first person to donate money to build a hall at this temple, but the hall was destroyed at a later time. In 977, or the second year of the Taping Xingguo reign of the Northern Song Dynasty, a temple and a pagoda of considerable size were built on

Longhua Pagoda in front of the Longhua Temple

the site with donations from Qian Shu, king of Wuyue, but these structures were razed to the ground towards the end of the Yuan Dynasty. The buildings extant today were mostly built during the Guangxu reign (1875-1908) of the Qing Dynasty. More buildings were added during the Republican years, but it did not become an influential temple until the 1930s. The Longhua Temple today is famed for its time-honored history and as a major tourist attraction in Shanghai. A solemn atmosphere prevails over the buildings of the temple. Incense sticks burn everywhere in this temple, and a constant stream of pilgrims and visitors come and go on a daily basis.

Yufo Temple

Yufo (Jade Buddha) Temple on Anyuan Road, Putuo District, is named after a jade statue of the Buddha inside it. The temple is relatively young, built as it was only a century ago, but it leads its counterparts in Shanghai in terms of scale and interior decoration, and it enjoys a worldwide reputation. The 1.9-meter-high statue of the Buddha, carved out of a whole piece of jade with a crystal-clear texture in state-of-the-art craftsmanship, was purchased with donations from Myanmar during the Guangxu reign of the Qing. Despite its short history the temple has changed its venue three times. At first it was a small affair close to the Jiangwan Railway Station. After the Revolution of 1911, the temple was occupied and used for other purposes, and the monks had no choice but to have a new temple built on present-day Huai'an Road. Later, with its influence outgrowing its size, the temple was moved to its present site. The temple as it stands today has a methodical layout, and its main buildings, including the Maitreya Hall, the Mahavira Hall, and the Jade Buddha Chamber are regarded as splendid paragons of classical Chinese architecture. Yufo Temple is definitely the foremost Buddhist establishment in Shanghai, due partly to its being the site of the Shanghai Buddhist Seminary and partly to its possession of a collection of different versions of the Tripitaka. During Buddhist festivals and the Lunar Chinese New Year, tens of thousands of pilgrims arrive to burn incense sticks and do devotionals. No Buddhist visitor leaves Shanghai without going to this temple. Food lovers, too, take great fancy in this temple, which operates a restaurant that serves all sorts of vegetarian's delicacies.

Shandong

Xingguo Temple

Xingguo Temple perches on Qianfo Mountain in south Jinan. When it was established during the Kaihuang reign (581-604) of the Sui Dynasty, however, it was known by another name: the Qianfo (Thousand-Buddha) Temple. Only after it was rebuilt

A view of the Yard of Xingguo Temple

during the Zhenguan reign (627-649) of the same dynasty was it given its present name. It was expanded during the Song Dynasty (960-1279), only to be destroyed by war in the early Ming Dynasty. Its reconstruction took place in 1468 (4th year of the Chenghua reign, Ming Dynasty). After the Jiaqing reign (1796-1820) of the Qing Dynasty, new halls were added until the temple grew into an impressive affair with seven halls and four courtyards. The layout is well-disciplined, and the architecture awesome enough to hush the visitor into noiseless reverence. Access to this temple is by a stone stairway of more than 300 steps. The southern wall of the temple is elevated on the top of a cliff, into which a beehive of caves are scooped, with those at the foot of the cliff enshrined with Buddhist statues. This is none other than the well-known Thousand-Buddha Grottoes that has been there for more than 1,400 years. Many of the statues in these caves were crafted during the Zhenguan reign (627-649) of the Tang Dynasty, and some one hundred and thirty of them are still in good shape today. The grottoes naturally came under protection as a site of foremost historical interest in Shandong Province. Qianfo Mountain is a favorite with tourists not only because of the temple and its grottoes but also for its pleasant scenery.

Zhanshan Temple

Zhanshan Temple was built in modern times. Sitting on the southwest foot of Zhanshan Mountain and facing the sea to the east of Qingdao, the temple itself is a favorite tourist attraction. Its front gate is guarded by a pair of exquisitely chiseled stone lions that once belonged to the mansion of the Prince of Qingzhou of the Ming Dynasty. Its edifices, including the Hall of Deva-kings, the Mahavira Hall, the Trinity Hall, and the Tripitaka Pavilion on an axial line, are imitation Ming structures that form a mingled picture of architectural pomp and religious solemnity. The statues of saints in these halls are marked for their graphic imagery and spiritual resonance. The two-storied Tripitaka Pavilion houses a Qianlong version of the *Tripitaka* on the ground floor and a Buddhist sarira on the second floor. The brick pagoda outside the temple is a seven-floored octagonal structure, with a staircase leading to three of these floors that offer a picturesque view of the seascape.

Jiangsu

Jiangtian Temple

Popularly known as the Jinshan Temple, it sits atop Jinshan Hill in the suburbs of Zhenjiang, a city by the Yangtze River. Jiangtian Temple is none other than the Zexin Temple built in 325, eight years after the founding of the Eastern Jin Dynasty. The prestige of this temple is associated with the fact it used to be the domain of Foyin, a celebrated monk of the Song Dynasty. The temple was renamed the "Longyou Temple" during the Tianxi reign (1017-1021) of the Song Dynasty, and during one of his south China tours, Emperor Kangxi of the Qing Dynasty changed it to the "Jiangtian Temple." Jinshan Hill used to be an isle in the Yangtze River, but during the Daoguang reign (1821-185) of the Qing Dynasty, the river course was gradually silted up to turn the island into a peninsula. The buildings of the Jiangtian Temple are laid out along the contours of the hill and look unique in architectural style. The temple is so cleverly tucked away in the depth of the woods that its buildings are invisible when observed from a distance, yet close at hand the spectator gets the impression that all he sees are magnificent buildings and the hill itself seems invisible. The landscape is indeed fabulous and mesmerizing. The place is studded with scenic spots and sites of historical and cultural value. Among the major ones are: 1) the Cishou Pagoda built during the Liang (502-557) Dynasty, a seven-story structure poised atop Jinshan Hill with staircases providing access to each of its seven floors; 2) the Fahai Cave, the legendary dwelling of Fahai, the legendary monk who was endowed with divine power and who once dug gold from underneath the hill to be used to rebuild the temple; 3) the Miaogao Terrace, also known as the Sutra Sunning Terrace, reportedly built by the famous Song-Dynasty monk Foyin; 4) the Lanka Terrace, also known as Sujing Altar, which was built during the Qiandao reign (1165-1173) of the Southern Song Dynasty; and 5) the Liuyun Terrace, also called the Pavilion to See the River and the Sky at a Glance, which is perched on the northern corner of the hilltop and commands a scenic overview of the surroundings, a must for travelers to the Jinshan Temple.

Dinghui Temple

The predecessor of the Dinghui Temple on Jiaoshan Isle in the Yangtze River to the northeast of Zhenjiang was the Puji Convent said to have been built in 194 AD, or the first year of the Xingping reign of the Eastern Han Dynasty. It was renamed the "Puji Temple" during the Song Dynasty and the "Jiaoshan Temple" during the Yuan Dynasty. During the Ming Dynasty, with the addition of a good number of halls, it became a major Buddhist sanctuary south of the Yangtze. The Mahavira Hall was rebuilt during the Xuande reign (1426-1435) of the Ming Dynasty, and when the Hall of Deva-kings, the Tripitaka Pavilion, the Thousand-Buddha Chamber, and the Haiyun Chamber were built during the Zhengtong reign, the temple acquired almost the same impressive size as the Jin Shan Temple. It was not until 1703, the 42nd year of the Kangxi reign of the Qing Dynasty, that the temple was renamed the Dinghui Temple. The buildings as we see them today have retained their Ming-Dynasty layout and architectural style. Jiaoshan Isle itself is a place with a picture-perfect landscape and a pleasant climate. Whenever the emperors Kangxi and Qianlong sailed down the Beijing-Hangzhou Grand Canal on south China tours, they never failed to stop over at Jiaoshan Hill, which today is known for its 16 breathtaking scenes and sights.

Tianning Temple

Tianning Temple in the city of Changzhou was known as the "Guangfu Temple" when it was founded during the Tianfu reign (901-904) of the Tang Dynasty, and was given its present name in 1111, the first year of the Zhenghe reign of the Song Dynasty. In its former days the temple was billed as the best in southeast China because of its size — its halls, chambers and pavilions totaling more than 500 bays and covering an area of more than 130 *mu* (8.67 hectares). The buildings at the site today were built during the Qing Dynasty and include a Mahavira Hall, a Vajra Hall, a Samantabhadra Hall, a Manjusri Hall, a Guanyin Hall, and an Arhats' Chamber. The Mahavira Hall is a dignified 33-meter-high structure propped by pillars that are 30 meters tall. The 500 arhats of the temple are a rare example of high artistic attainment and lifelike images.

Zhejiang

Lingyin Temple

Also known as Yunlin Temple, the Lingyin Temple nestles at the foot of the mountain of the same name north of West Lake in Hangzhou. It was first built during the Eastern Jin Dy-

nasty (317-420), and reached its zenith during the Five Dynasties Period (907-960) with nine chambers, 18 towers, 72 halls, and more than 1,200 domiciles that accommodated 3,000 monks. However, Lingyin Temple has had its fill of ups and downs in the intervening years. The few buildings that remain are mostly a Qing legacy. The tallest of them is the Mahavira Hall at 33.6 meters and with its roof covered with glazed tiles. It is the shrine for the first Buddhist statue built after

Mahavira Hall in Lingyin Temple

the founding of New China, a wooden sculpture of Sakyamuni 9.1 meters tall and gold-plated all over. Behind this statue is a sculpture of the Guanyin Mountain, with a likeness of Guanyin sitting in a cave, and Sudhana (善财童子, one of the bodhisattvas) and the 53 wise ones mentioned in the *Huayin Sutra* occupying every rock on the mountain. Along the side walls of the Mahavira Hall are arrayed the sculptures of the 20 devas in lifelike images. The front of the temple is screened by an artificial hill piled up with rocks in strange forms and shapes, which is a representation of the Lesser Grdhrakuta 小灵鹫山 which flew over all the way from India. Lingyin Mountain itself is the site of a number of cave-shrines for Buddhist statues. Lingyin Temple is a famed tourist attraction, visited by large numbers of tourists on a daily basis. In front of the temple, ancient trees rise to unbelievable heights, heaping up rich piles of foliage that block the sun and provide shade for visitors. A spring runs gurgling past the front gate. Taking a stroll under the shade of the woods is a most refreshing experience.

Jingci Temple

Jingci (Pure Compassion) Temple at the foot of the Nanping Mountain by West Lake in Hangzhou was known as the Bao'en Guangxiao Monastery when it was built in 954, or the first year of the Xiande reign of the Zhou (one of the Five Dynasties). It was renamed the Huiri Yongming Monastery after it collapsed and was rebuilt within a short time. During the Northern Song Dynasty (960-1127), Emperor Taizong (Zhao Jiong) named it the "Shouning Monastery." It was not until the Southern Song Dynasty (1127-1279) that it was named the Jingci Monastery and acquired a sizeable scale with 32 halls, chambers, and pavilions, and a population of more than 1,000 monks. What remains of the Jingci Monastery are three halls, among which the Mahavira Hall was rebuilt in recent years. To the west of the temple is the Well for Timber Transportation. As legend has it, when Monk Daoji was rebuilding the monastery during the Song Dynasty, he had all the timber shipped in from below this well, and the last piece of this still remains inside it today. As a Buddhist establishment in the old tradition, Jingci Monastery is a must for travelers to Hangzhou.

Seven-Pagoda Temple

Five kilometers east of downtown Ningbo sits the Seven-Pagoda Temple, originally the Dongjin Monastery (later renamed Xixin Temple) founded in 858, or the 12th year of the Dazhong reign of the Tang Dynasty. During the Song Dynasty the temple was known as the "Chongshou Temple," a name that was briefly replaced by "Wanshou Palace" (sounding like a Taoist establishment) before being restored. During the Ming Dynasty it was once called the "Botuo Temple." By the Qing Dynasty, it was renamed after the seven pagodas engraved in a brick engraving on the façade of its gate hall, a name that has remained. The temple's more than 1,000 years of ups and downs culminated in its destruction at the hands of the Heavenly Kingdom peasant uprising. The temple as it stands today is the result of reconstruction during the Guangxu reign of the Qing Dynasty, an immense complex of lofty buildings including a Hall of Deva-kings, a Trinity Hall, a Mahavira Hall, a Jade Buddha Chamber, a Huayan Chamber, a Scripture Repository, and a Cloud-and-Water Hall. What is special about Seven-Pagoda Temple is that its Mahavira Hall is the domain of Guanyin with 1,000 Hands instead of Sakyamuni, and because of this it used to be called the "Lesser Putuo Temple." The importance of this temple is evidenced by the fact that pilgrims make it a point to stop and pay homage at the Seven-Pagoda Temple before crossing the sea to visit the island known as Mount Putuo.

Tiantong Temple

Tiantong Temple at the foot of Taibai Mountain in Yinxian County, and 30 kilometers from Ningbo, owes its birth to a thatched hermitage built on the mountain by a monk named Yixing in 300, or the first year of the Yongkang reign of the Western Jin Dynasty. The hut became the site of a temple that came under construction in 732, or the 20th year of the Kaiyuan reign of the Tang Dynasty. Twenty-five years later, a monk chose a new site and built the Tiantong Temple as we see it today. In 759, or the second year of the Qianyuan reign of the Tang Dynasty, Emperor Xiaozong renamed it the "Tiantong Linglong Temple," which was then replaced by "Tianshou Temple" by Emperor Yizong in 869 (10th year of the Xiantong reign, Tang Dynasty). In 1007 (fourth year of the Jingde reign, Northern Song Dynasty) it received yet another name, "Jingde Monastery." It was not until 1392 (20th year of the Hongwu reign, Ming Dynasty) that it was officially given the name it has today. The buildings of the temple were the result of reconstruction done during the Qing Dynasty. In 1979, with the support of the People's Government, the temple underwent large-scale repairs, and emerged as a major Buddhist temple in southeast China. The time-honored history of the Tiantong Temple is testified to by its impressive trove of cultural artifacts. The vicinity of the temple is marked for its scenic beauty.

Anhui

Mingjiao Temple

Mingjiao Temple in the city of Hefei stands on a platform

that protrudes five meters from the ground. Its predecessor was the Tiefo (Iron Buddha) Temple founded during the Tianjian reign (503-519) of the Liang Dynasty, but it was destroyed towards the end of the Sui Dynasty. During the Dali reign (766-779) of the Tang Dynasty, a six-meter-tall iron statue of the Buddha was unearthed at the site. When Emperor Daizong (reign 762-779) got wind of this, he had the temple rebuilt and he named it the Mingjiao Monastery. During the Ming Dynasty it was renamed the "Mingjiao Temple." The temple crumbled as a result of war and turmoil in 1853 (3rd year of the Xianfeng reign, Qing Dynasty) but it was later gradually restored. The Mahavira Hall and the Posterior Hall have retained their original forms dating back to 1886 (12th year of the Guangxu reign, Qing Dynasty). As the Mingjiao Temple is in downtown Hefei and the site of such tourist attractions as the "well atop a house" and "pavilion to hear pines sighing in the wind," it is visited by tourists and pilgrims every day.

Yingjiang Temple

The Yingjiang (River-Greeting) Temple stands, as its name suggests, by the Yangtze River in the city of Anqing. One of the famous Buddhist sanctuaries in Anhui Province, it was established in 974 (7th year of the Kaibao reign, Northern Song Dynasty) and rebuilt and renamed the "Yongchang Monastery for Protection of the State" in 1619 (47th year of the Wanli reign, Ming Dynasty), only to be renamed once again as the "Emperor-mandated Yingjiang Monastery" in 1650 (7th year of the Shunzhi reign, Qing Dynasty). After being repeatedly repaired and expanded, it was razed to the ground during the war in 1853 (3rd year of the Xianfeng reign, Qing Dynasty). In 1870 (9th year of the Tongzhi reign, Qing Dynasty) and expanded in 1892 (18th year of the Guangxu reign, Qing Dynasty) it was rebuilt to attain its present size, a 2,400 and 60-square-meter complex whose five main buildings (Hall of Deva-kings, Mahavira Hall, Zhenfeng Pagoda, Vairocana Hall, and Tripitaka Pavilion) combine with the Yiyuan Garden, the Dashi Pavilion, the Ciyun Pavilion, the Riverside Chamber, and the Garden of Miniature Landscapes to form something that is both a solemn religious sanctuary and a scenic resort. The gate hall of the Yingjiang Temple is flanked by a pair of iron anchors weighing three tons apiece, which probably symbolize that the temple is a veritable ship anchored rock-firm in the Yangtze River. The temple's seven-floored Zhenfeng Pagoda with a staircase installed inside it, is an octagonal structure that rises to a height of 82.47 meters and commands an overview of the Yangtze and the city of Anqing.

Jiangxi

Youmin Temple

The predecessor of the Youmin Temple in Nanchang was the Dafo (Great Buddha) Temple founded in 547 (1st year of the Taiqing reign, Liang Dynasty). Legend has it that the temple's large statue of the Buddha was cast by the dragon that dwelled underneath the town well. In the intervening years the temple has assumed a succession of names: "Chengtian Temple," "Nengren Temple," "Yongning Temple" during the Ming Dynasty, and "Youqing Temple" after it was burned down by fire and rebuilt during the Shunzhi reign (1644-1661) of the Qing Dynasty. It was not until the Republican years that it assumed its present name. The Youmin Temple had played a major role in disseminating the doctrines of the Chan school of Chinese Buddhism. After the celebrated monk Mazu (709-788) achieved enlightenment as a disciple of the Chan master Huai Rang (677-744) at

Southern Holy Mountain and arrived in Hongzhou (present-day Nanchang), he settled in the Youmin Temple (then known as "Kaiyuan") and devoted himself to preaching the Chan discipline. He eventually acquired a following of more than 130 disciples who helped spread Huai Rang's theories in the Yangtze River valley and formed a school of their own — the Hongzhou school of Chinese Buddhism with the Youmin Temple as its cradle. Only a small number of buildings of the Youmin Temple today are of the Qing legacy; the others were built in recent years. The temple is in a place of fabulous scenic beauty with the limpid Nanhu Lake right beside it, which is thronged with visitors on weekends and during holidays. It is also the headquarters of the Jiangxi Provincial Buddhist Association.

Donglin Temple

Donglin Temple on Mount Lushan, Jiangxi Province, was founded more than 1,600 years ago by Huiyuan (334-416), a renowned monk of the Eastern Jin Dynasty, and had its heyday

An overall view of Donglin Temple

during the Tang Dynasty when it emerged as a colossal establishment with more than 300 halls and dormitories. The temple was ruined during the Shaoxing reign (1131-1162) of the Song Dynasty, and rebuilt once during the Ming Dynasty and twice during the Qing Dynasty. Some of the buildings on the premises were built during the Ming and Qing dynasties, and the others were constructed in recent years. The Donglin Temple was converted into a cradle of the Pure Land school of Chinese Buddhism thanks to the efforts of Huiyuan, who gathered 123 disciples under him to form the White Lotus Society. During Huiyuan's more than three decades of stay on Mount Lushan, "his person never moved from the mountain, and his footprints were never found in the mundane world." He never went beyond the Tiger Stream in front of the temple whenever he was sending off a guest. For his high moral integrity he was greatly esteemed. Among his friends were the famous poet Tao Yuanming, the well-known personage Liu Yiming, and the great man of letters Xie Lingyun. That's why the Donglin Temple abounds in anecdotes about these celebrities. Once, Tao Yuanming and Lu Xiujing arrived at Mount Lushan and joined Huiyuan in a discussion about Buddhism, Confucianism, and Taoism. The entire day passed quickly. When Huiyuan was walking with his two friends out of the temple and sending them off, they continued their discussion. In no time they crossed the Tiger Stream, and it was not until the God of Tiger started howling that Huiyuan realized that he had violated his taboo. He could not help laughing loudly. Such is the origin of the story "Three Laughs over the Tiger Stream."

Nengren Temple

The predecessor to the Nengren Temple east of the city of Jiujiang was the Chengtian Monastery that was established during the Liang Dynasty (502-557), rebuilt during the Dali reign (766-779) of the Tang Dynasty, destroyed by troops during the Yuan Dynasty, and rebuilt again in 1379 (12th year of the Hongwu reign, Ming Dynasty). It assumed its present name in 1489 (2nd year, Hongzhi reign). More buildings were erected during the Chongzhen reign (1628-1644), but the temple collapsed once again in war in 1853 (3rd year of the Xianfeng reign, Qing Dynasty). It was rebuilt in 1870 (9th year of the Tongzhi reign, Qing Dynasty) and has remained largely intact since. Along the axial line are three courtyards containing a Hall of Deva-kings, a Mahavira Hall and a Tripitaka Pavilion respectively, with the anterooms serving as the patriarch's hall, the preaching hall, the abbot's mansion, and the monks' residential quarters. The entire complex is laid out according to an impeccable plan. There are a host of historical and cultural relics in the temple, the better known of them being the "Eight Scenes of the Nengren Temple." These include a 43-metere-high pagoda, which is a seven-storied hexahedronal brick-and-masonry structure with a door built into each of its six sides (three of them merely ornamental), and a stone stairway inside it leading all the way to its top floor. The others are a Rain-perforated Stone, a Stone Boat, an Iron Buddha, an Ice Mountain, a Snow Cave, and a Hai'er Spring.

Fujian

South Putuo Temple

The South Putuo Temple in Xiamen (Amoy) was originally the Puzhao Temple established during the Tang Dynasty. It was renamed the "Sizhou Monastery" when it was reconstructed during the Five Dynasties, but was restored to its original name during the Song Dynasty. It was demolished during the Yuan Dynasty. When it was rebuilt during the Hongwu reign (1368-1398) of the

South Putuo Temple, lying at the South of Mount Putuo and facing the Sea

Ming Dynasty, an Avalokitesvara Hall was added to it, but all this was burned down towards the end of the Ming Dynasty. Because the temple is situated south of Mount Putuo in Zhejiang Province, it was renamed the "South Putuo Temple" after it was reconstructed during the Kangxi reign (1662-1722) of the Qing Dynasty. The temple enjoyed its peak of popularity during the 1920s and the 1930s, when the South Fujian Buddhist Seminary headquartered in the temple turned out large numbers of professional monks. The seminary was forced to close down after Japan launched an aggressive war against China in 1937, and it was not reopened until recent years. A good number of new structures have been added over the last few years, turning the South Putuo Temple into the foremost Buddhist sanctuary in Xiamen. On any given day the temple is crowded with visitors.

Yongquan Temple

The Yongquan (Gurgling Spring) Temple on Gushan Mountain in the eastern suburbs of Fuzhou is another famous Buddhist establishment in Fujian Province. The name of the temple, which was founded during the Five Dynasties, is derived from a gurgling spring in front of it. In 999 (2nd year of the Xianping reign, Song Dynasty), Emperor Zhenzong bestowed a name board in his own handwriting on the temple, calling it the "Gurgling Spring Temple on the White Peak of Gushan Mountain." During the Ming Dynasty the name was abbreviated as the "Yongquan (Gurgling Spring) Temple." During the period from 1408 (6th year of the Yongle reign) to 1542 (21st year of the Jiaqing reign) during the Ming Dynasty, the temple caught fire twice, but on both occasions it was rebuilt. Significant expansions were made during the Qing Dynasty so that despite the temple's thousand-year long history, the buildings remaining are mostly a Qing legacy. The temple is hailed as a fine example of classic Chinese architecture. All its main structure — the Hall of the Deva-kings, the Mahavira Hall, and the Preaching Hall — as well as its ancillary halls and domiciles are integrated by a labyrinth of corridors to form a gigantic engineering phenomenon that covers the entire length of a mountainside. Among the Yongquan Temple's collection of precious artifacts are three renowned treasures: a fireproof almsgiving table made of iron wiring and wood that dampens whenever it is raining; a thousand-year-old sago cycas (*Cycas revolute*) that blossoms every year, and 657 volumes of Buddhist scriptures written with blood. The picture-perfect mountains around the temple are favorite tourist destinations.

Chongqing

Luohan Temple

Built during the Zhiping reign (1064-1066) of the Song

Front gate of Luohan (Arhat) Temple

Dynasty, the Luohan (Arhat) Temple on Minzu Road in the Central District of the city is renowned for its history of nearly 1,000 years. As its name suggests, the temple is the site of an arhats' cave and a hall of 500 arhats. However, "Luohan" was not the original name of the temple. During the Ming Dynasty, it was renamed the "Gufoyan (Ancient Buddhist Rock) Temple" in 1462 (6th year of the Tianshun reign, Ming), the "Luohan Temple" in 1465 (1st year of the Chenghua reign), the "Cangjing (Scripture Repository) Pavilion" in 1506 (1st year of the Zhengde reign), and the "Xihu (West Lake) Monastery" in 1628 (1st year of the Chongzhen reign). The temple was given its present name in 1886 (12th year of the Guangxu reign, Qing Dynasty). The Luohan Temple used to be a large affair, but having had many ups and downs, only the compound with the Pavilion of Scripture Repository has remained. As if all this was not enough, an air raid launched by the invading Japanese reduced it to shambles. The temple as it stands today was gradually brought into being in the last half century. Probably because of its old history, the Luohan Temple is still regarded as an ancient Buddhist center, its elegantly designed buildings being perennial attractions to pious pilgrims and curious visitors from all over the world.

Ciyun Temple

Ciyun (Cloud of Benevolence) Temple stands picturesquely on Shizi (Lion) Mountain on the northern bank of the Yangtze River, where the Jialing River empties into it, and opposite Chaotian Gate across the river. Its predecessor was the tiny Guanyin Temple established during the Tang Dynasty. It was rebuilt in 1757 (22nd year of the Qianlong reign, Qing Dynasty). A major expansion project undertaken in 1927 transformed it into a large monastery that was given its present name. The expansion project was done to accommodate pilgrims who came and went by way of the harbor at the foot of the mountain on which the temple stood. All the buildings of the Ciyun Temple are found on the mountain. Access to the Mahavira Hall behind the gate hall is by several flights of stone steps. Chinese tradition is blended with Western influence in the architectural style of this temple. Glazed-tile roofs with upturning eaves mingle with multi-floored chambers and terraces to form an awesome landmark that is set off nicely by the tumbling rivers. The artificial mountain behind the temple is built of numerous rocks of exotic shapes and images, and landscaped, through the clever hands of the builders, with a series of fixtures. These include the Gazing-at-the-River Kiosk, the Moon Pavilion, the Golden Fish Pond, the Lotus Pool, and something that belongs only to the lore

Gufo Pavilion in Ciyun Temple

Ciyun Temple, lying at the convergence of the Yangtze River and
Jialing River, and gathering miraculous power

of Buddhism — an imitation of the pond in which nine dragons
spat water to bathe the newborn baby who is to become Prince
Siddhartha — as well as the Pond of Eight Merits.

Sichuan

Wenshu Monastery

Wenshu (Manjusri) Monastery by the Northwest Drilling
Ground in Chengdu is a major Buddhist sanctuary in Sichuan.
Its predecessor was the Xinxiang Temple founded during the
Sui Dynasty. It was expanded during the Song, only to crumble
in war and turmoil towards the end of the Ming Dynasty. When
the temple was rebuilt in 1697 (36th year of the Kangxi reign,
Qing Dynasty), a horizontal name board was bestowed on it.
Inscribed on the board in the emperor's personal handwriting
was the temple's new two-character name, *kong lin*, meaning

"Void Forest." That is why, for a time, people called the monastery the "Konglin Temple." The Wenshu Monastery today covers an area of 5,000 square meters. Visitors are invariably impressed by its well-disciplined layout and the classic forms of its 200-odd buildings, including main halls and monastic residential quarters, which are uniform carpentry-masonry structures. A few years ago, a pagoda was erected there, the "Thousand-Buddha Pagoda of Peace," and 999 Buddhist figurines are carved into the stone walls on each of its 11 floors.

A view of the yard of Wenshu Monastery

Baoguang Temple

Legend has it that the predecessor of the Baoguang (Precious Light) Temple in Xindu County, 19 kilometers from downtown Chengdu, was the Dashi (Big Rock) Temple established during the Han Dynasty. This was where Emperor Xizong of the late Tang Dynasty took refuge after the capital city of Chang'an fell into the hands of peasant uprising led by Huang Chao. One night during his stay in the temple, the emperor saw a light

Skyscraping Baoguang Temple

emitting from a Buddhist sarira enshrined in one of its halls, and he issued instructions to give the temple a new name: Baoguang Temple, meaning the Temple of Precious Light. During the Song Dynasty, it was renamed the Dajue (Great Enlightenment) Temple, and towards the end of the Ming Dynasty it was razed to the ground by war. The Baoguang Temple as it stands today was rebuilt in 1670 (9th year of the Kangxi reign, Qing dynasty), an impressive complex of 80,000 square meters that contains a pagoda, five main halls, and 16 compounds. The centerpiece consists of a Hall of Deva-kings, a Sarira Pagoda, a Seven-Buddha Hall, a Mahavira Hall, and a Tripitaka Pavilion. All the flank rooms and quadrangles are connected by corridors. The magnitude of the entire cluster is vastly enhanced by an ocean of roofs covered with green-glazed tiles and decorated with vermilion-painted eaves.

A view of the Hall of Arhats in Baoguang Temple

In the Hall of 500 Arhats, all the sculptures stand about two meters tall and every arhat looks lifelike with different expressions and postures. On public display in the temple are a vast collection of precious scrolls of calligraphy, traditional Chinese paintings, and other valuable artifacts.

Guizhou

Hongfu Temple

The people of Guiyang regard the Hongfu Temple, situated on Qianling Mountain 1.5 km west of downtown Guizhou and built in 1672 (11th year or the Kangxi reign, Qing Dynasty), as primary Buddhist sanctuary for their city. But the temple did not acquire its present size without repeated repairs and expansions that have been undertaken in the intervening years. During the decade-long chaos of the "cultural revolution" (1966-1976), the Hongfu Temple fell victim to wonton vandalism. The temple as we see it today was restored to its former glory in 1978 with the support of the local government and the donations of Buddhists from all walks of life. In terms of size, Hongfu Temple compares unfavourably with major counterparts in other parts of the province, but in Guiyang it is definitely the largest. The temple is in possession of 30 halls and monks' dormitories, the major ones being the Frontal Hall, the Middle Hall, the Mahavira Hall, the Guanyin Hall, the Preaching Hall, and the Tripitaka Pavilion. In each of these halls a complete array of the deities of the Buddhist pantheon are presented in finely crafted statues. A Qianlong edition of the *Tripitaka* is found in the collection of scriptures of the Tripitaka Pavilion. The vicinity of the temple is strewn with sites of cultural interest, including the Unicorn Cave, the Old Buddha Cave, the Alms Bowl Washing Pool on Qianling Mountain, and the "Holy Spring" behind the mountain. The temple itself is in the sequestered repose of towering trees that have been growing there for ages, and it draws droves of pilgrims and travelers from all over the world on a yearly basis.

Yunnan

Yuantong Temple

Yuantong Temple in Kunming had its beginning as the Bu-tuluo Temple founded during the Nanzhao Period (738-902). During the period from 1301 (5th year of the Dade reign, Yuan Dynasty) to 1319 (6th year of the Yanyou reign, Yuan Dynasty), the temple was reconstructed and given its present name, and a new Guanyin Hall was added to it. Repeated repairs were done during the Ming and Qing dynasties. According to historical records, Yuantong Temple was converted into a Taoist temple for

Yuantong Temple

a brief period, and as a result both Buddhist and Taoist influences are seen in some buildings, stele inscriptions, and religious statues. The topography of Yuantong Temple is that its front towers over its rear on a mountain slope so that one can peep through its front gate and get a panoramic view of the entire temple with its posterior perched on the edge of a cliff. The archway in front of the temple stands on a base that is ten meters higher than that of its Mahavira Hall. Few temples in this country are built this way. As behooves Kunming as a city where it is spring all the year around, the layout of the Yuantong Temple is combined with horticulture and landscaping, turning the place into both a religious center and a botanical garden of blossoming flowers and green trees.

Huating Temple

When Huating Temple, situated 15 kilometers southwest of Kunming, was established remains dubious to this day. It is known, however, that the first reconstruction of it dates back to 1320 (7th year of the Yanyou reign, Yuan Dynasty) and at the time it was known as the Yuanjue Temple. The temple was rebuilt and renamed the "Greater Yuantong Temple" during the Jingtai reign (1450-1456) of the Ming Dynasty, only to succumb to a major fire towards the end of that dynasty. During the Qing Dynasty, it was rebuilt in 1687 (26th year of the Kangxi reign), partially destroyed in 1857 (7th year of the Xianfeng reign), and restored again in 1883 (9th year of the Guangxu reign). In 1922, the temple received a major facelift when its old halls were refurbished and more halls were built, and for a time it was called the "Yunxi Monastery for the Stabilization of the Country." Huating Temple is tucked away in an ocean of bamboo groves in Kunming's Western Hill Scenic Resort. Its glazed-tile rooftops gleam in the rich verdure of ancient-looking cypresses and pines, and all the buildings are scattered about in an orderly way. Huating Mountain rises in the background and the vast Dianchi Lake extends an arm right beyond the front gate. The vivid and individually different images of the 500 Arhats in the Huating Temple never fail to draw appreciative comments from its visitors.

Shaanxi

Wolong Temple

Dating back to the Han Dynasty, the Wolong Temple in Xi'an was named the Fuying Monastery during the Sui Dynasty and the Guanyin Temple during the Tang Dynasty. In the founding year of the Song Dynasty, 960, it became the Wolong Temple, named after Weiguo, the abbot and celebrated monk who styled himself "Wolong (Sleeping-Dragon) Monk." In the past the Wolong Temple was an enormous complex that had been destroyed and rebuilt during the Ming Dynasty. By the Qing Dynasty, it had emerged as the leading Buddhist sanctuary in Xi'an. During the Republican years it suffered major destruction until it was rebuilt in 1931. The Wolong Temple as it is today is a compound of dignified halls with a methodical layout. It is one of the eight major temples in Shaanxi Province to be opened to foreign visitors.

Xingjiao Temple

The Xingjiao Temple, or Temple for Promoting Buddhism, was founded in 669 (2nd year of the Zongzhang reign, Tang Dynasty) on the Shaoling Tableland 20 kilometers from Xi'an, when Emperor Gaozong had the tomb of Xuanzang moved there and a temple and a pagoda built in memory of this great Buddhist master. He named it the "Great Tang Temple for Protecting the Country and Promoting Buddhism." During his reign,

Emperor Xiaozong of the Tang Dynasty inscribed a horizontal board with the two Chinese characters *xing jiao*, meaning "promoting Buddhism," and endowed this on the temple. However, the temple fell into disrepair 100 years later. The temple was restored in 828 (2nd year of the Taihe reign, Tang Dynasty), fell into dilapidation during the war-torn Tongzhi reign (1862-1874) of the Qing Dynasty, and was rebuilt in 1922 (11th year of the Republic). After the founding of the People's Republic, the People's Government had the temple repaired on two occasions, enabling it to emerge as one of the major Buddhist sanctuaries in this country. The complex of the Xingjiao Temple contains a front gate hall, bell and drum towers, a Mahavira Hall, a preaching hall, a meditation chamber, and monks' dormitories. Standing in front of it are three pagodas. The Xuanzang Pagoda in the center of the cluster is a 13-meter-high, five-floor structure with a statue of Xuanzang enshrined on the ground floor. The two flanking pagodas, both being five metres in height, are dedicated to Xuanzang's two famous disciples, Kuiji and Yuance. The temple is in possession of more than 10,000 volumes of Buddhist canons, and many other precious cultural artifacts. A series of stone tablets in it are inscribed with the full text of the *Diamond Sutra.*

图书在版编目（CIP）数据

中国佛教/郑立新 著

北京: 外文出版社, 2007 年

ISBN 978-7-119-04490-3

I. 中 ... II. 郑 ... III.佛教－概况－中国－英文 IV.B928.2

中国版本图书馆 CIP 数据核字（2006）第 111286 号

撰　　稿：郑立新
翻　　译：凌　原
英文审定：Foster Stockwell　郁苓
责任编辑：蔡跃蕾
封面设计：蔡　荣
印刷监制：张国祥

中国佛教

©外文出版社

外文出版社出版

（中国北京百万庄大街 24 号）

邮政编码 100037

北京外文印刷厂印刷

外文出版社网址：http://www.flp.com.cn

外文出版社电子信箱：info @ flp.com.cn

sales @ flp.com.cn

中国国际图书贸易总公司发行

（中国北京车公庄西路 35 号）

北京邮政信箱第 399 号 邮政编码 100044

2007 年（大 32 开）第 1 版

2007 年第 1 版 第 1 次印刷

（英）

ISBN 978-7-119-04490-3

06800（平）

7-E-3493P